DOCTOR FAUSTUS

broadview editions
series editor: L.W. Conolly

DOCTOR FAUSTUS

A 1604-Version Edition

Christopher Marlowe

SECOND EDITION

edited by Michael Keefer

broadview editions

Library and Archives Canada Cataloguing in Publication

Marlowe, Christopher, 1564-1593.
  Doctor Faustus : a 1604 version edition / edited by Michael Keefer. — 2nd. ed.

(Broadview editions)
Previous ed. published in 1991 under title: Christopher Marlowe's Doctor
    Faustus.
Includes bibliographical references.
ISBN 978-1-55111-210-7

  I. Keefer, Michael H.   II. Title.   III. Title: Christopher Marlowe's Doctor Faustus.
IV. Series.

PR2664.A2K43 2007   822'.3   C2006-904074-5

Broadview Editions

The Broadview Editions series represents the ever-changing canon of literature in English by bringing texts long regarded as classics with valuable lesser-known works.

Advisory editor for this volume: Michel Pharand

Broadview Press is an independent, international publishing house, incorporated in 1985. Broadview believes in shared ownership, both with its employees and with the general public; since the year 2000 Broadview shares have traded publicly on the Toronto Venture Exchange under the symbol BDP.

We welcome comments and suggestions regarding any aspect of our publications—please feel free to contact us at the addresses below or at broadview@broadviewpress.com.

North America:	UK, Ireland, and continental Europe:	Australia and New Zealand:
PO Box 1243, Peterborough,	NBN Plymbridge	UNIREPS,
Ontario, Canada K9J 7H5	Estover Road	University of New South Wales
PO Box 1015, 3576 California Road,	Plymouth PL6 7PY UK	Sydney, NSW, 2052 Australia
Orchard Park, NY, USA 14127		
Tel: (705) 743-8990;	Tel: 44 (0) 1752 202300	Tel: 61 2 9664 0999
Fax: (705) 743-8353	Fax: 44 (0) 1752 202330	Fax: 61 2 9664 5420
E-mail: customerservice@	E-mail: enquiries@nbnplymbridge.com	E-mail: info.press@unsw.edu.au
broadviewpress.com		

Broadview Press acknowledges the financial support of the Government of Canada through the Book Publishing Industry Development Program (BPIDP) for our publishing activities.

www.broadviewpress.com

Book design and composition by George Kirkpatrick
PRINTED IN CANADA

Contents

Preface to the Revised Edition, 2006

Fifteen years have passed since my edition of this play first appeared. This revised edition incorporates a substantially rewritten introduction, updated explanatory notes, and a small number of alterations to the edited text.

When my 1991 edition was first published, I expected that its most controversial feature would be its re-location of two comic scenes which my textual analysis showed to have been displaced in the early quartos of *Doctor Faustus* (and one or both of which had remained displaced in all subsequent editions of the play). The innovation was accepted by most textual scholars—among them David Bevington and Eric Rasmussen, who in their *Revels Plays* edition (1993) expressed the hope that this and other agreements between our editions might be "indicative of a new consensus, not only in the editing of this play but of others as well" (x).

What proved controversial was my practice, in a critical edition based upon the 1604 quarto (or A text), of printing readings from the 1616 quarto (or B text) in a number of closely parallel passages where I found reason to believe that the 1616 text preserves earlier and more authentic readings. Bevington and Rasmussen indicated the current limits to any "new consensus" when they contrasted their own (not wholly consistent) attempts to avoid any conflation of the 1604 and 1616 texts with the manner in which my "generally laudable edition makes the mistake of moving back and forth for its verbal choices in a way that implies a single underlying text and procedurally seems at times arbitrary" (Bevington and Rasmussen x). In this revised edition I have provided explanations in my notes of all points where I have adopted readings of the 1616 text; and in the fifth section of my introduction and in my Note on the Text I have indicated more clearly than before the editorial principles and textual evidence that have guided my choices.

Let me give an anticipatory glimpse of what is at issue—and hence, in broad terms, of the differences between the 1604-version text offered here and the texts of Bevington and Rasmussen (and of the other more recent editors who have followed their lead). Bevington's and Rasmussen's edition, no less than my own, presupposes that at some point around 1589 there was indeed a "single underlying text" of *Doctor Faustus*. Their aim, like mine, has been to produce a contemporary text that brings readers as close to the moment of originary textual production as the surviving textual and contextual evidence permits. We agree that the 1604 quarto (or A text) provides the best evidence for the play-text's earliest shape, and we agree that the 1616 quarto (or B text) is a composite or sedimented text that incorporates censorship and large-scale revisions dating from the first decade of the seventeenth century.

We differ, however, in our understanding of what the relationship might be between the originary "underlying text" and the 1604 and 1616 quartos of *Doctor Faustus*. Bevington and Rasmussen believe the connection between the earliest manuscript of the play and the A text to be very close indeed: in their view, the 1604 quarto was printed from that manuscript, "the original foul papers of Marlowe and his collaborator" (Rasmussen 31).[1] But as I have indicated in my Note on the Text—and as I have argued at greater length in a recent article (Keefer 2006) and in the full critical edition of the 1604 and 1616 versions that is being published by Broadview Press simultaneously with the present Broadview Editions text—their own textual evidence does not support this conclusion. Moreover, there is compelling evidence that at several points where the A and B texts are closely parallel, the 1616 quarto preserves readings that are demonstrably earlier and better than those of the 1604 quarto.

It follows from this analysis that the early history of the play must be more complex than contemporary textual critics have been willing to acknowledge. The occasional local superiorities of the B text lead to the conclusion (which I arrived at in 1991) that while the 1604 quarto preserves *Doctor Faustus* in a version that is both earlier and more authentic than the version of the play preserved in the textually composite and sedimented 1616 quarto, and while the 1604 text is in most places superior to the

---

1 The term "foul papers" refers to the manuscript of a play provided by the playwright, or playwrights, to a company of actors (in contrast to derivative manuscripts prepared by the acting company as theatrical promptbooks).

revised and censored 1616 text, the 1616 quarto incorporates some elements of a text of the play that is earlier and better than the text provided by the 1604 quarto.

The task of the critical editor may correspondingly be more complicated than we have tended to assume—though such a conclusion is unlikely to please textual critics of this play, who have historically displayed a strong preference for simple solutions. For much of the twentieth century, the 1616 quarto was regarded as being very close to the true Marlovian thing; the current orthodoxy has awarded the same prize to the 1604 quarto. In both cases, the out-of-favor text has been dismissed and thought to possess little if any substantive value.

As A.E. Housman intimated a century ago, an editor confronted by two divergent recensions of a text, both of which appear to make plausible claims to authenticity, may well feel caught, like the donkey in Jean Buridan's conundrum of choice, midway between two bundles of hay (Housman 35): but this is not a predicament that can properly be resolved by the expedient of kicking one bundle out of reach.

In my own renewed labors with the Marlovian hay-bales I have benefited from the kindness of librarians in the British Library, the Newberry Library, and the University of Guelph's McLaughlin Library. I have drawn in my revised introduction upon essays published in *Elizabethan Theatre XV,* eds. A. Lynne Magnusson and C.E. McGee (2002), in *Fantasies of Troy,* eds. Alan Shepard and Stephen D. Powell (2004), and in the *Papers of the Bibliographical Society of America* (2006). I am grateful to Luke Hill and Dave Hudson for their careful scholarship as research assistants, and to Jacqueline Murray, Dean of the University of Guelph's College of Arts, for the financial support that made their work possible. Thanks as well to Daniel Fischlin, Alan Shepard, Frank Baron, and Gordon Lester for friendship and collegial good sense; to Don LePan, for patient understanding; to my sons Tom and Chris, for unstinting comradeship; and, once more, to Janice Kulyk Keefer, my love, for her patience and love.

Preface to the First Edition, 1991

Marlowe's *Doctor Faustus* survived the Elizabethan age in two quite distinct versions, the earliest extant editions of which, printed in 1604 and 1616, differ in length by more than six hundred lines. The modern-spelling text offered here is based on the more authentic and dramatically superior 1604 version of the play, while also incorporating readings from parallel scenes in the 1616 text in places where the 1604 text and its early reprints are clearly deficient.

All but a few of the many editions of *Doctor Faustus* produced between the early 1930s and the late 1970s used the longer 1616 or B text as copy-text, and although the view that this was the more original version of the play was decisively overturned more than fifteen years ago, new editions relying on the 1604 or A text have only begun to appear during the past half-dozen years. The first such edition, that of David Ormerod and Christopher Wortham (1985), has since been followed by Roma Gill's new modern- and old-spelling editions (1989, 1990). While I have diverged in various ways from the work of these and earlier editors, I am nonetheless indebted to them—sometimes most deeply so at those points where I have most strenuously disagreed with their conclusions.

The present text of *Doctor Faustus* is shorter, harsher, more focused and more disturbing than that version of the play which readers and play-goers have for much of this century been taught to regard as Marlowe's. It also differs from previous A-version texts for, on the basis of a fresh analysis of the relations between the two substantive texts, I have departed from previous editorial practice by restoring two displaced comic scenes to their proper places, thus eliminating a discontinuity which appears in both the 1604 and the 1616 quartos.

The present edition differs in other respects as well from earlier editions of this play. The career of the historical Dr. Faustus and the manner in which his legend took shape are of greater relevance to Marlowe's play than has often been supposed. In my introduction I have therefore both drawn upon and supplemented the work of scholars like Frank Baron who have made available a new understanding of the historical Faustus and of the originary contexts of his legend. Marlowe was aware of these contexts; we need to be as well, if we wish to understand how this play reshapes and subverts an originally homiletic narrative.

My introduction also seeks to make visible certain links between recent developments in textual scholarship and in literary interpretation. The reversal of editorial opinion with regard to the two versions of *Doctor Faustus* has been accompanied by reversals in the interpretation of this play, and these parallel developments have in turn been part of a broader shift in the paradigms both of interpretation and of textual criticism which has taken place during the past two decades. An awareness of these connections can help one to see how intimately related textual decisions are to critical and ideological orientations—in the present edition as much as in previous ones.

Recent studies of *Doctor Faustus* and of the legend which it dramatizes point to the importance of a contextualized understanding of the play. I have therefore supplemented the play-text with four appendices. These are offered with the aim of bringing into focus the relations between Doctor Faustus and the ideological currents which it interrogates, as well as those by which the play was subsequently deformed. Appendix A contains those scenes in the 1616 text which deviate from the earlier version, and which, as part of a post-Marlovian re-visioning of the play, turn it back towards the moralistic, homiletic mode of Marlowe's principal source, a prose chapbook commonly referred to as the English Faustbook. Excerpts from that text, *The History of the damnable life and deserved death of Doctor John Faustus*, appear in Appendix B.

The writings of Henricus Cornelius Agrippa and Jean Calvin excerpted in Appendices C and D cannot properly be described as "sources" for Marlowe's play. However, they do form an important part of its context—in the root sense of *contextus*, as things inextricably woven into its texture. The names of Agrippa and of Faustus had already been linked by polemicists against Renaissance magic; and in expressing his desire to be "as cunning as Agrippa was" (I. i. 118), Marlowe's Faustus alerts us to the parodic echoes of

Agrippa's two best-known books, *Of the Vanity and Uncertainty of Arts and Sciences* and *Of Occult Philosophy*, which resonate through his first soliloquy. Calvin's theology, which in Marlowe's lifetime had become the ruling orthodoxy of the Elizabethan Anglican church, is present throughout the play in a more pervasive manner—as the limiting doctrine against which Faustus rebels and by which, paradoxically, he is constituted.

Spelling and punctuation have been modernized in the text of *Doctor Faustus* and in the four appendices (as well as in quotations from Renaissance texts in the notes); in the Introduction old spelling is retained except with regard to u/v and i/j. The name of Faustus's attendant spirit is given in this A-version text as "Mephastophilis," that being the form which occurs most frequently in the A text; I have used the spelling "Mephostophilis," which is the normal B-text form, only when discussing that text, as well as in Appendix A. In those parts of my introduction which discuss the distinctive features of the A and B texts I have identified quotations by means of their line numbers in W.W. Greg's parallel-text edition as well as their act, scene and line numbers in the present edition; elsewhere quotations are keyed to the present edition alone.

In editing the play-text I have had recourse to the single surviving copies of the 1604 and 1616 editions held by the Bodleian Library and the British Library respectively, and also (for the sake of convenience) to the Scolar Press facsimile of these unique copies. The excerpts from the *English Faustbook* [in Appendix B] have been edited from the unique copy of the 1592 edition in the British Library. In Appendix C, occasional errors in the Elizabethan translation of Agrippa's *De vanitate* have been corrected by reference to the first Latin edition of 1530; my translations of passages from *De occulta philosophia* were made from the first complete edition of 1533. And in modernizing the punctuation in Thomas Norton's translation of Calvin's *Institutes*, I have referred both to the McNeill-Battles translation of the 1559 Latin text and to Jean-Daniel Benoît's edition of the 1560 French text.

During the preparation of this edition I have benefited from the kind co-operation of librarians in the Bibliothèque Municipale de Dijon, the Warburg Institute, the British Library, the Bodleian

Library, the University of Sussex Library, and the Bibliothèque de l'Université Sainte-Anne. I am grateful also to the editors of the *Journal of English and Germanic Philology*, *The Dalhousie Review*, *University of Toronto Quarterly*, *Renaissance Quarterly*, and *Mosaic* for permission to draw upon articles of mine on *Doctor Faustus* and related subjects which appeared in those journals.

I owe special thanks to Tony Nuttall (whose presence and example in the early stages of my work were decisive), as well as to Don Beecher, Andreas Buss, Jonathan Dollimore, and James Quinlan; to the Social Sciences and Humanities Research Council of Canada, which in 1988-89 liberated me from my teaching duties with a generous research grant and research-time stipend; to the University of Sussex, which during that year gave me a most stimulating environment in which to work; and—most of all—to Janice Kulyk Keefer,

> *Ma douce Hélène, non, mais bien ma douce haleine:*
> *Seul je te choisi, seule aussi tu me plais.*

Introduction

Christopher Marlowe, 1564-1593

Born in 1564, in Canterbury, the son of a shoemaker, Christopher Marlowe was murdered twenty-nine years later in Deptford, near London. One way of understanding his life is as a sequence of interactions among three institutions: the church, the state, and the theater.

Nothing is known about Marlowe's early education. But at Christmas in 1578 he became a scholar at the King's School, which still occupies the old priory buildings in the precincts of Canterbury Cathedral; and in December 1580 he entered Corpus Christi College, Cambridge, where his way was paid by one of the scholarships established five years previously by the will of Archbishop Matthew Parker. These scholarships were normally of three years' duration, but could be renewed for a further three years by students who intended to take holy orders (Bakeless i. 49). Yet after a full six years as a Parker scholar—he received his B.A. early in 1584, and (in very unusual circumstances) his M.A. in July 1587—Marlowe moved into an association with the theater rather than the church, possibly taking with him some sense of what it meant to be, in Faustus's words, "a divine in show" (I. i. 3).

By the time of his departure from Cambridge Marlowe was already active as a poet: his translation of Ovid's *Amores* in *All Ovid's Elegies*, and his play *Dido Queen of Carthage*, are thought to have been written before 1587; and Robert Greene's remarks in the preface to *Perimedes the Blacksmith* (1588) about "daring God out of heaven with that Atheist *Tamburlan*," and about "such mad and scoffing poets, that have propheticall spirits as bred of *Merlins* race," indicate that both parts of *Tamburlaine* were performed before the end of 1587 (Leech 4). (Greene's pun on Marlowe's name becomes more obvious if one knows that "Marlin" and "Marlen" figure among the variant forms of this name in the Cambridge records.)

Marlowe's Ovid translation effectively "revived the Roman poet's radical commitment to sexual licence and freedom of speech" (Riggs 104). And as Patrick Cheney has proposed, this translation, together with Marlowe's early plays, announced a project of "counter-nationhood" that stands in deliberate opposition to Edmund Spenser's repetition of a Virgilian poetic *cursus* devoted to the celebration of established power (Cheney 49-135). Perhaps not surprisingly, the books which in June 1599 the Bishop of London and the Archbishop of Canterbury ordered to be publicly burned included the selection from Marlowe's translation of Ovid which had been printed together with Davies's epigrams (Gill 1987: 7).

But it was for reasons unconnected with his writings that in the spring of 1587 Cambridge University proposed to deny Marlowe his M.A. degree. The university authorities were prompted rather by rumors arising out of the fact that he had been supplementing his scholarship money by working as an undercover agent of the state in Sir Francis Walsingham's counter-espionage organization. During this period, as Marlowe has the French king Henry III say in *The Massacre at Paris* (c. 1592-93), "a sort of English priests" were drawn "to the seminary at Rheims / To hatch forth treason 'gainst their natural Queen" (xxi, 101-3). The reference is to English converts to Catholicism, many of them graduates of Oxford or Cambridge, who were trained at the English College at Rheims to return to England as missionaries—and who, since the papacy was effectively at war with Queen Elizabeth, were regarded by her government as traitors. One of Marlowe's contemporaries at the King's School, "a most terrible puritan" who had been placed in charge of Roman Catholic prisoners in the Tower of London and was promptly converted by one of them, followed this path (Urry 49). The Cambridge authorities must have suspected Marlowe of similar intentions, for on 29 June 1587, Her Majesty's Privy Council, no less, intervened on his behalf, insisting "that he should be furthered in the degree he was to take this next Commencement: Because it was not her majestie's pleasure that anie one emploied as he had been in matters touching the benefitt of his Countrie should be defamed by those that are ignorant in th'affaires he went about" (Bakeless i. 77).

What these matters were remains uncertain. During some of the absences attested to by the Buttery Book of Corpus Christi College, Marlowe may have carried secret dispatches to and from English diplomats in the Low Countries (Bakeless i. 71-75, 83-84).

The rumors of his intended defection, however, suggest that he was assigned the task of infiltrating recusant groups and spying on them. Continued employment of one or both kinds would explain his presence at Flushing on the Isle of Walcheren in January 1592, where he was denounced by one Richard Baines, a Cambridge M.A. who appears to have been Marlowe's precursor as a spy and infiltrator: Baines had defected to Rheims in 1578, and was ordained as a Roman Catholic priest in 1581, but in the following year was arrested as a traitor on the orders of Dr. William Allen, the president of the English College, and was only released in 1583 after making a lurid confession of penitence for his impiety and treachery. Baines and Marlowe accused one another of counterfeiting money and of intending to go over to the Spaniards or to Rome; Marlowe was arrested by Sir Robert Sidney, the governor of Flushing, and sent back to England, where the accusation of counterfeiting was dismissed.

The dating of Marlowe's plays is largely a matter for conjecture. But by the time of his first denunciation by Richard Baines, he was already famous for his *Tamburlaine* plays, and in addition to the early *Dido Queen of Carthage* had also probably written *Doctor Faustus, Edward II,* and *The Jew of Malta*.[1] During the last year of his life Marlowe wrote *The Massacre at Paris,* and also, no doubt because an outbreak of plague—or of social disorder represented by the authorities as plague (see Freedman)—had resulted in the closing of the theaters, that delicious poem *Hero and Leander.*

Marlowe's friends and acquaintances were not predominantly of the Baines type: they included Thomas Watson, who was a spy as well as a poet, but also the poets Matthew Roydon and Thomas Kyd and the mathematician Thomas Harriot; moreover, at the time of his arrest in Flushing, Marlowe claimed familiarity with the Earl of Northumberland and with Lord Strange, patron

---

1 *The Jew of Malta* may have provided Richard Baines with one reason for disliking Marlowe. Dr. Allen had in 1583 printed the confession in which Baines acknowledged having contemplated wiping out the entire religious community of the English College at Rheims by poisoning its water supply (Kuriyama 1988a: 346-47, Nicholl 123-24, 127-29). The scenes in which Marlowe's Jew effortlessly commits an analogous crime, poisoning all the occupants of a nunnery (III. iv. vi), may well have reminded contemporaries of Baines's confession and exposed him to mockery.

of the company which staged his plays. He was also a member of Sir Walter Ralegh's circle, and enjoyed the patronage of Thomas Walsingham, a nephew of Queen Elizabeth's Principal Secretary, Sir Francis Walsingham (Urry 70-73).[1]

Harriot, Ralegh and Northumberland were all suspected of holding heterodox opinions; Marlowe, with none of their discretion, trumpeted his abroad. As David Riggs has indicated, the government of Elizabeth I felt itself in 1592-93 to be facing converging threats from the Catholic powers and their English agents, from religious radicals who rejected royal and episcopal control over the Anglican church, and from "atheists" or skeptics who it was feared might undermine loyalty to the established order (see Riggs 315-37). The result was a surge of repression well beyond the violent norm of the period.

As a student at Cambridge, Marlowe had undergone a prolonged immersion in the hard paradoxes of Calvinism, many of which have to do with the inscrutable hidden will of a God whose basic motive, as disclosed by his Genevan prophet, is not unlike that of the princes studied by Machiavelli: the promulgation of his own glory. Marlowe had probably also read Machiavelli; more importantly, he had witnessed his precepts in action and knew that "such as love [him] guard [him] from their tongues" (*Jew of Malta*, Prologue 6). While yet a student he had been inducted, in the service of his monarch and the defence of true religion, into a murky world of deceit, betrayal and role-playing, where the pretence of converting to the enemy's beliefs may have taught him how easily interchangeable they were with the ones he was being paid to defend. The name of Lightborne in *Edward II*, and his dissembling expressions of concern (reminiscent, perhaps, of the handling of the Babington conspirators by Marlowe's acquaintance Robert Poley),[2] might be taken to suggest that the poet

---

1   For a detailed account of the circles of patronage, male friendship and acquaintanceship with which Marlowe was associated, see Kuriyama 2002: 85-95.

2   Anthony Babington was one of a group of Catholic gentry who plotted in 1586 to overthrow Elizabeth and place Mary Queen of Scots on the throne. Poley and other agents of Sir Francis Walsingham penetrated and exposed the plot, which because of Mary's complicity provided the pretext for her execution in February 1587 (see Riggs 143-55).

recognized the demonic character of those whose double role was to incite subversion and to stand as its accuser.

Marlowe's subversive opinions were thus arguably conditioned by what he had witnessed as an agent of the state in its war against political and religious subversion. In this light it seems significant that one Richard Cholmeley, who had been "imployed by some of her Majesties prevy Counsaile for the apprehension of Papistes, and other daungerous men," professed to have been converted by Marlowe to atheism: Cholmeley reportedly spoke "all evill of the Counsell; saying that they are all Athiestes and Machiavillians" (Boas 1940: 253-54, Nicholl 268-81).

As this example may suggest, the notion of atheism was strongly marked in this period by asymmetries of power. "Atheism"—an attribute of others, almost never of oneself—was commonly deduced as a logical consequence of disaffection from the state church, or of a critical awareness of the manner in which religion served, in Marlowe's supposed words, "to keep men in awe" (Maclure 37). Richard Cholmeley's accusation is thus paradoxical, for whatever Privy Councillors may have thought or said in private, or whatever one might deduce from their actions, they had a vested interest in suppressing any public demystification of religious authority. Marlowe, as an oppositional voice, was open to the charge of being an "atheist"; they could not be, so long as they continued to exercise power.

Given that the theatricality of power was a commonplace of the period, it seems peculiarly appropriate that Marlowe's sardonic representations and interrogations of power took theatrical form. Calvin, whose theology largely shaped that of the Anglican church, and who labored to clear from any imputation of evil a God whose will determines every act of "the divel & al the rout of the wicked" (Calvin 1587: fol. 66; I. xvii. 11), also described the world as a theater in which we are set as spectators of the works of God (I. vi. 2). A related sense of the theatricality of sovereign power appears in Elizabeth's statement to the House of Commons that "we Princes [...] are set on stages"; and there is a momentary awareness of the ethical cost of this display in the remark of her spymaster Sir Francis Walsingham: "I hold them happiest in this government that may be rather lookers-on than actors" (Shepherd xvii). Marlowe, who was employed rather in the cellarage or the tiring-house than on the stage of Elizabethan politics, was able to view at close range and from an unaccustomed angle the processes of political and religious legitimation implied by these theatrical metaphors. And when it came to writing for an actual stage, he developed a whole range of rhetorical and dramatic effects which interrupt, parody or mock the theatrics of legitimation.

In his conversation, "in table talk or otherwise" (Maclure 35), Marlowe seems to have striven more openly against "known truth"—or against what one might now call the hegemonic ideologies of the day. As a direct consequence of his indiscretions, he was made, after his violent death, into a prominent exhibit in another kind of theater: the puritan clergyman Thomas Beard, author-translator of a miscellany of moral exempla entitled *The Theatre of Gods Judgements* (1597), wrote of this "Poet of scurrilitie" that "hee even cursed and blasphemed to his last gaspe, and togither with his breath an oath flew out of his mouth" (Maclure 41-42).

On 12 May, Thomas Kyd was arrested and imprisoned on suspicion of involvement in posting "divers lewd and mutinous libels" which sought to stir up xenophobic violence against Protestant immigrants from Holland and France (Nicholl 42-43, Riggs 318-19); under torture, he appears to have denounced Marlowe as an atheist and named him as the owner of heretical papers found in his chambers (though Kyd's written statements to this effect were composed after Marlowe's death). On 18 May, the Privy Council issued a warrant for Marlowe's arrest, and two days later, treating him with what may seem surprising mildness, ordered him "to give his daily attendaunce on their Lordships untill he shalbe lycensed to the contrary" (Boas 1940: 242-44). Richard Baines's very detailed denunciation of Marlowe's "Damnable Judgement of Religion, and scorn of God's word" appears to have been delivered to the Privy Council around 27 May (Riggs 326)

Marlowe spent the last day of his life, 30 May 1593, in Deptford, on the bank of the Thames less than a mile from the royal palace at Greenwich, in the company of three very shadowy figures. One of them, Robert Poley, a confidential messenger, informer and double agent, has been described as "the very genius of the Elizabethan underworld," a man whose life exudes "an evil odour of fraud, crime and double dealing" (Urry 68); his major accomplishment had been the entrapment and betrayal of the Babington conspirators in 1586 (Bakeless i. 171-80). Another, Nicholas Skeres, appears to have moved from a life of theft and burglary into the lower reaches of the secret service, where he was involved in the Babington plot and subsequently used as a messenger by Sir Francis Walsingham (Bakeless i. 180-82; Urry 87-88). Although there is no evidence that the third, Ingram Frizer, was involved in espionage, he was in the employ of Thomas Walsingham, himself a secret agent as well as Marlowe's patron.

The four men shared most of a day and two meals together in a house in Deptford which was until quite recently thought to have been a tavern. But as Richard Wilson has demonstrated, this house and its associations add an important further twist to the story. The house's owner, Eleanor Bull, was no Mistress Quickly: "the supposed ale-wife or bawdy-house keeper of Deptford dockside came of an ancient armorial family with members close about the queen" (Urry 86); and her husband Richard, who had died in 1590, was bailiff of the Clerk of the Greencloth, "the local official responsible for receipt of goods into the royal household" (Wilson 123). Not far from Richard Bull's offices on Deptford Strand stood the warehouse of the Muscovy Company, the first English venture into the form of the joint-stock corporation; from 1576 to 1599 the Company's London agent, who controlled all of its import-export dealings, "was Anthony Marlowe, long identified as a Crayford relative of Christopher Marlowe, and a cause, we may infer, of the dramatist's fatal connection with the Deptford docks" (Wilson 122).

The Muscovy Company, described by Wilson as "in reality a cartel of Kent families" (123), was the engine of a huge semi-clandestine arms trade in which England, hoping by this means to outflank Turkish control of the Silk Road trade-route to the far East, supplied the governments of Ivan the Terrible and his successors with the high-quality artillery and explosives that made possible the expansion of the Muscovite empire into central

Asia—and received in return the Russian cordage and cable with which the fleet that defeated the Spanish Armada was rigged (120-22, 129-31). Christopher Marlowe's *Tamburlaine* plays resonate powerfully with the Company's involvement in the struggle for access to and control of Asian trade routes and commodities that nineteenth-century British imperialists called "the great game." So close, indeed, are the parallels between Ivan and Tamburlaine that Wilson can plausibly call Marlowe's stage epic "a prospectus for London's first joint-stock enterprise," reflecting, by implication, the Muscovy Company's geopolitics (Wilson 120).

Wilson has no theory as to the precise nature of the connections he suspects between the workings of the Muscovy Company and the bloody business that transpired in Eleanor Bull's house. But he does note that in 1587, the year that *Tamburlaine the Great* was first staged, Anthony Marlowe and Richard Bull were complicit, along with other insiders, in "a gigantic fraud devised by the Company governor, George Barne, a Woolwich broker, with his brother-in-law, the spymaster, Francis Walsingham" (122).

Christopher Marlowe was thus killed at the focal point of the Elizabethan armaments trade, after a day spent in the company of agents of Walsingham's secret service, in a setting whose recent history included England's inaugural insider-trading scandal. His family connections, his employment, and his writings link him with all three of these. But by the official story at least, the struggle which resulted in Marlowe's death was provoked by a falling-out over a very minor transaction indeed.

According to the testimony accepted by the coroner's inquest, Marlowe quarreled with Ingram Frizer over "le recknynge" for the eight meals the men had consumed; attacking him from behind, he was killed by Frizer in self-defence (Bakeless i. 155-56). Frizer was pardoned for the killing on 28 June; within a matter of days, he and Nicholas Skeres set about cheating a witless young country gentleman out of thirty pounds in a classic Elizabethan loan-and-commodity fraud. The nature of the commodity, "a certayne nomber of gunnes or greate Iron peeces," suggests that they were backed in this scheme by someone connected to the Muscovy Company—and indeed, when Frizer and Skeres went on to fleece their victim of a further two hundred pounds, they acted with the open connivance of Frizer's master Thomas Walsingham (Bakeless i. 167-68).

Robert Poley, in the mean time, continued to attend to the Queen's business. According to a warrant of payment signed on 12 June by the Queen's Vicechamberlain, he had left the royal court at Croydon on 8 May, carrying "lettres in poste for her Majesties speciall and secret afaires [...] to the towne of the Hage in Hollande," and reported back to the royal palace of Nonesuch "with lettres of aunswere" on 8 June. This warrant very conveniently specifies that Poley had been "in her majesties service all the aforesaid tyme" (Boas 1940: 267)—a formula which would silence any awkward questions about his detour in Deptford on the return journey.

The eagerness with which Thomas Kyd's interrogators pursued his statements about Marlowe's blasphemies is a reminder that the two poets were arrested at the height of Archbishop Whitgift's violent campaign against religious dissidence. Two leading nonconformists, John Greenwood (whom Marlowe had known at Cambridge) and Henry Barrow, had been hanged in April 1593 (Urry 81). John Penry, another Cambridge contemporary who shared their views and who was suspected of having helped to produce the Marprelate tracts, was executed on 29 May, the day before Marlowe's death, "at St. Thomas a'Watering, about two and a half miles from the house in Deptford where Marlowe was killed" (Kuriyama 2002: 122). But Penry would have been as horrified as his persecutors by the ribald blasphemies attributed to Marlowe by Thomas Kyd, and by Richard Baines. Kyd, reflecting back to 1591 or earlier, wrote that "it was his custom when I knewe him first & as I hear saie he contynewd it in table talk or otherwise to jest at the devine scriptures gybe at praiers, & strive in argument to frustrate & confute what hath byn spoke or wrytt by prophets & such holie men." The first instance Kyd offers of Marlowe's blasphemies, though muted in transmission by his own fear, is also the boldest: "He wold report St John to be our saviour Christes Alexis I cover it with reverence and trembling that is that Christ did love him with an extraordinary love" (Maclure

35).[1] Baines, who was not himself under suspicion, writes more directly and more coarsely:

> He affirmeth that Moyses was but a jugler & that one Heriots [Harriot] being Sir W Raleighs man Can do more then he. [....]
>
> That the first beginning of Religioun was only to keep men in awe. [....]
>
> That Christ was a bastard and his mother dishonest.
>
> That he was the sonne of a Carpenter, and that if the Jewes among whome he was borne did Crucify him theie best knew him and whence he Came. [....]
>
> That if he were put to write a new Religion, he would undertake both a more Exellent and Admirable methode and that all the new testament is filthily written.
>
> That the woman of Samaria & her sister were whores & that Christ knew them dishonestly.
>
> That St John the Evangelist was bedfellow to Christ and leaned alwaies in his bosom, that he used him as the sinners of Sodoma.
>
> That all they that love not Tobacco & Boies were fooles. [....] (Maclure 37)

A fog of uncertainties remains. The authorities of church and state had good reason to wish Marlowe silenced. He was evidently loathed by Richard Baines, and his connections with Walsingham's spy network, or possibly with large or small-scale frauds run by the Walsinghams and by the Muscovy Company, may in other ways have rebounded upon him. Alternatively—or in some connected way—Marlowe may have been a victim, as Charles Nicholl argued, of factional power struggles within the Elizabethan court. Although Nicholl's theory that the Earl of Essex and his followers were the responsible agents has been strongly challenged, the basic intuition that Marlowe's death was most probably a politically motivated murder seems plausible,

---

1 Alexis is the boy loved by the shepherd Corydon in Virgil's Second Eclogue, a poem which was an important exemplar for early modern expressions of homoeroticism; see Bray 63-65 and Smith 80-84, 89-97.

even if the agencies behind the deed, and their precise reasons for arranging it, remain obscure.

The extent to which the testimony of Marlowe's enemies and accusers should be allowed to affect interpretations of his writings is bound to remain a matter for debate. But even if we set their words aside, it can fairly be said that he stands out among Elizabethan poets as one who, in giving voice to the discursive extremes of his era, never appears to suggest with any conviction the possibility of a center in which these might meet and be reconciled. The comparative scarcity in his plays of the analogies to natural processes favored by other Elizabethan writers, and his preference for imagery drawn from the elemental, the astronomical, or the spiritual and daemonic levels of the cosmos (rather than from the level of organic nature, where his contemporaries found a reservoir of social and behavioral norms): these are signs of "extremism"—which is also to say of a divorce from the commonplaces of natural morality and natural law. Marlowe's characters thus move through a polarized, decentered world of warring elements, glittering artifacts, and fetichized objects of desire, "heaven and earth the bounds of [their] delight" (*Dido*, I. i. 32). In the lapidary ironies of *Hero and Leander* Marlowe is the most exaggeratedly civilized poet of the age—and, in the savageries of *Tamburlaine*, its most superbly barbaric one. And just as the "feral otherness" (Wilson 17) of his individual texts denies their audiences or readers the security of a moral center or of a fixed interpretive stance, so also Marlowe's *oeuvre* as a whole resists any attempt to compose at its heart the image of a consistent creative intelligence—unless it be that of the sexual outlaw and blasphemer who stares insolently at us from the files of the Elizabethan thought police.

The Historical Dr. Faustus, c.1466–c.1537

Given the obviously legendary or mythic quality both of Marlowe's play and of its principal source, the prose *Historie of the damnable life, and deserved death of Doctor John Faustus*, the fact that there was a historical Doctor Faustus may come as a surprise. Like

Christopher Marlowe, this man was a trangressor both of sexual and of ideological codes.

Until quite recently, research into the traces of this historical figure was bedeviled by several puzzling facts. Sixteenth-century accounts give the man two different names, Georgius and Johannes, leading some scholars to suppose that there might have been two distinct magicians named Faust (a common German surname) or Faustus. Faustus appears to have claimed the academic titles of Magister, or of Doctor—but while a Magister Georgius Faustus was practising various arts of divination in Gelnhausen, Würzburg, and Kreuznach in 1506 and 1507 (Palmer and More 84-86), the records of German universities mention only a single Johannes Faust or Fust who entered Heidelberg in December 1505, and received a bachelor's degree in January 1509 (Palmer and More 86-87).

However, as Frank Baron showed in *Doctor Faustus from History to Legend* (1978), the early accounts of Faustus divide under critical analysis into two groups: those written between 1507 and the mid 1530s as immediate responses to his activities, and those composed during the half-century between his death (c. 1537) and the publication in 1587 of the *German Faustbook*. In the former texts, which have documentary value, his first name, when it is mentioned, is Georgius; in the latter, which show unmistakable marks of legend-formation, the name has become Johannes. Baron also sorted out the puzzle of the university records: in brief, there are no records of the magician Faustus for the very good reason that that was not his name—at least until some time after his graduation.

In January 1483 a young man from the nearby village of Helmstadt enrolled at the University of Heidelberg in the nominalist *via moderna*[1] of the arts faculty; his name appears variously

---

1 The arts faculties in northern European universities in the fifteenth century were commonly divided between exponents of the *via antiqua*, a philosophy of metaphysical realism developed in the thirteenth century by Albertus Magnus and Thomas Aquinas and their successor Duns Scotus, who thought of universal metaphysical categories and the relationships among them as existing independently of our experience or knowledge of them; and exponents of the *via moderna*, a critical and sometimes corrosively sceptical nominalism, developed in the fourteenth century by William of Ockham, Nicholas of Autrecourt and Jean Buridan.

in the university records as Georgius Helmstetter, Georio de Helmstadt, or some variant thereof. He received his bachelor's degree within less than the prescribed minimum of a year and a half of study, but took longer than most students to earn the master's degree, which he was granted only in 1487—having been held back, most probably, by a requirement that a *magister artium* be at least twenty or twenty-one years old. The fact that he was one of only two students in a class of sixty-seven who gave no indication of a family name or patronymic suggests that he may, like Erasmus, have been illegitimate. If, as the university statutes required, he taught for two years in the faculty of arts as a Master of Arts, he would have remained at Heidelberg until at least the summer of 1489 (Baron 1978: 16-18).

In addition to the scholastic learning of the nominalist *via moderna* to which he was exposed in his formal course of studies, Georgius Helmstetter would also have encountered at Heidelberg both the speculative (which is to say occultist) and the philological sides of the new humanist learning. During the 1480s the city was home to a number of distinguished humanists, who tended to ally themselves with the exponents of the *via moderna*. According to Heiko Oberman, one consequence of the modernists' rejection of the universal terms deployed by Aquinas and the other theologians of the *via antiqua* was "a craving to experience and apprehend the world free from the tutelage of faith"—a craving, however, which soon "proved irreconcilable with the platonically inspired humanist propensity for a *sancta philosophia*" (Oberman 38). In the interim, though, there seems to have been a period in the late fifteenth century during which young German scholars, perhaps especially those trained in the *via moderna*, were able to find a substitute for the theological speculations challenged by nominalism in that syncretic compendium of Hermetic theosophy, Neoplatonic theurgy and Christian Cabala which interested speculative humanists.[1]

An exchange of letters whose significance was first recognized by Frank Baron makes it clear that this Heidelberg graduate

---

[1]   Important studies of this then-emergent tradition include those of Garin, Walker 1972 and 1975, Yates 1964 and 1979, Couliano, Tomlinson, and Grafton.

practised some at least of the arts of divination which commonly interested speculative humanists. In October 1534, Dr. Petrus Seuter, a lawyer living in the city of Kempten, enclosed two documents in a letter he sent to his friend Nicolaus Ellenbog, a monk with humanist interests in the monastery of Ottobeuren. One of these, an academic oration delivered by a Heidelberg professor to the Emperor Maximilian (who reigned from April, 1487 to January, 1519), may date from the period of Seuter's own studies at Heidelberg, which began in March, 1490. The other, a horoscope prepared for Seuter by "magister Georgius Helmstetter" according to the judgment of the astrological, physiognomic and chiromantic art (Baron 1989: 298), may also date from the same period: if Helmstetter remained at Heidelberg beyond the statutory two years after his graduation, he could have been one of Seuter's teachers in the Faculty of Arts.

Since a doctoral degree was obtainable only in the disciplines of law, medicine, and theology, Georgius Helmstetter's proper academic title was the one used by Seuter: *magister*. But by the convention of the time he would have been able, outside academic circles, to call himself Doctor (Baron 1982: 17). It seems likely that he did so—and that this was the same man whose public career as a diviner and magician, beginning in the early years of the sixteenth century, made the name of Doctor Faustus notorious throughout Germany.

In August 1507, the humanist Johannes Trithemius, himself a graduate of Heidelberg, and an occult philosopher and magician as well as a Benedictine abbot, wrote a long letter to his friend Johannes Virdung von Hassfurt, an astrologer at Heidelberg who had an active interest in magic and divination. In this letter Trithemius described the activities over the preceding year of a man who announced himself in what was probably a printed sheet of self-advertisement as "Magister Georgius Sabellicus, the younger Faustus, chief of necromancers, astrologer, the second magus, palmist, diviner by earth and fire, second in the art of divination by water" (Baron 1978: 96; cf. Tille 2, Palmer and More 84). "Sabellicus" is probably a humanist cognomen incorporating a learned allusion to Numa Pompilius, the second king of Rome, whose origins were among the Sabines or Sabellici, and who as the supposed inventor of divination by water could be regarded as a pagan prophet (Baron 1978: 32). "Faustus" seems also to be a humanist cognomen, chosen for its meaning ("auspicious"), and as alluding to one or more of the earlier bearers of the name—most probably the Manichaean bishop with whom St. Augustine debated, or the Faustus who in a widely-read patristic text, the pseudo-Clementine *Recognitions*, is briefly a disciple of the Gnostic heresiarch and magician Simon Magus (Wentersdorf; Richardson). "The second magus" may be a bow in the direction of Zoroaster, whom Renaissance genealogies of wisdom commonly list as the first inventor of magic. But Faustus is not being modest: this admission of secondariness puts him ahead of Hermes or Mercurius Trismegistus, the usual number two in accounts of the magical *prisca theologia* or "ancient theology" (see Walker 1975: 23, 93, and Yates 1964: 15, 131). Moreover, "magus secundus," in conjunction with claims to astrological competence and primacy in necromancy, might reinforce the suggestion of an affiliation with Simon Magus—who in the *Recognitions* is denounced as a necromancer, and is closely associated with belief in astrology (*Recognitions* II. 13-15, IX. 12 ff., X. 7 ff.).

The man, as Trithemius describes him, was clearly transgressive: a braggart, a blasphemer, and a pederast. He apparently boasted that if the writings and doctrines of Plato and Aristotle were wholly lost and forgotten, he "would be able to restore them all with increased beauty," just as the prophet Ezra had restored the lost books of the Law (cf. 2 *Esdras* 14: 20-26). He claimed "that the miracles of Christ the Saviour were not so wonderful, that he himself could do all the things that Christ had done, as often and whenever he wished." And when in 1507 Faustus was appointed schoolmaster in Kreuznach, he promptly indulged "in the most abominable kind of fornication with the boys," and fled to escape punishment (Baron 1978: 96-97; Tille 1-3; Palmer and More 83-86).

In 1513 another distinguished humanist, Conrad Mutianus Rufus, wrote of the recent arrival in Erfurt of a chiromancer named "Georgius Faustus, Helmitheus Hedebergensis, merus ostentator et fatuus"—"a mere braggart and fool," who babbled at an inn and was marvelled at by the ignorant. But his claims, "like those of all diviners, are idle, and such physiognomy has no more weight than a water spider" (Palmer and More 87-88).[1]

Later notices support the identification of the Heidelberg graduate Georgius of Helmstadt with the magician Doctor Faustus. In July 1528 Kilian Leib, prior of Rebdorf (near Eichstätt) in Bavaria, recorded that on the fifth of June "Georgius faustus helmstetensis" had said "that when the sun and Jupiter are in the same constellation prophets are born (presumably such as he)"; and on June 17 of the same year, a soothsayer who called himself "Dr. Jörg Faustus von Heidelberg" was banished by the council of the nearby city of Ingolstadt, and being invited "to spend his penny elsewhere, ... he pledged himself not to take vengeance on or make fools of the authorities for this order" (Palmer and More 89-90).

Georgius Faustus's expulsion from Ingolstadt may suggest that he enjoyed a somewhat dubious reputation. However, transgressions and indiscretions of the kind reported by Trithemius, Mutianus and Leib did not prevent him from being hired in February 1520 to cast the horoscope of Georg Schenk von Limburg, the Prince-Bishop of Bamberg (Palmer and More 88-89), or from being consulted in 1536 by a close associate of Erasmus's to predict the fortunes of a colonizing expedition to Venezuela (Palmer and More 92, 95-96, Baron 1978: 48-66). One may wonder whether Faustus guessed that Georg Schenk had little more than two years to live (he died in May 1522, aged fifty-two), or whether he would have been indiscreet enough to share such a guess. But he did foretell disaster for the Venezuela expedition—a prognostication borne out by events, much to the discomfiture of the Nuremberg humanist Joachim Camerarius, who had prophesied "an entirely propitious outcome" (Baron 1978: 59).

The only other records of Faustus's activities are negative in tone. In May 1532 the city council of Nuremberg refused a safe-conduct

---

1 This odd title "Helmitheus Hedebergensis" may be a mistranscription of "Hemitheus Hedelbergensis" ("the demi-god of Heidelberg"), or possibly of "Helmsteten[sis] Hedelbergensis" ("from Helmstadt near Heidelberg"). But "Helmitheus" appears rather to be a literary allusion to a patristic text that we have already seen Faustus may have known: in the pseudo-Clementine *Recognitions*, as first printed in 1504, a statement to the effect that Pyrrha and Erymetheus were the parents of Helen and Prometheus is garbled through scribal error into the claim that Pyrrha and Prometheus were the parents of "Helmitheus" (Richardson 141-42).

to "Doctor Faustus, the great sodomite and necromancer" (Palmer and More 90). And in 1539, not long after his death, a contemporary wrote that "The number of those who complained to me that they were cheated by him was very great.... his deeds, as I hear, were very petty and fraudulent" (Palmer and More 94-95).

The Legend of Faustus

Conspicuously absent from the accounts of Georgius Faustus written during his lifetime is any suggestion that he had a pact with the devil, an attendant spirit, powers of flight, the ability to devour a cartload of hay, detachable legs, or an affair with Helen of Troy. Yet some fifty years after his death a legend which included all of these features, and which in addition recounted in lurid detail the lamentations and terrors of his final hours, was in print as the *Historia von D. Johann Fausten* (1587). This *German Faustbook* is evidently Lutheran in inspiration: its demonology, some of its episodes and many of its turns of phrase are lifted from Martin Luther's writings and table-talk (Baron 1978: 70-82; 1982: 67-74).

The notoriety of Georgius Faustus made him an apt candidate for demonization by the orthodox. The first cue for this development was given in 1537 by Martin Luther himself. Prompted, it may be, by news of Faustus's death, or possibly by the publication in the previous year of a collection of Johannes Trithemius's letters which included his 1507 account of Faustus, a conversation at Luther's dinner table on the subject of scoffers (*ludificatores*) and the magic art turned to "Faustus, who called the devil his brother-in-law" (Palmer and More 93; *WATr* no. 3601)—and who must therefore, it is implied, have cohabited with a succubus demon. Luther made this the occasion for a string of carnivalesque anecdotes—about a sorcerer who devoured a peasant, together with his horse and wagon, a monk who offered another peasant a penny for all the hay he could eat and then consumed half a wagon-load before being beaten off, and a man who frightened away his Jewish creditor by making it seem he had pulled off the debtor's leg (*WATr* no. 3601). These stories reappear in the *Historia* as exploits of Faustus himself; so also does Luther's tale of a magician (identified in one report of the conversation as the abbot Trithemius) who entertained the Emperor Maximilian by having demons take on the forms of Alexander the Great and other monarchs (*WATr* no. 4450).

Luther's belief that all magicians have a pact with the devil was confirmed for him in 1537 by a Wittenberg student who confessed to have foresworn his faith in Christ and promised himself to "another master" (*WATr* no. 3618A-B, 3739). Fifteen years later, recounting this same incident, Philipp Melanchthon added the detail of a written pact with the devil; and in 1585 Augustin Lercheimer (a pen name for Hermann Witekind, who had studied under Melanchthon) combined this story in his *Christian Synopsis of Magic* (an important source for the 1587 *Historia*) with the first published reference to Faustus's demonic pact (Baron 1985: 535-36).

Luther may also have contributed more directly to the launching of the legend through the stories he helped to spread when his former Wittenberg colleague and later radical opponent, Andreas Bodenstein von Karlstadt, died in Basel on Christmas Eve, 1541. In early 1542, Luther and his correspondents in Basel and elsewhere claimed successively that Karlstadt had left behind him a noisome spirit, and that his death had been caused, not by the plague—Karlstadt was himself a plague to God's church—but by his terror when the devil materialized to carry him off (*WABr* ix. 621-22, x. 12-14, 24-30, 49). Johannes Gast, a Protestant clergyman of Basel, appropriated these same motifs of a noisome spirit and of a death at the devil's hands as organizing features of the first clearly legendary account of Doctor Faustus, which he published in his *Tomus secundus convivalium sermonum* (Basel, 1548). Paolo Giovio had claimed in his *Elogia doctorum virorum* (1546) that the humanist and occult philosopher Henricus Cornelius Agrippa had a black dog who was actually a devil.[1] Not to be outdone, Gast declared that the necromancer Faustus's dog, and his horse as well, were both devils. And Faustus did not simply die in despair: "he was strangled by the devil and his body on its bier kept turning face downward even though it was five times turned on its back. God preserve us lest we become slaves of the devil" (Palmer and More 98).

---

1 See Nauert 327. James Sanford, who in 1569 translated Agrippa's *De vanitate* into English, repeats the story in his preface (Agrippa 1974: 4).

Further elaborations of the legend were produced by a succession of Lutheran writers, among whom the most influential was Philipp Melanchthon. His references to Faustus in lectures delivered at Wittenberg during the 1550s are of particular interest for what they suggest about the legend's antecedents and ideological motivation. Linking Faustus with the first-century magician and heresiarch Simon Magus (both attempted to fly up to heaven), he reminds his auditors that in the apocryphal *Acts of the Apostles Peter and Paul* Simon is represented as the apostles' great opponent (Palmer and More 99). He makes a point of claiming that he himself knew "Ioannes" Faustus, whose birthplace he identifies as Kundling (now Knittlingen—a village some half-hour's walk from Melanchthon's home town of Bretten); and he states that Faustus studied magic in Cracow.[1] He gives a circumstantial account of Faustus's death at the devil's hands in a village in the Duchy of Württemberg, and as though to confirm that the man was a servant of Satan, he adds that during his life he "had with him a dog which was a devil, just as that scoundrel who wrote *De vanitate artium*"—the humanist Henricus Cornelius Agrippa—"likewise had a dog that ran about with him and was a devil." After telling how Faustus twice escaped arrest, presumably by demonic means, Melanchthon concludes by refuting the boast of this same "Faustus magus, a most filthy beast and a sewer of many devils," that all of the Emperor Charles V's victories in Italy had been won by his magic (Palmer and More 102-03).

Like several of his first-century contemporaries, Simon Magus, the magician and Gnostic heresiarch to whom Melanchthon likened Faustus, professed to be God. Simon makes a cameo appearance in the canonical *Acts of the Apostles*: acclaimed by his followers as "the power of God that is called great" (*Acts* 8: 10), this Samaritan magician is converted by the apostle Philip, and then, after seeking to buy the power of the Holy Spirit, cursed

---

1   This detail is suggestive. In his youth Melanchthon was acquainted with a Johannes who was deeply interested in magic, who practised physiognomic and astrological divination, who had studied at Cracow, and who was associated both with Heidelberg and also with Georgius Faustus. The man in question was Johannes Virdung von Hassfurt, the recipient of Trithemius's 1507 letter about Faustus; he taught at Heidelberg and was court astrologer to the Elector Palatine—and had also cast the young Melanchthon's horoscope.

by the apostle Peter (*Acts* 8: 15-24). But he appears to have been a more substantial figure than the polemical narrative in *Acts* would suggest. The doctrines of Simon and the sect he founded are refuted at length by patristic writers, including Hippolytus and Irenaeus—according to whom this apostate, antichrist and agent of the devil gave visible form to his heresies by cohabiting with a woman whom his followers knew variously as Helena, Minerva, or Luna. Appropriating a motif from the apocryphal Wisdom literature, which he conflated with the Greek myth of the birth of Athena, goddess of wisdom, from the head of Zeus, Simon described this woman as his own divine First Thought. The evil archons whom she had absent-mindedly engendered, and who then created the world, imprisoned her within it in a series of human forms, among them that of Helen of Troy; but Simon, the originary God, had now descended to save her and all who believed in him (Irenaeus I. 23).

The reappearance of Helen in the *German Faustbook* of 1587 is one sign of the Faustus legend's affiliation to the patristic accounts of Simon. But Simon Magus and "Faustus magus" (as Melanchthon called him) have more in common than this. Both could be described (to borrow a phrase from Hart Crane's poem "For the Marriage of Faustus and Helen") as "bent axle[s] of devotion" (Crane 29)—in the sense that their transgressions against orthodoxy were recuperated by the legends which formed around them in such a way as to legitimize that orthodoxy.

The role of Simon Magus in the legitimation of orthodoxy is evident in the pseudo-Clementine *Recognitions*, where St. Peter, who defeats Simon Magus in a series of public debates, explains human history in terms of a sequence of pairs appointed by God: the first of each pair to manifest himself is an emissary of evil, the second an emissary of the true prophecy (III. 59). Thus Cain was followed by Abel, Esau by Jacob, Pharaoh's magicians by Moses, "the tempter" by the Son of Man, and Simon Magus by Peter himself (III. 61).

During the 1530s, Martin Luther developed a view of his own function which is clearly indebted to this pseudo-Clementine master-narrative. In his *Annotations on Matthew* (1538), Luther speaks of Satan's perpetual invention of new calumnies, and (alluding to his own radical opponents), of those "cunning and pestilential men" among his contemporaries who have served Satan in this respect, but who are confuted by the Holy Spirit. He promptly identifies the same pattern in the age of Jesus and the apostles: "Thus Christ always conquered the cleverest contrivances of the Pharisees, Peter those of his magician Simon, and Paul those of his Pseudoapostles" (WA xxxviii, 501).

Melanchthon's construction of a parallel between "Faustus magus" and Simon Magus, who by his very presence testified to the apostolic mission of St. Peter and St. Paul, may thus lead one to suspect that he is hinting, with all due modesty, at a similar guarantee through demonic opposition of his own and Luther's quasi-apostolic role. Such a suspicion is strengthened by Melanchthon's claim to have known Faustus, not just by reputation but in person—and also by a story about an encounter between them which appeared in Augustin Lercheimer's Christian Synopsis of Magic (1585).

Lercheimer tells us that when Faust, as he calls him, was in Wittenberg, "he came at times to the house of Philipp [Melanchthon]," of all people, where he received both hospitality and admonitions. Resenting the latter, he told his host one day as they descended to dinner that he would make all the pots in his kitchen fly up through the chimney. To which Melanchthon replied, with less than his usual eloquence, "Dass soltu wol lassen, ich sch[e]isse dir in deine kunst" (Baron 1985: 532)—"You'd better lay off; I shit on your art!" The sorcerer did indeed lay off. For, as Lercheimer added in 1597, in the third edition of his Christian Synopsis, "the devil was unable to rob the kitchen of this holy man" (Palmer and More 122).

There is perhaps an echo of Luther's and Melanchthon's logic of legitimation in the Historia as well. Lercheimer followed his story about Melanchthon's ability to resist Faust's devilish tricks with one about an elderly neighbor's attempt to convert the sorcerer. The two together seem to have inspired the story of the Old Man's intervention with Faustus in chapters 52 and 53 of the Historia—where, although Philipp Melanchthon has disappeared, a trace of him remains in the Old Man's exhortation to remember how St. Philip's preaching converted Simon the supposed God to faith in Christ (EFB 102 [ch. 52]). It is left to the reader to remember how promptly Simon Magus lapsed from his faith—as Faustus likewise does in this same chapter.

If Faustus could in this peculiar sense be at once a precursor, an enemy and a guarantor of the Lutheran faith, so also could the celebrated humanist and occult philosopher Henricus Cornelius Agrippa, that "scoundrel" to whom Melanchthon likened him. In 1522 the reformer Wolfgang Capito wrote to Agrippa, and in an attempt to persuade him to commit himself openly to the Reformation, reported a conversation with an admirer who had declared that "what Luther sees now, Agrippa saw long ago" (Agrippa 1970: ii. 729-30). There is some truth to this: Agrippa had been involved in bitter controversies with the theologians of the Franciscan and Dominican orders since 1509.

But Agrippa was a well-known exponent of what Frances Yates termed the Hermetic-Cabalistic tradition—a current of thought to which Georgius Faustus was also, if more peripherally, attached. This tradition, while encouraging purported restorations of originary discourses in a manner that in some ways anticipated the Reformers' project of returning to the forms of early Christianity, differed from the latter in its wholesale syncretism, its willingness to believe in the underlying congruity of all originary discourses, whether Christian, Jewish, Muslim or pagan, and also in its view of human empowerment through magical practices understood as a common element of these discourses. Moreover, while this Hermetic-Cabalistic tradition preceded the Reformation by at least a generation, it also encouraged radical evangelical opposition to Luther's doctrines.

During the decades immediately preceding the Reformation the newly available and supposedly ancient texts of Hermes Trismegistus and the Kabbalists, which it was thought could contribute to a restoration of the pristine verities of Christianity, aroused considerable excitement. However, the occultist tradition's emphasis on spiritual autonomy and on a deification achieved through spiritual rebirth was diametrically opposed to Luther's biblical exclusivism and his rejection of free-will; while this tradition undoubtedly helped to create a favorable climate for the reception of his early writings, it subsequently contributed to radical reforming tendencies which outflanked or subverted the positions of the magisterial reformers.

The Hermetic-Cabalistic tradition encouraged more extreme forms of prophetic and magical delusion as well. Georgius Faustus, whose blasphemies Johannes Trithemius reported in 1507, was still claiming two decades later to be a prophet (Palmer and More 89). Trithemius also wrote about the visit of a similarly boastful Italian magician, Joannes Mercurius de Corigio, to the court of Louis XII of France in 1501. From other sources (among them his own writings) it is clear that this magician announced himself as a wonder-working Hermetic-Christian redeemer; Trithemius's suppression of this aspect of his claims raises the interesting possibility that he also knew more about Georgius Faustus's Hermetic-Cabalistic affiliations than he was willing to reveal (Keefer 1989: 85-86).

In the course of the Faustus legend's narrative exfoliation, the anti-Catholic overtones which had been present in its earliest forms became more pronounced, and the legend acquired, in inverse form, many of the features of the popular genre of saints' lives—a genre which it also helped to displace (Allen 13-41). At the same time, the carnivalesque elements evident in Luther's anecdotes about magicians were taken up and amplified.

But whatever it contained of anti-Catholic polemic or of folktale, the legend remained a repressive narrative—one which sought to legitimize Protestant orthodoxy through a terrifying representation of the wages of transgression. It is no coincidence that the period between 1560 and the late 1580s, during which the Faustus legend received its full narrative elaboration, also saw the first major outbreak of witch-hunts in Western Europe—an outbreak in which, with the vehement approval of orthodox intellectuals, thousands of people, most of them women, were imprisoned, tortured, and judicially murdered.[1]

---

1   In those parts of Germany where records of the witch-persecutions have received the most detailed study (present-day Baden-Württemberg and Bavaria), there was a sharp increase of witchcraft trials after 1560, peaking in the 1580s, and a further wave of persecutions between 1585 and 1595 (Behringer 11, 13). Monter notes that a "rapid intensification of persecution" in the territories, both Catholic and Protestant, from Geneva and Savoy north to Alsace and Lorraine began "sometime between the 1560's and the 1580's" (Monter 35). A similar pattern is evident in south-eastern England, where witchcraft indictments on the Home Circuit Assizes rose from less than 40 in the 1560s to 109 in the 1570s and 166 in the 1580s (Sharpe 108-09). Across Western Europe, the number of witch trials increased greatly "after about 1550" (Klaits 48).

Marlowe's *Doctor Faustus*: Source and Contexts

The first canonical version of the legend of Faustus was the so-called *German Faustbook*, the *Historia von D. Johann Fausten* (1587), a huge popular success that was reprinted some twenty times before the end of the century. A free English translation of this text, *The Historie of the damnable life, and deserved death of Doctor John Faustus* (which has been dated to 1588), was Marlowe's principal source.

It is important to recognize that the *German Faustbook* was written in Lutheran Germany within a context defined by what the late-nineteenth-century historian W.E.H. Lecky, with the commendable frankness of his age, termed "religious terrorism" (Lecky i. 37-38, 78-82).[1] Lecky's opinion that a train of developments culminating in the Reformation "diffused through Christendom a religious terror which gradually overcast the horizon of thought" (i. 81) has been amply confirmed by the work of present-day historians. Gerald Strauss, for example, has proposed that "only the most denominationally committed scholar would now speak of the age of state churches and orthodoxy as a time of religious emancipation," for during the sixteenth century "life for all but the most inaccessibly situated men and women in urban and rural Germany became more rule-bound, more closely surveyed, and more rigorously directed ... than it had been at any time in the recent or distant medieval past" (Strauss 28-29).

The Reformers' ethic of "decency, diligence, gravity, modesty, orderliness, prudence, reason, self-control, sobriety, and thrift" (Burke 213, qtd. by Strauss 29), was supported by church and state through evangelical preaching and catechization, and harsh practices of surveillance and punishment—which in Germany

---

1   As the *Oxford English Dictionary* reminds us, the word "terrorism" initially referred to exercises of state power, specifically the "Government by intimidation as directed and carried out by the party in power in France during the Revolution of 1789-1794"; this meaning was subsequently generalized to the senses of "A policy intended to strike with terror those against whom it is adopted; the employment of methods of intimidation; the fact of terrorising or condition of being terrorized" (*OED*, "terrorism," 1-2). All of these senses are active in Lecky's analysis of late fifteenth- and sixteenth-century "religious terrorism"; so also is one of the meanings of "terrorist," current in the nineteenth century: "One who entertains, professes, or tries to awaken or spread a feeling of terror or alarm" (*OED*, "terrorist," 2).

were supplemented by a massive outpouring of writings designed to inculcate godly discipline through fear of the devil. Written by Lutheran pastors to show Satan's loathing of humanity, these *Teufelsbücher* also encouraged readers to fear that any lapse in their obedience to church and state might lead them to be identified as agents of the devil in his war against God's people. The latter fear was not an idle one at a time when the continental practice of torturing suspected witches could produce wildly multiplying accusations once a process of inquisition had been initiated.

The German devil-literature of the mid and late sixteenth century has attracted the attention of historians on account both of its scale and its social function. Strauss quotes as exemplary the dedication of the *German Faustbook*, in which "'des Teuffels Neid, Betrug und Grausamkeit gegen dem menschlichen Geschlecht' ['the Devil's envy, deceit, and cruelty against humankind'] is shown to be the root cause of every ill done or suffered in the world," and he remarks that the estimated quarter of a million copies of these *Teufelsbücher* that were circulating in the latter half of the sixteenth century had a clearly definable impact: "the late-sixteenth- and seventeenth-century fixation on the devil did not originate as a popular notion deep in the grassroots of society. Instead, it was a position developed by the educated and spread by them to the populace" (Strauss 31).

To us it might seem madness that theologians, lawyers and other intellectuals committed to an ethic of decency and reason should have set about inculcating belief in satanic pacts, werewolves, and witches' sabbats. But, as Strauss observes, "bedeviling the world.... facilitated social control and strengthened authorities in their endeavor to bring people into line with the abstract, written, urban, civilized, academic, legal, and theological norms of the great tradition" (Strauss 31-32).

The *German Faustbook* was rendered into English by a translator, "P.F. Gent[leman]," who "took any amount of liberties" with the original (Butler 1952: 33), and who possessed "three qualities notably lacking in the German author: a flair for pungent expression, a vivid visual imagination and a taste for ironic humour" (*EFB* 12). In his hands, both Mephostophiles and Faustus become more imposing figures, and he brings out in Faustus what E.M.

Butler calls a "latent titanism," especially evident in the prominence given to his "burning desire for knowledge" (Butler 1952: 37). But although the *English Faustbook* is "grander, loftier, more intense and tragic than the by no means paltry original" (Butler 1952: 34), it retains the moralizing tendency of the *German Faustbook*, presenting Faustus as an example from which "the stiff-necked and high-minded may ... learn to fear God and ... not invite the devil as a guest, nor give him place as that wicked Faustus hath done" (*EFB* 181).

John Henry Jones has plausibly identified P. F. as one Paul Fairfax, who claimed to hold a medical degree from the university of Frankfurt on the Oder, and who came to the attention of the Royal College of Physicians in 1588 as a result of having practised medicine in London from June until late September of that year. Fairfax was fined as an unlicensed practitioner—and, on refusing to pay his fine, was imprisoned by the College, which declared his credentials "vehemently to be suspected" (*EFB* 31-32).

If Paul Fairfax and P.F. were indeed one and the same person, this likeness might explain "the affinity of the author for his protagonist and the motivation for his labours" (*EFB* 33-34). P.F.'s expansions of those chapters of the German *Historia* that recount Faustus's Grand Tour give evidence, Jones argues, of personal knowledge of parts of Germany, Poland and Italy—and according to the College of Physicians, Paul Fairfax was likewise a man who "by travel ... seemeth to have gotten some kinds of language and therewithal hath boldly put himself into some empirical practice, most dangerous in truth to the patient than in any wise commendable to the practitioner" (*EFB* 32).

The *English Faustbook* has been commonly represented as the sole source of *The Tragical History of Doctor Faustus*. However, there are grounds for asserting that Marlowe was not merely adapting the *Faustbook* for the stage, but was also actively reshaping the legend—and subtly undermining its repressive orthodoxy—through an exploration of its historical and ideological roots. In the eyes of some at least of his contemporaries, Marlowe was in his own way as openly transgressive a figure as the historical Faustus had been. And there is plentiful evidence that when in 1588 he turned his attention to the legend of Faustus he gave it a subversive twist.

Without altering its sequence of apostasy, despair and damnation, he foregrounded the question of human autonomy, stripped away the layers of moralizing commentary which in the German and English *Faustbooks* mask the ethical problems raised by Lutheran and Calvinist doctrines of predestination, and made the story into an expression of the most intimate fear of sixteenth-century Protestants: that of predestined damnation to eternal torment. A legend which had buttressed Lutheran orthodoxy in Germany thus became a means of interrogating the quite similar Calvinistic orthodoxy of late sixteenth-century England.

In this swerve away from a repressive orthodoxy, Marlowe reconfigured Faustus, in Jonathan Dollimore's words, as a figure whose "mode of transgression [is] identifiably protestant in origin: despairing yet defiant, masochistic yet wilful. Faustus is abject yet his is an abjectness which is strangely inseparable from arrogance, which reproaches the authority which demands it, which is not so much subdued as incited by that same authority ..." (Dollimore 1993: 115). Marlowe was thus arguably producing what Dollimore terms a "transgressive reinscription," in which the abjection and masochism that figure in the orthodox story of Christ's suffering are redeployed in Faustus (Dollimore 1991: 286).

But it would be misleading to attribute this transgressive reinscription solely to the quirks of one idiosyncratic sensibility: the play nudges its audience into confronting issues that were already circulating in Elizabethan public discourse. The central question of the ethics (and the implicit politics) of the doctrine of predestination had been foregrounded in William Lawne's dialogue-form *Abridgement of Calvin's Institutes of the Christian Religion* (1583) when Lawne voiced the objection that for God "to adjudge to destruction whom he will, is more agreeable to the lust of a tyrant, than to the lawful sentence of a judge"—only to give it the standard obscurantist non-response of Elizabethan Anglicanism: "It is a point of bold wickedness even so much as to inquire the causes of God's will" (qtd. by Sinfield 1983: 141).

As recent critics have proposed, *Doctor Faustus* can best be understood as responding—with unprecedented forthrightness—to the harshly predestinarian teachings of the Elizabethan state church and the anxieties they provoked. In John Stachniewski's words, "the consciousness invested in Faustus ... [is] a passionately detailed concentration of literal contemporary experiences of subjectivity in a theological culture so repressive that it created the rebel state of mind it reprobated" (Stachniewski 10). The extinction of this consciousness is "terrible" rather than "bleakly deserved," A.D. Nuttall writes, "because the narrative of just punishment for sin is fused with another narrative of predestined damnation and future everlasting torment. Calvin was very willing to say that God is terrible but would never say that he is wicked—only that he is inscrutable. Marlowe conversely finds in the terror of God a space for moral criticism, a space for the special blasphemy of Christian tragedy" (Nuttall 1998: 41).

Operating within the limits of a censorship that suppressed any overt challenge to official doctrine but left room for strategies of indirection or insinuation (Patterson 17), Marlowe's *Doctor Faustus* does not invite its audience to imagine any secure alternative to the orthodoxy which it questions. Faustus's brief pretense of "manly fortitude" (I. iii. 85) is shown in an ironic light, and he dies in a state of abject terror, self-loathing and despair. Yet his perseverance in despair is as distinct a sign of divine reprobation as Calvin held perseverance in grace to be one of divine election, and the insistent suggestions of the A text that his repeated inability to will his own salvation may be due to the workings of another will, anterior to his and subjecting him to its determinations, make Faustus's "torture" deeply unsettling. A Calvinistic orthodoxy may appear to win out at the end of this play, but it does so at the cost of being exposed, in the moment of its triumph, as intolerable.

Faustus's desire to be "as cunning as Agrippa was" (I. i. 118) provides one clue to the manner in which motifs from other texts are woven into this play. Agrippa's rhetorical demolition of all the orthodox forms of knowledge in *De vanitate* was suspected, despite the evangelical orientation of that book, of having been designed to prepare readers for the magical doctrines espoused in *De occulta philosophia*: although in *De vanitate* he claimed to be "Professinge Divinitee" (Agrippa 1974: 12 [cap. 1]), he was thought by some to be doing so hypocritically (cf. Thevet ii. fol. 544r-v).

This is very much the pattern of Faustus's first speech.

Announcing his intention to be "a divine in show" (I. i. 3), he launches into a sophistical survey of the academic disciplines, of which there is no hint in *EFB*, and then into a rapturous praise of magic, which is parallelled in *De occulta philosophia* but not in the *Faustbooks*. By the time he mentions Agrippa, Faustus is thus already emulating him, if in a parodic manner.

The Hermetic-Cabalistic notion of spiritual rebirth and deification which figures in both of Agrippa's best-known works (Keefer 1988: 620-39) is also ironically echoed in this play. Faustus initially declares: "A sound magician is a mighty god: / Here tire, my brains, to get a deity!" (I. i. 63-64). He thus announces a project of a self-begotten rebirth into divine form which would deliver him into "a world of profit and delight, / Of power, of honor, of omnipotence" (I. i. 54-55). In his last soliloquy, however, he wishes futilely that he might evade eternal punishment by being "chang'd / Unto some brutish beast" (V. ii. 100-01), and he calls upon the stars that reigned at his nativity to

> draw up Faustus like a foggy mist
> Into the entrails of yon laboring cloud,
> That when you vomit forth into the air
> My limbs may issue from your smoky mouths,
> So that my soul may but ascend to heaven.
>
> (V. ii. 85-89)

In what can be read as a violently physical reversal of spiritual rebirth, Faustus proposes an abject surrender of bodily integrity in exchange for the salvation of his soul: having once aspired to "rend the clouds" (I. i. 60), he now begs for physical dissolution in their entrails, for resorption into a dismembering womb, followed by regurgitation and dispersal.

It would appear that Marlowe saw a connection between Renaissance occultist traditions and the Simonian resonances of the legend. When Faustus cries out, "Sweet Helen, make me immortal with a kiss; / Her lips suck forth my soul, see where it flies!" (V. i. 92-93), his playful attribution to his apparently demonic paramour of the power to confer at least one of the attributes of a god is also, it would seem, an allusion to the Cabalist idea that the human soul "can be ravished by God in a mystical union referred to [...] as 'the death of the kiss'" (Mebane 127; cf. Yates 1964: 99). This blasphemous conceit is linked to Marlowe's evident awareness of the patristic legend of Simon Magus. For while in the *Historia* and the *English Faustbook* Helen is a straightforwardly erotic figure, his Faustus transforms her, like Simon's Helena, into a parodic image of the figure of divine Wisdom. In the words of Solomon, Wisdom "is more beautifull then the Sun, and above all the order of the starres, and the light is not to be compared unto her. [....] I have loved her, and sought her from my youth: I desired to marry her, such love had I unto her beauty" (*Wisdom of Solomon* 7:26, 29; 8: 2 [*Geneva Bible*]). Faustus's echo of this passage is unmistakable:

> O, thou art fairer than the evening air
> Clad in the beauty of a thousand stars;
> Brighter art thou than flaming Jupiter
> When he appear'd to hapless Semele,
> More lovely than the monarch of the sky
> In wanton Arethusa's azur'd arms,
> And none but thou shalt be my paramour.
>
> (V. i. 103-09)

The theological dimensions of the play's context, obscurely hinted at in the Prologue's suggestion of a heavenly conspiracy (lines 21-22), first become evident in the syllogism with which Faustus dismisses theology:

> *Stipendium peccati mors est.* Ha! *Stipendium, etc.*
> The reward of sin is death? That's hard.
> *Si pecasse negamus, fallimur,*
> *et nulla est in nobis veritas:*
> If we say that we have no sin
> We deceive ourselves, and there's no truth in us.
> Why then belike we must sin,
> And so consequently die.
> Ay, we must die, an everlasting death.
>
> (I. i. 39-47)

In more than one sense these lines offers a lesson in the importance of contextualizing. Faustus misreads the words of St. Paul (*Romans* 6: 23) and St. John (*1 John* 1: 8) because he has lifted them out of their contexts, failing in each case to notice that the words he quotes form only the first half of an antithetical construction. The second clause of *Romans* 6: 23 ("but the gifte of God is eternal life through Jesus Christ our Lord") and the next verse in the epistle of John ("If we acknowledge our sinnes, he is faithful and just, to forgive our sinnes, & to clense us from all unrighteousnes") conditionally withdraw the condemnations which are all that Faustus sees.

Readers who wish to interpret *Doctor Faustus* as a morality play, and its protagonist as no more than a witless incompetent, need go no further in their restorations of context. However, further consideration may suggest that to dismiss Faustus in this manner is not an adequate response to this passage. A more suitable reaction than contempt might be the proverbial "There, but for the grace of God, go I."

Marlowe scholars have long been aware that Faustus succumbs to the same diabolical logic that was used by Despair in Spenser's *Faerie Queene* to lead Redcrosse Knight towards suicide, and, some decades previously in a dialogue written by Thomas Becon, by Satan in an attempt to undermine the faith of another Christian Knight. Both knights, unlike Faustus, escape this logic in what for sixteenth-century Protestants was the only possible way, by transcending it through an appeal to divine grace. Becon's knight, admitting his condemnation under the Law, turns to the Gospel, "that is to say, grace, favour, and remission of sins, promised in Christ" (Becon 629); Spenser's is saved by the intervention of Una:

> In heavenly mercies hast thou not a part?
> Why shouldst thou then despeire, that chosen art?
> Where justice growes, there grows eke greater grace....
>   (I. ix. 53)

But while Becon's knight is able to appeal to God's mercy, and while Una is there to remind Redcrosse of this same grace and mercy, the notion of divine mercy is no more than hinted at in *Doctor Faustus* until after Faustus has committed apostasy and signed his pact with the devil, and it is strikingly absent from this first scene. Faustus is reminded by his Good Angel of a quite different aspect of the divine nature:

> O Faustus, lay that damned book aside,
> And gaze not on it, lest it tempt thy soul
> And heap God's heavy wrath upon thy head!
> Read, read the Scriptures; that is blasphemy.
>
> (I. i. 71-74)

Although this may seem very much the sort of thing that a Good Angel ought to say, these words, addressed to a man whose soul has evidently already been tempted by the necromantic book he is holding, are less akin to the intervention of Spenser's Una than to the persuasions of Despaire from which she saved Redcrosse Knight:

> Is not the measure of thy sinfull hire
> High heaped up with huge iniquitie,
> Against the day of wrath, to burden thee?
>
> (I. ix. 46)

One may well wonder why the Good Angel neither suggests to Faustus the sort of question that George Herbert asks—"Art thou all justice, Lord? / Shows not thy word / More attributes?"—nor tries to prompt him to the request which follows from it: "Let not thy wrathfull power / Afflict my houre, / My inch of life..." ("Complaining," lines 11-13, 16-18). The answer would seem to be that Faustus is not among those chosen by God's inscrutable will for salvation. If this is so, the function of the Good Angel's exhortation is not to convert Faustus, but rather (in terms which readers of Calvin will find familiar) to render him inexcusable (see Institutes III. iii. 10-11).

In the passage from which Faustus lifted the major premise of his syllogism, St. Paul contrasts a state of bondage to sin with one of bondage to God in a manner that seems to exclude any overtone either of autonomy or of free-will:

For when ye were the servants [*douloi*, i.e., slaves] of sinne,
ye were freed from righteousness. What frute had ye then in
those things, whereof ye are now ashamed? For the end of
those things is death. But now being freed from sinne, and
made servants unto God, ye have your frute in holines and
the end, everlasting life. For the wages of sinne is death: but
the gifte of God is eternal life.... (*Romans* 6: 20-23)

Responding perversely to the passages from which he quotes,
Faustus concludes (to borrow the wording of *Romans* 6: 21) that
"the end of those things is death." And in reducing Christian
theology to a doctrine of necessity, he goes one step further:

What doctrine call you this? *Che sarà, sarà,*
What will be, shall be? Divinity, adieu!

(I. i. 48-49)

This sounds very much like a parodic reduction of the Calvinistic
teachings on predestination which were the official doctrine of
the Anglican church throughout the reign of Elizabeth I.

The Calvinist theology to which Marlowe is alluding is thoroughly equivocal. God summons the reprobate to repent, and
therefore 'wants' them to—but they do not receive the grace
which would enable them to repent, and the fact that he has
willed their damnation is eventually manifested in their lack of
faith. The willful self-estrangement of the reprobate from God
is said to make their condemnation just—but what is this human
will? The Calvinist apologist Du Plessis-Mornay wrote that "God
therefore to shew his power in our freedome and libertie, hath
left our willes to us; and to restreyne them from loosenesse, he
hath so ordered them by his wisedome, that he worketh his owne
will no lesse by them, than if we had no will at all" (Du Plessis-
Mornay 221).[1]

When Faustus, having signed his pact, wonders whether it is
not too late to repent, the Good Angel equivocates in a simi-

---

1   Calvin makes a similar argument in the passages from *Institutes* I. xvii. 5, I. xvii. 11,
II. ii. 6-7, and III. iii. 5 excerpted in Appendix D.

lar manner: "Never too late, if Faustus can repent" (II. iii. 81). Enfolded in that conditional clause is the brute question of fact on which the doctrine of double predestination hinges. If Faustus is going to be able to repent, then he is eternally out of trouble and it is never too late; but if he cannot, it will always have been too late.[1] Someone with an eye for theological nuances altered the B text to read "if Faustus *will* repent" (my emphasis)—thus deflecting our attention to the question of Faustus's willingness to will his own salvation. But what immediately follows confirms in a spectacular manner the A text's insinuation that the issue is not his to decide: when Faustus calls on Christ, he is answered by the appearance of a demonic trinity.

There is a sense in which Faustus's handling of scriptural texts, in addition to being a gross misreading, is also the appropriate, indeed inevitable, response for someone in a state of bondage to sin. The Bible came to sixteenth-century Protestants equipped with a theory of reading (and of misreading). Thus Elizabethan Anglicans prayed to God for "grace to love thy holie word fervently, to search the Scriptures diligently, to reade them humblie, to understand them truly, to live after them effectually" (*Prayer Book* 150). The operative word is "grace"—lacking which, scriptural study could only result in misinterpretation and mortal sin. For (to quote from another of the "Godly Prayers" printed with many editions of the *Book of Common Prayer*), "If man trust to himselfe, it cannot bee avoyded, but that hee must headlong runne and fall into a thousand undoings and mischiefs" (*Prayer Book* 148-49).

But this insistence upon divine grace and upon human weakness and perversity would seem to have produced a tendency to separate, if only for purposes of emphasis, the two halves of the very texts from which Faustus quotes. Faustus's truncation of *1 John* 1: 8-9 is paralleled in Article XV of the Church of England, which ends with these words: "If we say we have no sin, we deceive ourselves, and the truth is not in us" (see Kastan 244). Full

---

1 A.D. Nuttall has commented on the future-perfect verb in this sentence (which appeared also in my 1991 introduction) in the course of his very astute analysis of the strangely proleptic temporal logic of Calvinism. See Nuttall 1998: 33-41.

stop. Nothing remotely like *1 John* 1: 9 appears in the following articles, or indeed anywhere among the *Thirty-Nine Articles*. In Calvin's *Institutes of the Christian Religion* there occurs a similar truncation, this time of the words of St. Paul. Calvin is here fulminating against the Roman Catholic distinction between mortal and venial sins:

> Will they imagin the wrath of God to be so disarmed, that punishment of death shall not foorthwith follow upon them? [....] The soule (saith he) that sinneth, the same shall die [*Ezekiel* 18: 4. 20]. Againe, which I even now alleaged, the reward of sinne is death [*Romans* 6: 23] [....] let the children of God learne this, that all sinne is deadly, because it is a rebellion against the wil of God, which of necessitie provoketh his wrath, because it is a breach of the lawe, upon which the judgment of God is pronounced without exception: and that the sinnes of the holy ones are veniall or pardonable, not of their owne nature, but because they obtaine pardon by the mercie of God. (Calvin 1587: II. viii. 59, fol. 132v-133)

Calvin has chosen to emphasize the tautological nature of the Pauline doctrine: all sins without exception are mortal, he says, except those of the saints, which are forgiven not because they are intrinsically saints but because they are forgiven. One can imagine a graceless reader asking, "What doctrine call you this? *Che sarà, sarà?*"

What I have spoken of as contextual is in fact embedded in this play at the most intimate level of its rhetoric. Faustus may experiment with the third-person self-objectification practised by Marlowe's Tamburlaine. But his habitual, his characteristic mode of speech is second-person self-address: "Settle thy studies Faustus" (I. i. 1); "Then fear not, Faustus, but be resolute" (I. iii. 14); "Now, Faustus, thou art conjurer laureate" (I. iii. 32); "Now, Faustus, must thou needs be damn'd" (II. i. 1); "What art thou, Faustus, but a man condemn'd to die?" (IV. ii. 33).

This mode of apostrophic self-address is, very largely, what constitutes Faustus's dramatic identity. At the same time as his apostrophic self-reflections enact a split between the speaking subject's perverse willfulness and the fearful, speechless and strangely passive selfhood which his words invoke and to whom they are addressed, they also construct a trap of self-authenticating predication. The despairing self-definitions of Faustus would cease to be true if only he could cease from making them; but conversely, he could only cease from making them if they were not true—or rather, if he were not constituted as a victim and self-victimizing subject by this very pattern of apostrophic self-address.

What Faustus simultaneously recognizes as his destiny and struggles to escape is also gradually revealed as the true shape of what he has desired. An eschatological awareness burns up through even his most splendid effort at forgetfulness. Helen's "sweet embracings" are to "extinguish clean" (V. i. 85) the motions of penitence and despair that have wracked him, but the very language of the escapist fantasy which he constructs around her expresses through a strange inversion his actual relation to this spirit: "Brighter art thou than flaming Jupiter / When he appear'd to hapless Semele..." (V. i. 105-06).

Faustus began by "level[ing] at the end of every art" (I. i. 4)—that is, by challenging both the purposes and the limits of the disciplines which he had studied. Discovering in the first scene that the end of Divinity, for those who lack the grace to apply to themselves the scriptural offers of forgiveness, is "everlasting death," he opposed to this depressing conclusion the fantasies of unconditioned autonomy and limitless power inspired by the "metaphysics of magicians" (I. i. 47, 50). But what C.L. Barber defined as an unstable appropriation of the divine for the human (Barber 98-101) quickly collapses in this play. When in his final soliloquy Faustus begs God to "Impose some end to my incessant pain," there is a horrible irony to the ensuing recognition: "O, no end is limited to damned souls" (V. ii. 93, 96). This concern with *ends*, in all of the related senses so skillfully analyzed by Edward Snow—of intention, reason for being, *telos*, finality, limit, and eschatological termination—resonates through the play, and is perhaps one reason for the place it occupies in our literary canon.

Marlowe's play reverses the crushingly homiletic orientation of its principal source, not indeed by glorifying Faustus, whose pretensions are undermined through a sequence of mordant ironies, but rather by insistently implying that his perverse willfulness has itself been willed by higher powers. The intimate manner in which the protagonist's damnation is unfolded makes a detached judgment of him difficult, and the absence of that moralistic authorial condemnation which in the *English Faustbook* and its German original had masked the issue of predestination throws into question the nature of the divine power by whose will the action is implicitly shaped.

The original version of *Doctor Faustus* thus gave interrogative form to a narrative that had previously been, in Lecky's sense, "terroristic" in tendency. As I have observed below in my Note on the Text, much of the play's subsequent textual history, and much of the history of its modern and contemporary critical receptions, has been made up of repeated attempts to reimpose upon this dissident play-text one or another form of theological, critical—or textual-critical—orthodoxy.

Ideological Motives in the B-text Revisions.

The issue of censorship in early modern English literature, and in Marlowe's *Doctor Faustus* in particular, has attracted renewed attention in recent years (see Patterson, Clare, Dutton, Empson). It has long been recognized that B is a censored text, and there is now general agreement that some of the textual variants which W.W. Greg took to exemplify memorial corruption in A are more probably the result of censorship in B. However, the ideological motivations of this censorship, and the systemic differences it created between the A and B versions of the play have yet to be widely acknowledged.

The revisionary processes out of which the B version of the play emerged included two distinct, if sometimes overlapping, kinds of censorship. The one most commonly understood is more superficial in its effects, and usually easier to detect. I refer to the changes, often involving the substitution of single words, but occasionally amounting to the deletion of whole lines at a time, which appear to have been made in response to the 1606 Act of Abuses. It seems likely that the B-text deletions of Faustus's description of "Divinitie" as "Unpleasant, harsh, contemptible and vilde" (Greg A: 141-42; I. i. 109-10), and of his promise "Never to name God, or to pray to him, / To burne his Scriptures, slay his Ministers, / And make my spirites pull his churches downe" (Greg A: 726-28; II. iii. 96-98), were of this kind.

The other more significant form of censorship can be seen in ideologically-motivated revisions which obscure or remove the Calvinistic implications of the A text, usually by substituting an emphasis on Faustus's perverse willfulness for indications that his thoughts are influenced or controlled by external agencies. (Although this tendency is consistent enough in B to indicate a deliberate re-orientation of the play, it does not go uncontra-dicted: the B-text additions also include Mephostophilis's parting declaration to Faustus that "'Twas I, … when thou wer't i'the way to heaven, / Damb'd up thy passage, when thou took's the booke, / To view the Scriptures, then I turn'd the leaves / And led thine eye" [Greg B: 1989-92; B: V. ii. 90-93].)

The following brief discussion moves from instances of textual alteration in which these two forms of censorship appear to be combined, to others in which the motivating factor is clearly ide-ology rather than the avoidance of blasphemy.

The impact of censorship on the B text is most obvious in the last scene of the play, where Faustus's magnificent outcry in the A text—

> O Ile leape up to my God: who pulles me downe?
> See see where Christs blood streames in the firmament,
> One drop would save my soule, halfe a drop, ah my Christ
> (Greg A: 1462-64; V. ii. 70-72)

—is reduced in B to the barely intelligible

> O I'le leape up to heaven: who puls me downe?
> One drop of bloud will save me; oh my Christ....
> (Greg B: 2048-49; B: V. ii. 142-43)

Another desperate plea in the same speech—

Oh God, if thou wilt not have mercy on my soule,
Yet for Christs sake, whose bloud hath ransomd me,
Impose some end to my incessant paine
             (Greg A: 1483-85; V. ii. 91-93)

—is transformed into something at once less vivid and more moralistic:

O, if my soule must suffer for my sinne,
Impose some end to my incessant paine....
             (Greg B: 2067-68; B: V. ii. 160-61)

More has been excised here than the name of God and the blood of Christ: the alarming implication of a refusal of divine mercy has disappeared from the B text, to be replaced by an acknowledgment of the due connection between sinfulness and suffering.

In the immediately preceding scene a similar effect can be noted. The Old Man tells Faustus in the A text that the "stench" of his "most vilde and loathsome filthinesse"

      corrupts the inward soule
With such flagitious crimes of hainous sinnes,
As no commiseration may expel,
But mercie Faustus of thy Saviour sweete,
Whose bloud alone must wash away thy guilt.
             (Greg A: 1308-13; V. i. 41-46)

Like the Good Angel's first speech, this is not a comforting intervention; for although the Old Man wishes to guide Faustus "unto the way of life" (Greg A: 1303; V. i. 36), what his words convey most distinctly is a violent revulsion from him. Faustus already believes that God "loves [him] not" (Greg A: 447; II. i. 10); the same is apparently true of God's spokesman in this scene.

The B text gives the Old Man an altogether different speech, which provides a striking contrast to the loveless rhetoric of his A-text counterpart:

It may be this my exhortation
Seemes harsh, and all unpleasant; let it not,
For gentle sonne, I speake it not in wrath,
Or envy of thee, but in tender love,
And pitty of thy future miserie.
                    (Greg B: 1823-27; B: V. i. 44-48)

The theology of the B-text speech is also different. Christ's blood
has again been effaced, and the A-text's suggestion that an unmerited divine mercy is Faustus's only hope of salvation gives way
to the implication that it is within his own power to repent:

Though thou hast now offended like a man,
Doe not persever in it like a Divell;
Yet, yet, thou hast an amiable soule,
If sin by custome grow not into nature....
                    (Greg B: 1816-19; B: V. i. 37-40)

Faustus responds to the Old Man's intervention with an out-
burst of despair—"Where art thou Faustus? wretch what hast thou
done? / Damnd art thou Faustus, damnd, dispaire and die" (Greg
A: 1314-15; V. i. 47-48)—the second line of which is deleted in B.
To the suicidal gesture which follows, the Old Man reacts in both
texts with the vision of an angel that hovers over Faustus, "And
with a violl full of precious grace, / Offers to powre the same into
thy soule" (Greg A: 1321-22; V. i. 54-55). But in neither case does
Faustus seem to receive this grace: the Old Man leaves him, in A,
"with heavy cheare, / fearing the ruine of thy hopelesse soule"
(Greg A: 1327-28; V. i. 60-61)—and in B, "with griefe of heart,
/ Fearing the enemy of thy haplesse soule" (Greg B: 1841-42; B:
V. i. 62-63). Faustus then asks himself, in A, "Accursed Faustus,
where is mercie now?" (Greg A: 1329; V. i. 62)—a question for
which B, re-using an earlier line, substitutes "Accursed *Faustus*,
wretch what hast thou done?" (Greg B: 1843; B: V. i. 63).
    These variants result in a distinct shift in the meaning of this
passage: where A implies that there is a link between Faustus's
despair or hopelessness and the divine mercy which hovers just be-

yond his reach, B emphasizes instead his own perverse agency and that of the "enemy" whose hapless victim he has made himself.

Whether the above alterations be ascribed to the 1602 revisions or to a subsequent censoring of the play, they are consistent in substituting for A's foregrounding of the harshness of Calvinist theology an orientation that might be described as semi-Pelagian. In these passages in B the view that Faustus has the capacity to repent, and is therefore wholly responsible for his sinful failure to do so, supplants the A text's insistent suggestion that his despairing inability to will his own salvation is due to the withholding of divine grace.

Although the disturbing notion of a refusal of divine mercy was thus removed from the last act of the B text, it remains in evidence elsewhere, most notably in Act Two, where, encouraged by his Good Angel to repent, Faustus calls on Christ—only to be answered by the terrifying entrance of a demonic trinity: Lucifer, Belzebub, and Mephastophilis. Not surprisingly, in this passage also there are signs, though less obtrusive, of revision in the B text.

Faustus cries in his brief prayer: "Ah Christ my Saviour, / seeke [B: Helpe] to save distressed Faustus soule" (Greg A: 711-12; II. iii. 83-84). Greg cited this variant as one of several in which—sure evidence of memorial corruption—the reading of A implies a definite misunderstanding of the theological situation. "To seek to do something," he wrote, "implies a doubtful issue: but whereas it is heretical to question Christ's power to save, it is true belief that that power is only exercised in aid of the sinner's own endeavour" (Greg 46).

In at least two respects this statement is curiously revealing. It implies, first, that theological orthodoxy can be used—in this of all plays—as a textual criterion. This naivety is compounded by a strange disregard of historical context in Greg's definition of "true belief." Given that the theology of the Anglican church in the latter decades of the sixteenth century was overwhelmingly Calvinistic in orientation, most educated Anglicans of Marlowe's time would have rejected this definition as arrant Pelagianism: to them it was axiomatic that a sinner was powerless to help himself until Christ's saving power was exercised on his behalf.

Greg's words amount to saying that the reading of the 1616 text in this line is authentic because he agrees with its theological implications. But since there may be better reasons for preferring the reading of the 1604 text, it is worth lingering a moment longer over Faustus's prayer. Greg's perception of an undertone of doubt in the A text's "seeke to save" is acute, but should, if anything, serve to confirm the appropriateness of this expression in the mouth of one whose problem is precisely that he lacks faith. More obviously, though, "seeke" carries two other implications: first, that it is primarily up to Christ to save Faustus's soul; and second, that he has not previously been trying to.

A simple cry for help—the B text's "Helpe to save"—does not imply anything about the previous stance of the person to whom it is addressed, but the A text's imploring "seeke" contains an element of persuasion which can only suggest that at some level Faustus thinks persuasion to be necessary. It takes no leap of the imagination to see how the reviser or censoring editor who in the final scene substituted Faustus's bland B-text acknowledgment of sin for the A text's refusal of divine mercy might have recognized these implications. On the other hand, there is no reason for accepting Greg's belief that an actor's faulty memory might have effected the reverse substitution.

The words I have quoted from Greg's commentary represent, not a momentary aberration, but rather the basic orientation of his approach to the play. I have remarked that Faustus's prayer in II. iii. was preceded by the Good Angel's encouragement to repent: but the precise nature of this encouragement needs closer examination. When, having broken angrily with Mephastophilis, Faustus wonders aloud whether it is not too late, his Good Angel reassures him with the words: "Never too late, if Faustus can [B: will] repent" (Greg A: 708; II. iii. 80). Here again, Greg argues that the reading of A is corrupt: "A is wrong in making the Angel doubt Faustus' ability to repent if he has the will to do so" (Greg 338). But this is not what the line means. The Angel does not oppose ability and will in this manner; rather, he is suggesting that Faustus is perhaps unable to will to repent. Greg writes: "It is not a question of the possibility of repentance—that is assumed—but of the will to repent" (Greg 45). One must ask: assumed by whom?

Far from being a theological absurdity, as Greg's words seem to imply, the A-reading would have been immediately comprehensible to Marlowe's audiences: for the predicament of the reprobate, of those who have not been chosen by God for salvation (and therefore, as Calvin would insist, have been actively rejected by God, and chosen for the opposite fate), is quite simply that they cannot repent; or, more precisely, that they are unable to will to repent.

To our minds this may seem paradoxical: the very notion of will is commonly taken to imply freedom and autonomy. But, as Calvin wrote, "[if] this, that it is of necessitie that God doe well, doe not hinder the free will of God in doing well, if the divell which cannot but do evil yet willingly sinneth, who shall then say that a man doeth therefore lesse willingly sinne for this that hee is subject to necessitie of sinning?" Greg's belief that the possibility of repentance and the will to repent are separate matters could only indicate to Elizabethan Anglicans that he had fallen into the error of Peter Lombard, who, in Calvin's words, "could not distinguish necessitie from compulsion," and thus "gave matter to a pernicious errour" (Calvin 1587: fol. 88v; II. iii. 5).

The Good Angel's words in the 1604 text suggest a question that may already have occurred to members of the audience. Can Faustus repent? It would seem that Anglican theologians of the period, if consulted on the matter at this point in the play, would have responded with a unanimous negative. Faustus, one remembers, abjured the Trinity in his invocation of Mephastophilis in the third scene of the play (see my note to I. iii. 16-17), thus denying the very foundation of the Christian faith. In Richard Hooker's opinion,

if the justified err, as he may, and never come to understand his error, God doth save him through general repentance: but if he fall into heresy, he calleth him either at one time or other by actual repentance; but from infidelity, which is an inward direct denial of the foundation, preserveth him by special providence for ever. (Hooker i. 49-50)

Faustus has not been so preserved—and if he is therefore not one of the justified, he cannot repent.

What then of the mental agonies which he undergoes? For Calvin and his followers, at least, the answer is brutally simple: "… that blinde torment wherewith the reprobate are diversly drawen, when they see that they must needes seeke God, that they may find remedy for their evils, and yet doe flee from his presence, is unproperly called Conversion and prayer" (Calvin 1587: fol. 201v; III. iii. 24).

The ethical discomfort induced by reflections such as these would appear to have been part of the intended effect of this play in its original version—an effect which the revisionary censorship that produced the B text managed largely to efface.

Christopher Marlowe: A Brief Chronology

Marlowe's Life and writings	Contexts
	1535 Death of Henricus Cornelius Agrippa.
c. 1536 Birth of Marlowe's father John.	
	c. 1537 Death of Georgius Faustus of Helmstadt.
	1548 Publication of Johannes Gast's *Sermones conviviales*, vol. 2, which contains the earliest legendary account of Faustus.
	c. 1554 Birth of John Lyly.
	c. 1557 Birth of Thomas Kyd.
	1558 Accession of Queen Elizabeth I.
	c. 1560 Birth of Robert Greene.
1561 Marriage of John Marlowe and Katherine Arthur in Canterbury.	1561 First English edition of Calvin's *Institutes* (translated by Thomas Norton).
	1563 Johannes Manlius's *Locorum communium collectanea* contains an account of Faustus from lectures by Philipp Melanchthon.
1564 Birth of Christopher Marlowe.	1564 Birth of William Shakespeare, death of Jean Calvin.
	c. 1572 Birth of Thomas Dekker.
	c. 1573 Birth of Ben Jonson.
	1576 Opening of James Burbage's playhouse, The Theatre.
1579 January: Marlowe admitted to the King's School, Canterbury (Jan. 1579, new style).	

Marlowe's Life and writings	Contexts
1580 Marlowe admitted to Corpus Christi College, Cambridge, December 1580.	
1584 Marlowe receives his B.A. degree.	
c. 1584-86 Writing of *Dido Queen of Carthage* and translation of Ovid's *Amores* (*All Ovids Elegies*).	1586 Death of Sir Philip Sidney.
1587 Marlowe receives his M.A. degree. A letter from the Privy Council to the Cambridge authorities makes it clear that he had been doing undercover work for the government.	c. 1587 Kyd, *The Spanish Tragedy.* 1587 Execution of Mary, Queen of Scots. 1587 *Historia von D. Johann Fausten.*
1587-88 *Tamburlaine*, parts 1 and 2 performed.	
1587 Greene's Epistle to *Perimedes the Blacksmith* insinuates that Marlowe is an atheist.	1588 English translation by P.F. of the *German Faustbook.*
1588-89 Writing and first performances of *Doctor Faustus.*	1588 Defeat of the Spanish Armada.
1589 18 September: Marlowe and the poet Thomas Watson involved in a duel in which Watson kills William Bradley, a London innkeeper's son.	1589 Greene, *Friar Bacon and Friar Bungay.*
1589-90 Writing and first performances of *The Jew of Malta.*	
1590 First edition of *Tamburlaine.*	1590 First editions of Sidney, *The Defence of Poesie,* and of Spenser, *The Faerie Queene*, Books I-III.
1591 Marlowe and Kyd share a room for writing; both are patronized by Ferdinando Stanley, Lord Strange. Marlowe also enjoys the patronage of Sir Walter Ralegh and of Thomas Walsingham (nephew of Sir Francis Walsingham, Queen Elizabeth's spymaster).	

1591-92 Writing and first performances of
         Edward II.

1592 26 January: At Flushing, the   1592 First performances of Shakespeare's
      central English outpost in the Low   *Titus Andronicus.*
      Countries, Richard Baines accuses   Death of Robert Greene
      Marlowe of counterfeiting and of   (September).
      planning to desert to the Spanish
      and Roman Catholic enemy.
      5 May: Marlowe is bound over to
      keep the peace by two London
      constables.
      15 September: A fight between
      Marlowe and William Corkine in
      Canterbury leads to legal charges
      and countercharges.

1592 Greene's *Groatsworth of Wit*
      attacks Marlowe as an atheist and
      Machiavellian.

1592-93 Composition of *Hero and Leander*,   1592-93 Composition of Shakespeare's
         translation of *Lucan's First Book*   *Venus and Adonis*; first

1593 Composition of *The Massacre at*   performances of Shakespeare's
      Paris.   *Richard III.*

1593 12 May: Thomas Kyd is arrested on
      suspicion of seditious libel.
      18 May: warrant issued for
      Marlowe's arrest by the Privy
      Council.
      20 May: Marlowe instructed by
      Privy Council to give "daily
      attendance."
      26 May: Possible date of delivery
      of Richard Baines's denunciation
      of Marlowe, recommending that
      he be silenced.
      30 May: Marlowe killed by Ingram
      Frizer in Deptford.

Marlowe's Life and writings	Contexts
1594 First editions of *Dido Queen of Carthage* and of *Edward II*.	1594 Nashe, *The Unfortunate Traveller*.
1598 First edition of *Hero and Leander*.	1597 Marlowe's death celebrated in Thomas Beard's *Theatre of God's Judgments* as an instance of divine retribution.
1599 Marlowe's translation of Ovid's *Amores* burned by order of the Bishop of London and the Archbishop of Canterbury.	
c. 1600 First (undated) edition of *The Massacre at Paris*.	
1604 First printing of the A version of *Doctor Faustus*.	
1616 First printing of the B version of *Doctor Faustus*.	
1633 First edition of *The Jew of Malta*.	

A Note on the Text

The Tragical History of Doctor Faustus was first printed in 1604, eleven years after Christopher Marlowe's death, and reprinted (with minor corrections and new typographical errors) in 1609 and 1611. A quite different and much longer version appeared in 1616; the title page of this version's 1619 reprint belatedly announced it as containing "new additions."

The 1604 and 1616 quartos, referred to by scholars as the A and B texts, differ very substantially from one another. They are quite closely parallel in most of Acts One and Two, diverge widely in Acts Three and Four, and converge again for much of Act Five. The B text is longer overall by 614 lines of print—but its first two acts, surprisingly perhaps, are shorter than A's by some 70 lines. (A significant part of the difference in Acts One and Two is due to cuts in the 1616 text: eighteen lines of indisputably Marlovian verse are missing in B, as well as thirteen lines of prose that can on good grounds be attributed to Marlowe.)

The play was collaboratively written. In the A text, the prologue, the first and third scenes of Act One, the first and third scenes of Act Two, both scenes of Act Five, and the final chorus are acknowledged to be Marlowe's work. Most if not all of the rest was written by collaborators who have yet to be securely identified. In the B text, the Marlovian parts of the play were preserved (though often retouched, and sometimes, as in Act Five, scene one, heavily revised), while with the sole exception of Act One, scene two, the scenes composed by Marlowe's original collaborators were discarded and replaced.

We know from the diary of the theatrical entrepreneur Philip Henslowe that in 1602 he paid William Birde and Samuel Rowley the substantial sum of four pounds "for ther adicyones in doctor fostes" (Greg 11). The text printed in 1604 would evidently have been the one that their work replaced, and it is now accepted that the B text incorporates the 1602 revisions. However, scholars have been slow to recognize the extent to which the B text also shows signs of a thorough and ideologically motivated censorship. As is well known, at some point, quite probably in response to the 1606 Act of Abuses (which imposed a heavy fine on each occurrence of stage blasphemy), most references to God and Christ were cut from what became the B text of the play, along with Faustus's more extended blasphemies—such as his dismissal of theology as "Unpleasant, harsh, contemptible and vile" (I. i. 110), and his promise to Mephastophilis "Never to name God or to pray to him, / To burn his Scriptures, slay his ministers, / And make my spirits pull his churches down" (II. iii. 97-99). In one B-text passage in Act Five this demon tells Faustus that he controlled the hapless man's turn away from theology. But at about a dozen other points where the A text implies that Faustus's fate is due to powers beyond his control, the B text makes alterations that put the blame on his own willful perversity, thereby turning a play that in its original version insistently interrogated the Calvinist orthodoxy of Elizabethan England into something at once tamer and more homiletic.

The early nineteenth-century editors who were the first in nearly two centuries to reprint *Doctor Faustus* were aware only of the longer B version—though once scholars rediscovered the 1604 quarto and its reprints they naturally assumed that it represented an early version of the play, and that the 1616 quarto was the result of a subsequent revision. By the late nineteenth century this had become the accepted view: all of the new scholarly editions of *Doctor Faustus* published between the 1880s and the 1920s were based on the 1604 version.

Toward the middle of the twentieth century, however, a contrary opinion gathered strength, as a result of the editorial and textual-critical work of F.S. Boas and Leo Kirschbaum (published in 1932 and 1946 respectively), and more distinctly as a result of W.W. Greg's magisterial parallel-text edition of the play, published in 1950. Greg's exhaustive textual analysis established a new orthodoxy, according to which the 1616 quarto was very close in shape and detail to the original form of the play, while the 1604 quarto was said to be an abbreviated version of that original, cut down for performance in provincial towns at a time in the early 1590s when the London theatres were closed because of plague, and based not on authorial manuscripts but on actors' far-from-adequate memories of their performances of the play. The success of Greg's analysis for rather more than a quarter-century is reflected in the fact that after 1950, with just one exception, every new edition published until the mid-1980s was based upon the 1616 version of the play.

This shift in textual-critical opinion was not without ideological, even political implications. The freethinker Havelock Ellis, whose 1887 edition of Marlowe's plays included an A-version *Doctor Faustus*, had identified Marlowe as a kindred spirit, a man whose "thirst for emancipation" was expressed in "acute and audacious utterances"—so Ellis characterized the violent blasphemies attributed to Marlowe by his contemporaries. Ellis added provocatively that the poet's opinions correspond closely to the views of "students of science and of the Bible in our own days" (Ellis xxxi, 430-31). Leo Kirschbaum, in contrast, defined *Doctor Faustus* (referring of course to the B version, which he ascribed to Marlowe) as "a quasi-morality in which is clearly set forth the hierarchy of moral values which enforces and encloses the play, which the characters in the play accept, which the playwright advances and accepts in his prologue and epilogue, which—hence—the audience must understand and accept" (Kirschbaum 1943: 229).

Two points can be made about this swing in textual-critical opinion. The first is that it embodies a deep historical irony. Marlowe and his collaborators had dramatized a repressive prose narrative written with the aim of frightening its readers into orthodoxy and obedience, turning it into a disturbingly interrogative play; the B text revisions and censorship silenced these subversive overtones, and returned the play to what Kirschbaum rightly recognized as a moralizing orthodoxy. The irony is that Kirschbaum's and Greg's textual-critical work effectively repeated that early act of censorship—conferring upon it the authority of the supposedly scientific 'new bibliography'.

The second point to be made is that the B-version editions which followed in Greg's wake were actually in nearly every case conflations of the A and B texts: they followed B's general shape, and printed its versions of the non-Marlovian scenes, but at the same time obscured B's reorientation of the play's deepest meanings by restoring lines which had been cut from the play during the processes of revision and censorship that had produced the B text. One can understand editors wanting to re-insert the Old Man's last speech, which was cut from B, or preferring Faustus's magnificent outcry in the A text's final scene—

> O, I'll leap up to my God: who pulls me down?
> See, see where Christ's blood streams in the firmament:
> One drop would save my soul, half a drop! Ah, my Christ
> (V. ii. 70–72)

—to B's barely intelligible revision:
> O, I'll leap up to heaven: who pulls me down?
> One drop of blood will save me; oh my Christ….
> (Greg B: 2048–49)

But the result was that these editions do not provide a reliable impression of what they claim is the more authentic of the play's two versions.

Beginning in 1973, the existing consensus was overthrown by a series of new textual-critical analyses: Fredson Bowers's groundbreaking study of the 1602 additions, Constance Brown Kuriyama's incisive 1975 re-examination of the external evidence adduced by Greg, Michael Warren's 1981 exploration of the re-working of the Old Man sequence, my own consideration in 1983 of the contradictions introduced by the B text's handling of verbal magic, and David Lake's discussion in the same year of colloquialisms that allow the B-text additions to be securely dated. On every major issue, Greg's analysis was shown to have been mistaken. New editions based on the A text substantiated this reversal of the field: David Ormerod's and Christopher Wortham's 1985 edition was followed in 1989 and 1990 by Roma Gill's modernized and old-spelling editions, in 1991 by my first Broadview Press edition, and in 1993 by the Revels Plays edition of David Bevington and Eric Rasmussen.

But the demonstration that the A text is both earlier and more authentic than the B text left two further questions unanswered. Given that A provides a more authentic version of the play than B, how closely is it related to the original manuscript produced by Marlowe and his collaborators? And if B is recognized as a thoroughly sedimented text, the most recent layers of which date from 1602 or later, does that mean it can be of no substantive value to editors of A-text editions?

Ormerod and Wortham answered the second of these questions by declaring that those superior readings which do occur in B in some parallel passages "can be put down to intelligent editorial emendation rather than access to a supposed manuscript by Marlowe" (Ormerod and Wortham xxviii). Gill, similarly, suggested that "For the most part the edited and censored B text is of historical interest rather than practical use in preparing a modern edition of *Dr. Faustus*" (Gill 1990: xvii). I argued for a more nuanced conclusion, noting that while the A version of the play is clearly more authentic, in several parallel passages the readings of the A text seem clearly to be secondary to those of B (Keefer 1991: lxi, lxvii–lxix).

In 1993, Eric Rasmussen proposed what looked like a definitive answer to the first question. In a modestly titled but important monograph, *A textual companion to "Doctor Faustus,"* published alongside the Revels edition, he argued on the basis of a detailed study of the typefaces and variant spellings of the 1604 quarto that this first edition of the play was printed from the authorial manuscript of Marlowe and his collaborators. Leah Marcus has written amusingly that the wish-fulfillment fantasy of Marlowe scholars would have to include the discovery of an authorial manuscript of *Doctor Faustus* (Marcus 38). Forget the fantasy: according to Rasmussen, something close to that object of desire has been staring us in the face all along—in the form of the 1604 quarto, "which must now be presented as the text with primary authority. Scholars who are chiefly interested in Christopher Marlowe will have to concentrate exclusively upon the A-text, which preserves the original version of what is arguably his supreme achievement as a playwright" (Rasmussen 93).

During the past several years I have returned to the problem of the A and B texts; the result, a new analysis of the issue which is being published concurrently with this edition (see Keefer 2006 and 2007), establishes two points of some importance to editors and readers of *Doctor Faustus*.

I have shown, first, that Eric Rasmussen's own evidence does not support the conclusions he drew from it. That evidence may indeed suggest that the non-Marlovian Acts Three and Four of the A text were printed from authorial manuscripts—but at the same time it actively undermines any such claim for the rest of the play.

And secondly, I have demonstrated that at four points in the play—in both of Act Two's Marlovian scenes, in the chorus to Act Three, and in Act Three, scene one—there are short passages in which the readings of the B text are clearly prior to the parallel readings of A. These local superiorities can be attributed to the consultation during the printing of B of a manuscript that contained readings which come from an earlier state of the play than those provided by the 1604 quarto—and in every Marlovian scene in B, except for the heavily revised Act Five, scene one, there is evidence of recourse to this hypothetical underlying manuscript.

This analysis has significant implications for editorial practice. David Bevington and Eric Rasmussen, and those more recent editors who have accepted Rasmussen's textual analysis, have followed the readings of the A text (even where these might seem problematic or, frankly, inferior to the readings of B), on the grounds that A was printed from authorial manuscripts. But if A's Marlovian scenes were not printed from authorial manuscript, and at certain points offer readings demonstrably inferior to those of B, a different procedure is called for in critical editorial work.

The present edition follows the A version of *Doctor Faustus*, but in parallel passages where my analysis has led me to conclude that the readings of the A text are secondary or corrupted, and that the B text preserves readings from an earlier state of the play, I have not hesitated to prefer these readings.

Given the fact that the B text underwent censorship as well as thoroughgoing revision, extreme caution is called for in such judgments. In critical editorial work of this kind, two opposite forms of error are possible. It is possible, on one side, to attribute to the A text an authority it does not have, and to print as Marlovian and authorial word choices that might more accurately be ascribed either to the actors or copyists through whose hands the manuscript passed, or else to the evidently careless compositors who set the type for the 1604 quarto. An uncritical conflation of A and B readings, on the other hand, could result in an editorial preferring of word choices that are actually those of early seventeenth-century revisers or censors, rather than of Christopher Marlowe and his original collaborator.

Most contemporary A-text editors have, I believe, succumbed to the former error. I hope to have avoided the latter one. The reasons for my choices have in every instance been provided in the notes to the full-scale edition of the two versions of *Doctor Faustus* that is being published by Broadview Press concurrently with this edition.

The major textual innovation of my 1991 edition was its relocation of the two comic scenes printed here as Act Two, scene two and Act Three, scene two. Both scenes were printed out of sequence in the 1604 quarto, and the first of them had not previously been correctly relocated. My innovation, which restored the structural integrity of the A version, has been accepted by all subsequent editors of the play, and is retained in this edition.

THE TRAGICAL HISTORY OF DOCTOR FAUSTUS

DRAMATIS PERSONAE

(in the order of their appearance, including *mutes)

CHORUS.

JOHN FAUSTUS, *doctor of theology.*

WAGNER, *a student, and Faustus's servant; also speaks the part of* CHORUS.

GOOD ANGEL.

EVIL ANGEL.

VALDES *and* CORNELIUS, *magicians.*

FIRST *and* SECOND SCHOLARS, *colleagues of Faustus at Wittenberg.*

MEPHASTOPHILIS.

CLOWN (ROBIN).

RAFE, *a second clown.*

LUCIFER.

BELZEBUB.

SEVEN DEADLY SINS.

POPE.

CARDINAL OF LORRAINE.

FRIARS.

VINTNER.

CAROLUS (CHARLES) THE FIFTH, *Emperor.*

KNIGHT.

*ATTENDANTS OF THE EMPEROR.

*ALEXANDER AND HIS *PARAMOUR.

HORSE-COURSER.

DUKE OF VANHOLT *and his* DUCHESS.

THIRD SCHOLAR.

HELEN OF GREECE.

OLD MAN.

*DEVILS.

PROLOGUE

Enter Chorus.

CHORUS.

Not marching now in fields of Thracimene
Where Mars did mate the Carthaginians,
Nor sporting in the dalliance of love
In courts of kings where state is overturn'd,
Nor in the pomp of proud audacious deeds   5
Intends our muse to vaunt his heavenly verse.
Only this, gentlemen: we must perform
The form of Faustus' fortunes, good or bad.
To patient judgments we appeal our plaud,
And speak for Faustus in his infancy: 10
Now is he born, his parents base of stock,
In Germany, within a town call'd Rhodes;
Of riper years to Wittenberg he went,

---

2. *Mars did mate*] Mars allied himself with or rivalled. Hannibal's Carthaginian army inflicted a crushing defeat upon the Romans at the battle of Lake Trasummenus in 217 BCE. According to Livy's *Historiae* XXII. i. 8-12, the battle was preceded by terrifying portents in which the war-god Mars figured prominently.

3-5.] These lines may refer to other plays by Marlowe: lines 3-4 to *Dido, Queen of Carthage* or (depending on the dating of *Doctor Faustus*) to *Edward II*, and line 5 to *Tamburlaine*.

4. *state*] Though *OED* cites this line as an instance of "state" in the obsolete sense of "high rank, greatness, power" (*OED* "state," 16.b), the word may also carry the modern meaning of "the supreme civil power and government" ("state," 29).

6. *our muse*] the poet. A metonymic equation of muse with poet is evident in Shakespeare, Sonnet xxi. 1-2, and Milton, *Lycidas*, lines 19-21.
vaunt] display proudly (*OED* 4). This B1 reading seems preferable to A1's "daunt" (meaning "quell" or "overcome"), which is probably a misprint (Greg 41).

7-8. *perform / The form*] a characteristically Marlovian jingle; compare II. iii. 42 ("whose termine is term'd"), *2 Tamburlaine* III. v. 27 ("brandishing their brands") and V. iii. 7 ("pitch their pitchy tents"), and *The Jew of Malta* I. i. 17 ("Haply some hapless man…").

8. *Faustus*] pronounced as spelled by Henslowe in his *Diary*: "Fostes."

9. *appeal our plaud*] appeal for our applause.

12. *Rhodes*] Roda (now Stadtroda), near Weimar.

13. *Wittenberg*] The University of Wittenberg was famous under Martin Luther and Philipp Melanchthon as a Protestant centre of learning. The A-text's "Wertenberg" is an error, prompted perhaps by a compositor's awareness of the Duchy of

Whereas his kinsmen chiefly brought him up.
15   So soon he profits in divinity,
The fruitful plot of scholarism grac'd,
That shortly he was grac'd with doctor's name,
Excelling all whose sweet delight disputes
In heavenly matters of theology,
20   Till swoll'n with cunning of a self-conceit,
His waxen wings did mount above his reach
And melting heavens conspir'd his overthrow:
For falling to a devilish exercise,
And glutted now with learning's golden gifts,
25   He surfeits upon cursed necromancy;

Württemberg as a state allied to England, or by knowledge that Melanchthon and others had claimed that Faustus was born and died in Württemberg (see Palmer and More 101-02, 105-07, 119-21).

14. *whereas*] where. Compare *Dido* I. ii. 28, and *2 Tamburlaine* III. ii. 66 and V. iii. 132.

17. *grac'd*] Cambridge degrees were and still are conferred by the "grace" or decree of the university Senate; Marlowe's name appears in the Grace Book in 1584 and in 1587 for the B.A. and M.A. degrees respectively.

18. *whose sweet delight disputes*] "Disputes" may be construed as a verb; more probably the expression is elliptical and means "whose sweet delight consists in disputes...." Bowers emends to "whose sweet delight's dispute." B1's "and sweetly can dispute" appears to be an attempt to clarify a difficult wording.

20. *swoll'n with cunning of a self-conceit*] The phrase implies that Faustus is "pregnant with self-engendered cleverness" (Hamlin 1996: 8). "Cunning" can mean knowledge or erudition, sometimes with negative connotations made explicit in Bacon's essay "Of Cunning" (1612): "We take Cunning for a sinister or crooked wisdom" (Bacon 434).

21. *waxen wings*] an allusion to the story of Icarus (cf. Ovid, *Metamorphoses* VIII. 183-235): escaping with his father Daedalus from Minos's island kingdom of Crete, Icarus ignored his father's warning about the wings he had made for them and flew too close to the sun. The episode was a favourite of Renaissance moralists and emblem writers.

22. *melting heavens conspir'd his overthrow*] Compare *1 Tamburlaine* IV. ii. 8-11, where the possibility of heaven conspiring refers to astrological causation as opposed to the will of "the chiefest god." In B1, a comma after "melting" alters the sense: the melting ceases to be an aspect of the heavens' active and conspiratorial power, and becomes instead a consequence of mounting above one's reach.

23. *falling to*] These words link the metaphors of an Icarian (or Luciferian) fall and of gluttonous surfeit. A distant secondary overtone in line 23 ("falling to" in the sense of eating, as in the B-version III. ii. 59, 61) comes suddenly to the fore in line 24 with "glutted now."

25. *necromancy*] The A-text spelling ("Negromancy," corrected in B to "Necromancie") reflects a common Medieval and early modern corruption of *necromantia* (divination by consultation of the dead) into *nigro-* or *negromantia* (black magic).

Nothing so sweet as magic is to him,
Which he prefers before his chiefest bliss:
And this the man that in his study sits.

Exit.

ACT I

— ACT I SCENE I —

Faustus in his study.

FAUSTUS.

Settle thy studies Faustus, and begin
To sound the depth of that thou wilt profess.
Having commenc'd, be a divine in show,
Yet level at the end of every art,
5   And live and die in Aristotle's works.
Sweet *Analytics*, 'tis thou hast ravish'd me:
Bene disserere est finis logices.

1-37.] As Jump, and Bevington and Rasmussen, have noted, these lines may be indebted
to two passages in Lyly's *Euphues*: "Philosophy, Physic, Divinity, shall be my study.
O the hidden secrets of Nature, the express image of moral virtues, the equal balance of Justice, the medicines to heal all diseases, how they begin to delight me. The
Axiomaes of *Aristotle*, the *Maxims* of *Justinian*, the *Aphorismes* of *Galen*, have suddenly
made such a breach into my mind that I seem only to desire them which did only
erst detest them" (Lyly i. 241); "If thou be so nice that thou canst no way brook the
practice of physic, or so unwise that thou wilt not beat thy brains about the institutes
of the law, confer all thy study, all thy time, all thy treasure to the attaining of the
sacred and sincere knowledge of divinity" (Lyly i. 251-52).

2. *profess*] affirm faith in or allegiance to; also "adopt as the subject of public teaching"
(Ward 129).

3. *commenc'd*] taken an academic degree.

be a divine in show] Faustus is advising himself to make a hypocritical profession of divinity (in a manner antithetical to the sincere piety advocated in Lyly's *Euphues*).

4. *level at the end of every art*] take aim at or challenge the final purpose or limit of every
discipline. Aristotle begins his *Nicomachean Ethics* by stating that "Every art and every
inquiry, and similarly every action and choice, is thought to aim at some good; and
for this reason the good has rightly been declared to be that at which all things aim"
(Aristotle ii. 1729 [1094a]). Faustus both echoes and perverts this doctrine: "level at"
here implies deliberate opposition, as in *2 Henry IV* III. ii. 243-44: "the foeman may
with as great aim level at the edge of a penknife."

5. *live and die in Aristotle's works*] This echoes a passage in Giordano Bruno's *La cena de
le Ceneri*, or *Ash Wednesday Supper* (1584), I. 34, which mocks those who, without
grasping even the titles of his books, "want to live and die for Aristotle" (Bruno
1995: 95).

6. Analytics] the name of two treatises on logic by Aristotle, whose works still domi-
nated the university curriculum.

7. bene … logices] "To argue well is the end or purpose of logic." This definition,
derived not from Aristotle but from Cicero, recurs in works on logic and dialectic

Is to dispute well logic's chiefest end?
Affords this art no greater miracle?
Then read no more, thou hast attain'd the end.   10
A greater subject fitteth Faustus' wit:
Bid *on kai me on* farewell; Galen come,
Seeing *ubi desinit philosophus, ibi incipit medicus.*
Be a physician Faustus, heap up gold,
And be eterniz'd for some wondrous cure!   15
Summum bonum medicinae sanitas:
The end of physic is our bodies' health.
Why Faustus, hast thou not attain'd that end?
Is not thy common talk sound aphorisms?
Are not thy bills hung up as monuments,   20
Whereby whole cities have escap'd the plague
And thousand desperate maladies been eas'd?
Yet art thou still but Faustus, and a man.
Couldst thou make men to live eternally,
Or being dead, raise them to life again,   25
Then this profession were to be esteem'd.
Physic farewell; where is Justinian?

---

by Petrus Ramus (1515-72), who hoped to supplant Aristotelian logic with his own dichotomizing method.

11. *wit*] understanding.

12. on kai me on] Bullen identified A1's "*Oncaymaeon*" as a transliteration of Greek words meaning "being and not being." The phrase is not Aristotelian; its source is a text of the sophist Gorgias preserved in the sceptic Sextus Empiricus's *Adversus mathematicos* VII. 65-86.

Galen] Claudius Galenus (c. 130-200), a Greek who served as the personal physician of several Roman emperors, is the most famous of ancient writers on medicine.

13. ubi ... medicus] "Where the philosopher leaves off, there the physician begins." Freely adapted from Aristotle, *Sense and Sensibilia* 436a (see Aristotle i. 693).

15. *be eterniz'd*] be immortalized. The implications can be religious, or wholly secular (in the sense of attaining worldly fame).

16. Summum ... sanitas] "The supreme good of medicine is health." Translated from Aristotle, *Nicomachean Ethics* 1094a (see Aristotle ii. 1729); a similar formulation occurs in Aristotle's *Politics* 1258a.

17. *physic*] medicine.

19. *sound aphorisms*] reliable medical precepts. Hippocrates' *Aphorisms* consisted of more than four hundred short sentences containing the basis of his teachings. The term came to refer to pithy sentences containing the gist of any subject.

20. *bills*] prescriptions, advertisements.

27. *Justinian*] A sixth-century Roman emperor responsible for compiling and codifying

Si una eademque res legatur duobus,
alter rem, alter valorem rei, etc.
30 A petty case of paltry legacies!
Exhereditare filium non potest pater, nisi—
Such is the subject of the *Institute*
And universal body of the law.
This study fits a mercenary drudge
35 Who aims at nothing but external trash—
Too servile and illiberal for me.
When all is done, divinity is best:
Jerome's Bible, Faustus, view it well.

Roman law. Gill notes that "His *Corpus Juris* consisted of four parts, the first of which was *Institutiones*, a manual intended for the use of students" (Gill 1990: 55).

28-29. Si … rei] "If one and the same thing is bequeathed to two persons, one of them shall have the thing, the other the value of the thing." This is derived in part from II. xx. 8 of Justinian's *Institutiones* or *Institutes*.

30. *petty*] inconsiderable, trivial. This word (from B1) often occurs in commercial, financial, or legal contexts: "petty traffickers" (*Merchant of Venice* I. i. 12), "petty charges … petty gettings" ("Of Expense," Bacon 54). Bevington and Rasmussen find B1's reading superior to A1's "pretty" (meaning "fine" or "admirable," spoken ironically).

31. Exhereditare … nisi—] "A father cannot disinherit his son except—." A loose rendering of a rule from Justinian's *Institutes* II. xiii (see Gill 1990: 56).

32-33. Institute / *And universal body of the law*] This is an instance of the rhetorical figure of hendiadys ("the figure of twins" [Puttenham 188]), making a double reference to the legal code of Justinian. "Institute," uncapitalized in A1 and B1 and meaning "founding principle," is recognized by most editors as referring also to Justinian's *Institutes*; B1's "body of the law" evokes the *Corpus Iuris Civilis* within which the *Institutes* was a founding text. A1's corrupt reading "body of the Church" may be the work of a compositor who, with Calvin's *The Institution of Christian Religion* in mind, understood "institute" as evoking an ecclesiastical context.

34. *This study*] Bevington and Rasmussen print A1's "His study," and gloss it as meaning "the study of Justinian." But Faustus takes up Aristotle, Galen, and Justinian as successive metonyms for logic, medicine, and law, and in turn dismisses "this art" (9), "this profession" (26), and—in B1's reading—"this study" (34). A1's reading, which requires a possessive pronoun to refer to an antecedent from which it is separated by six lines, is probably a compositorial error.

36. *Too servile*] A contrast between the liberal arts and "servile" or "mechanical" studies and practices is an Elizabethan commonplace. Greg noted a graphical resemblance between A1's nonsensical "The deuill" and B1's "Too seruile" which might suggest that A1's compositor misread the manuscript. A3, used in the printing of B1, reads "The Diuell"; B1's compositor probably had access to a manuscript that provided the correct reading.

38. *Jerome's Bible*] The *Vulgate*, prepared mainly by St. Jerome in the 4th century, was the Latin text of the Bible used by the Roman Catholic church. Faustus's quotations

Stipendium peccati mors est. Ha! *Stipendium, etc.*
The reward of sin is death? That's hard.   40
Si peccasse negamus, fallimur,
et nulla est in nobis veritas:
If we say that we have no sin
We deceive ourselves, and there's no truth in us.
Why then belike we must sin,   45
And so consequently die.
Ay, we must die, an everlasting death.
What doctrine call you this? *Che sarà, sarà,*
What will be, shall be? Divinity, adieu!
These metaphysics of magicians   50

---

in lines 39 and 41-42 differ from the wording of the *Vulgate*: the Latin appears to be
Marlowe's back-translation from English texts, in the first case probably the *Geneva
Bible* (1560), and in the second, *The Book of Common Prayer.*

39. Stipendium ... est] the first half of *Romans* 6: 23, a verse translated in the *Geneva Bible*
as follows: "For the wages of sin is death: but the gift of God is eternal life through
Jesus Christ our Lord."

etc.] Greg thinks that while in line 29 *et cetera* is part of the spoken text, it indicates
here that Faustus is to repeat and murmur to himself the words he has quoted from
Romans 6: 23. Alternatively, *et cetera* might be understood as something the actor
pronounces as a sign of dismissive impatience. As Gill 1990 notes, "It is certainly *not*
an indication that Faustus should appear to continue his reading" into the second
half of *Romans* 6: 23.

41-42. Si peccasse ... veritas] *1 John* 1: 8. Faustus has again quoted only the first half of
an antithetical statement. In the *Geneva Bible, 1 John* 1: 8-9 is rendered as follows:
"If we say that we have no sin, we deceive our selves, and truth is not in us. If we
acknowledge our sins, he is faithful and just, to forgive us our sins, and to cleanse us
from all unrighteousness."

43-47. If ... death] In Thomas Becon's *Dialogue Between the Christian Knight and Satan*
(1564), Satan attempts to reduce the Knight to despair with a similar syllogism; the
Knight, recognizing his guilt before the Law, appeals to the Gospel, "that is to say,
grace, favour, and remission of sins, promised in Christ" (Becon 628-29). In Spenser's
Faerie Queene, Una rescues Redcrosse Knight from the similar arguments of Despair
by asking him, "In heavenly mercies hast thou not a part? / Why shouldst thou then
despair, that chosen art? / Where justice grows, there grows eke greater grace" (I.
ix. 53). An appeal to divine grace and election was held to provide the only possible escape from what Luther called "the devil's syllogism"; see Snyder 1965: 30-31.

48-49. What ... adieu] Making a "despairing reference to the difficulties of the doctrine
of predestination" (Ward 135), these words amount to a reprobate's version of the
Calvinist teaching on this subject.

50. metaphysics] the science of the supernatural. The word originated as the title given
by later Greek scholars to Aristotle's fourteen books on ontology, which in the
traditional arrangement of his writings were placed following (*meta*) his works on

And necromantic books are heavenly!
Lines, circles, seals, letters and characters:
Ay, these are those that Faustus most desires.
O, what a world of profit and delight,
55   Of power, of honor, of omnipotence,
Is promis'd to the studious artisan!
All things that move between the quiet poles
Shall be at my command. Emperors and kings
Are but obey'd in their several provinces,
60   Nor can they raise the wind, or rend the clouds;
But his dominion that exceeds in this
Stretcheth as far as doth the mind of man!
A sound magician is a mighty god:
Here tire, my brains, to get a deity!

---

natural science (*ta physika*). But for Renaissance occult philosophers like Henricus Cornelius Agrippa the Latin word *metaphysica* referred to things above nature.

52. *lines*] a reference, Ormerod and Wortham suggest, to the occult art of geomancy, or divination by means of astrologically determined patterns of points and lines. See Agrippa, *In geomanticam disciplinam lectura* (Agrippa 1970: i. 506-07).

circles] See I. iii. 8-13. A primary function of magic circles was to protect the practitioner of ceremonial magic from evil spirits.

seals, letters and characters] talismanic symbols of the planets and of the angels, spiritual intelligences and daemons that were believed to govern them. "Seals," a conjecture recorded by Ward, is the emendation I would propose for A1's "sceanes," which makes poor sense (and may for that reason have been dropped from B).

54. *profit and delight*] There may be a parallel between what Faustus sees as the promise of magic and Horace's statement of the aim of poetry: "Aut *prodesse* volunt aut *delectare* poetae ..." (*Ars poetica* ll. 333; emphasis added: "Poets seek either to profit [the reader] or to delight ...").

56. *artisan*] practitioner of an art.

57. *quiet poles*] This could refer either to the motionless poles of the outermost celestial sphere or, more probably, to those of the earth. See the note to II. iii. 48-49.

60. *raise the wind, or rend the clouds*] a blasphemous echo of *Jeremiah* 10: 13 (which speaks of God's power over clouds, lightning and wind). Agrippa, in *De occulta philosophia*, III. vi, claims that magicians devoted to God and elevated by the theological virtues of love, hope and faith, can "command the elements, drive away mists, summon winds, collect clouds into rain, cure diseases, raise the dead..." (Agrippa 1970: i. 321).

61. *exceeds*] surpasses others, is preeminent, whether in a good or bad sense (*OED*, 5).

63. *mighty god*] This is the A1 reading; B1 prints "Demi-god," which may be a revision intended to avoid imputations of blasphemy.

64. *get*] beget. A1's reading ("Here Faustus try thy brains to gain a deity") appears secondary in two respects: the more difficult reading preserved in B1 ("to get a Deity") seems here to have been simplified, and as at II. i. 137, the vocative "Faustus" seems an addition.

Enter Wagner.

Wagner, commend me to my dearest friends,   65
The German Valdes and Cornelius;
Request them earnestly to visit me.

WAGNER.
I will, sir.

Exit.

FAUSTUS.
Their conference will be a greater help to me
Than all my labors, plod I ne'er so fast.   70

Enter the Good Angel and the Evil Angel.

GOOD ANGEL.
O Faustus, lay that damned book aside,
And gaze not on it, lest it tempt thy soul
And heap God's heavy wrath upon thy head!
Read, read the Scriptures; that is blasphemy.

EVIL ANGEL.
Go forward, Faustus, in that famous art   75
Wherein all nature's treasury is contain'd:
Be thou on earth as Jove is in the sky,
Lord and commander of these elements!

---

69. *conference*] conversation.

70.1. Good Angel … Evil Angel] Belief in such spirits was widespread. Agrippa writes:
"As therefore there is given to every man a good spirit, so also there is given to every
man an evil diabolical spirit" (*De occulta philosophia* III. xx, Agrippa 1993: 521).

73. *heap God's heavy wrath*] The Good Angel makes no mention of grace or election. His
words, addressed to a man whose soul has evidently already been tempted by the
necromantic book he is holding, seem less akin to the intervention of Spenser's Una
(see note to I. i. 43-47 above) than to the persuasions of Despair himself: "Is not the
measure of thy sinful hire / High heaped up with huge iniquity, / Against the day of
wrath, to burden thee?" (*Faerie Queene* I. ix. 53, I. ix. 46).

77. *Jove*] The substitution of the supreme god of the Roman pantheon for the Christian
God is common in Renaissance humanist texts and in Elizabethan poetry.

78. *these elements*] earth, water, air and fire, here used as a metonymy for the world constituted by the four elements and contained by the sphere of the moon.

Exeunt Angels.

FAUSTUS.

How am I glutted with conceit of this!
80   Shall I make spirits fetch me what I please,
Resolve me of all ambiguities,
Perform what desperate enterprise I will?
I'll have them fly to India for gold,
Ransack the ocean for orient pearl
85   And search all corners of the new found world
For pleasant fruits and princely delicates;
I'll have them read me strange philosophy
And tell the secrets of all foreign kings;
I'll have them wall all Germany with brass
90   And make swift Rhine circle fair Wittenberg;
I'll have them fill the public schools with silk
Wherewith the students shall be bravely clad;
I'll levy soldiers with the coin they bring,
And chase the Prince of Parma from our land

---

79. *conceit of this*] the thought, the notion of this.

80. *spirits*] Roberts (1996: 155-56) notes that in the *Heptameron* of Petrus de Abano (see note to I. i. 155), the aerial spirits associated with the seven days of the week are said to give gold and jewels, reveal secrets, provide soldiers, give victory in war, and teach the reconstructed principles of lost sciences (Agrippa 1970: i. 577, 579, 581, 583).

81. *Resolve me of all ambiguities*] This appears to echo Giordano Bruno's *La cena de le Ceneri* (1584), I. 34-35, where exponents of Bruno's "ancient philosophy" are said to be "miraculous in magic" and to "purge all doubts and clear away all contradictions." See Eriksen 1985: 464 and Bruno 1995: 96-97.

83. *India*] a name applied to "both th'Indias of spice and mine" (Donne, "The Sun Rising"); it could refer to the East Indies or to Spain's conquests in the Americas.

84. *orient pearl*] "lustrous; strictly, from the eastern seas" (Jump).

89. *wall ... brass*] an aspiration paralleled by Spenser's Merlin (*Faerie Queene* III. iii. 10) and by Greene's Friar Bacon (*Friar Bacon and Friar Bungay* ii. 30, 171).

91. *public schools*] the Cambridge term for the lecture halls where students of all colleges attended lectures and participated in academic disputations (Riggs 64).

silk] Dyce's emendation; A1's "skill" is a metathesis perhaps resulting from compositorial fatigue; the error was copied by A2 and A3, and followed by B1.

92. *bravely*] splendidly. University regulations forbade students to wear fine clothing: silk-lined hoods could only be worn by the holders of graduate degrees.

94. *the Prince of Parma*] Alessandro Farnese, Duke of Parma, a grandson of the emperor Charles V and the foremost general of his time. Parma, who served as Spanish

And reign sole king of all our provinces;   95
Yea, stranger engines for the brunt of war
Than was the fiery keel at Antwerp's bridge
I'll make my servile spirits to invent.
Come German Valdes and Cornelius,
And make me blest with your sage conference!   100

Enter Valdes and Cornelius.

Valdes, sweet Valdes, and Cornelius,
Know that your words have won me at the last
To practise magic and concealed arts:
Yet not your words only, but mine own fantasy,
That will receive no object, for my head   105
But ruminates on necromantic skill.
Philosophy is odious and obscure;
Both law and physic are for petty wits;
Divinity is basest of the three,
Unpleasant, harsh, contemptible and vile;   110
'Tis magic, magic, that hath ravish'd me.
Then, gentle friends, aid me in this attempt,
And I, that have with concise syllogisms
Gravell'd the pastors of the German church

---

governor of the Netherlands from 1578 until his death in 1592, was hated by
Protestants as a tyrant. He commanded the force that the Armada was to have transported across the Channel in 1588 to invade England.
96. *brunt*] assault, onset.
97. *fiery ... bridge*] On April 4, 1585 the Netherlanders sent two fire-ships loaded with explosives against the pontoon bridge over the river Scheldt which formed part of Parma's
siegeworks around Antwerp; one of them reached its target and destroyed part of the
bridge. Parma had the bridge rebuilt, and Antwerp subsequently surrendered.
104-06. *Yet ... skill*] According to Marsilio Ficino's influential theory of natural magic,
fantasy or imagination is the chief magical faculty. Faustus is saying that his rumina-
tions on necromancy block his perception of external things. B1 cuts these lines,
perhaps because of their obscurity.
106. *but ruminates on*] does nothing but reflect upon (Burnett).
109. *basest of the three*] "i.e., even baser than the other three" (Greg).
109-10.] B1 cuts these lines, no doubt to avoid imputations of blasphemy and the penal-
ties threatened by the 1606 Act of Abuses.
114. *Gravell'd*] confounded, perplexed. This usage is a nautical metaphor carrying implications of mental shallowness: one can be "gravelled for lack of matter" (*As You*

115	And made the flowering pride of Wittenberg
	Swarm to my problems as the infernal spirits
	On sweet Musaeus when he came to hell,
	Will be as cunning as Agrippa was,
	Whose shadows made all Europe honor him.
	VALDES.
120	Faustus, these books, thy wit, and our experience
	Shall make all nations to canonize us.
	As Indian Moors obey their Spanish lords,
	So shall the subjects of every element
	Be always serviceable to us three:
125	Like lions shall they guard us when we please,
	Like Almain rutters with their horsemen's staves,

Like It IV. i. 64) just as a ship lacking an adequate depth of water under it will be grounded or gravelled on a shoal (*OED*, "gravel," v. 3).

116. *problems*] questions proposed for academic discussion or scholastic disputation (*OED*, 2). A sample problem from the *Sophismata* of the influential scholastic Jean Buridan: "The claim 'God is unjust' (*Deum esse iniustum*) is to be denied by all the faithful." Buridan notes that affirming God to be unjust is heretical and false, and since heretical and false statements are to be denied, the proposition is true; but affirming God to be unjust amounts, because of his justice, to nothing, and because that which is nothing is neither to be asserted nor denied, the proposition is false. Clerical opponents might well be gravelled by Buridan's conclusion that the proposition is indeed false (see Buridan, *Sophisms* III. A, 97, 99-102).

117. *Musaeus*] the legendary pre-Homeric Greek poet, a pupil of Orpheus, to whom was ascribed the poem on which Marlowe based his *Hero and Leander*. In Virgil's *Aeneid* VI. 666-67, Musaeus is represented as standing in the midst of a crowd of spirits in the underworld, head and shoulders above the rest.

118-19. *Agrippa ... Whose shadows*] Henricus Cornelius Agrippa of Nettesheim (1486-1535) distinguished in *De occulta philosophia* III. xlii between two kinds of necromancy: *necyomantia*, the reviving of corpses by means of a blood sacrifice, and *scyomantia*, in which only the shadow of a dead person is invoked (Agrippa 1970: i. 437). Lyly wrote, in the court prologue to *Campaspe*: "Whatsoever we present, we wish it may be thought the dancing of *Agrippa* his shadows, who in the moment they were seen, were of any shape one could conceive..." (Lyly ii. 316).

122. *Indian Moors*] native peoples of the Americas, or "Muslims from the Spanish-controlled Portuguese East Indies" (Neill 273).

123. *subjects*] a word close in meaning to B1's "spirits" (which may be an editorial simplification). "Subjects" carries the additional implication of obedience or subjection to a sovereign will (here, that of the magician). Ward glosses "subjects" as "the bodily forms taken by the spirits belonging to the several elements."

126. *Almain rutters*] German cavalrymen.

staves] lances.

Or Lapland giants trotting by our sides;
Sometimes like women, or unwedded maids,
Shadowing more beauty in their airy brows
Than has the white breasts of the queen of love.   130
From Venice shall they drag huge argosies,
And from America the golden fleece
That yearly stuffs old Philip's treasury,
If learned Faustus will be resolute.

FAUSTUS.

Valdes, as resolute am I in this   135
As thou to live, therefore object it not.

CORNELIUS.

The miracles that magic will perform
Will make thee vow to study nothing else.
He that is grounded in astrology,
Enrich'd with tongues, well seen in minerals,   140

---

129. *shadowing*] harboring. Compare *1 Tamburlaine* V. i. 513-14.

130. *Than has the white breasts*] A1's "Than in their white breasts," which repeats "in their" from line 129, appears to be a compositorial error (as is A1's "For Venice" in line 131). Greg's emendation "in the," which produces the puzzling meaning that these spirits are "shadowing" beauty in the breasts of Aphrodite or Venus, is accepted by current A-version editors.

131. *argosies*] large merchant ships of the city of Ragusa (now Dubrovnik), on the Dalmatian coast, which was known to the English as Argouse, Argusa or Aragosa; by the late 16th century the word was applied to merchant ships of Venice and Spain as well as Ragusa.

132. *golden fleece*] "Perhaps the word 'argosies', often wrongly supposed to be derived from the name of Jason's ship, the *Argo*, suggested to Marlowe the use of the image of the golden fleece" (Jump).

133. *stuffs*] An annual plate-fleet shipped gold and silver from the Americas to Spain. Philip II of Spain died in 1598; A1's "stuffs" is revised in B1 to "stuff'd" to accommodate that fact.

139. *grounded in*] firmly established in. The usage reflects the widespread view of astrology as a foundational science which studied the celestial influences that supposedly affected the occult qualities of all earthly objects.

140. *enrich'd with tongues*] improved by knowledge of (ancient) languages. Latin was the common language of educated people in 16th-century Europe, while advanced humanist scholars would be expected to study Greek, Hebrew and possibly Aramaic and other languages as well.

well seen in minerals] well versed in the properties of minerals. Ward notes that "seen" here has "the same meaning as the Latin *spectatus*—of proved capacity, of a high reputation."

Hath all the principles magic doth require.
Then doubt not, Faustus, but to be renown'd
And more frequented for this mystery
Than heretofore the Delphian oracle.
145 The spirits tell me they can dry the sea
And fetch the treasure of all foreign wrecks,
Ay, all the wealth that our forefathers hid
Within the massy entrails of the earth.
Then tell me Faustus, what shall we three want?

FAUSTUS.

150 Nothing, Cornelius. O, this cheers my soul!
Come, show me some demonstrations magical,
That I may conjure in some lusty grove
And have these joys in full possession.

VALDES.

Then haste thee to some solitary grove,
155 And bear wise Bacon's and Albanus' works,
The Hebrew Psalter, and New Testament;
And whatsoever else is requisite
We will inform thee ere our conference cease.

CORNELIUS.

Valdes, first let him know the words of art,

---

143. *frequented*] sought out.

144. *Delphian oracle*] The oracle of Apollo at Delphi was the most famous and authoritative of ancient Greek oracles.

145-48.] According to Bevington and Rasmussen, "The pecuniary advantages of raising
a spirit are well attested to in Scot's *The Discovery of Witchcraft* (1584)"; they quote
from XV. xiii: "if thou wilt command him to tell thee of hidden treasures ... he will
tell it thee: or if thou wilt command him to bring thee gold or silver, he will bring it
thee" (Scot 347). Scot also states, however, that "He that can be persuaded that these
things are true ... may soon be brought to believe that the moon is made of green
cheese" (Scot 329 [XV. v]).

148. *massy*] solid and heavy, massive.

155. *wise Bacon's and Albanus's works*] Roger Bacon (c. 1214-94), an English Franciscan
philosopher, was reputed also to have been a magician (see Thorndike i. 659 ff., and
Greene's play *Friar Bacon and Friar Bungay*). "Albanus" is Pietro d'Abano or Petrus de
Aponus (c. 1250-1316), whose *Heptameron* was printed together with other works on
magic in editions of Agrippa's *De occulta philosophia*, with the author's name given as
"Petrus de Albanus" (Roberts 1996: 151, 154).

156. *Psalter, and New Testament*] Ward remarks that the book of *Psalms* and the opening
verses of the *Gospel of St. John* were thought to be particularly useful in conjurations.

And then, all other ceremonies learn'd,   160
Faustus may try his cunning by himself.

VALDES.

First I'll instruct thee in the rudiments,
And then wilt thou be perfecter than I.

FAUSTUS.

Then come and dine with me, and after meat
We'll canvass every quiddity thereof.   165
For ere I sleep I'll try what I can do;
This night I'll conjure though I die therefore.

Exeunt.

— ACT I SCENE II —

Enter two scholars.

1 SCH.

I wonder what's become of Faustus, that was wont to make
our schools ring with *sic probo.*

2 SCH.

That shall we know, for see: here comes his boy.

Enter Wagner.

1 SCH.

How now sirrah, where's thy master?

WAGNER.

God in heaven knows.   5

2 SCH.

Why, dost not thou know?

WAGNER.

Yes, I know, but that follows not.

---

164. *meat*] food.
165. *canvass every quiddity*] discuss every essential particular.
2. sic probo] "Thus I prove it"; the cry of triumph with which Faustus, in "gravelling"
    another theologian (I. i. 114) in disputation, would have clinched his argument.
4. *sirrah*] a term of address expressing contempt, or the addressee's social inferiority.
7. *that follows not*] an English equivalent, as Bevington and Rasmussen observe, of the

1 SCH.

Go to sirrah, leave your jesting, and tell us where he is.

WAGNER.

That follows not necessary by force of argument, which you,
being licentiate, should stand upon; therefore acknowledge
your error and be attentive.

2 SCH.

Why, didst thou not say thou knew'st?

WAGNER.

Have you any witness on't?

1 SCH.

Yes, sirrah, I heard you.

WAGNER.

Ask my fellow if I be a thief!

2 SCH.

Well, you will not tell us.

WAGNER.

Yes sir, I will tell you; yet if you were not dunces you would
never ask me such a question, for is not he *corpus naturale*,
and is not that *mobile*? Then wherefore should you ask me
such a question? But that I am by nature phlegmatic, slow

---

scholastic term *non sequitur*. (A syllogism of the form, "God in heaven knows where
Faustus is; we on earth do not know what God knows; therefore Wagner does not
know where Faustus is," is indeed one whose conclusion does not follow from its
premises.)

10. *licentiate*] licensed by an academic degree to proceed to further studies.
stand upon] insist on.

15.] A popular proverbial saying (see Tilley F177). Wagner means that the First Scholar's
support for his companion's statement is worth no more than one thief's testimony
to another's innocence.

17. *dunces*] Renaissance humanists opposed the hair-splitting complexity of scholastic
logic; the name of Johannes Duns Scotus (c. 1265-1308), one of the most subtle
medieval logicians, came to denote stupidity.

18-19. corpus naturale ... mobile] Ward explains *corpus naturale seu mobile*, i.e., "a body that
is natural or subject to change," as a scholastic adaptation of Aristotle's statement of
the subject-matter of physics (cf. *Physics* I. 2, 185a, in Aristotle i. 316). Giovanni Pico
wrote that "Corpus mobile est subiectum scientiae naturalis" ("Moveable body is the
subject of natural science"), which paraphrases the opening sentence of Aristotle's
On the Heavens (see Pico 216, and Aristotle i. 447). Wagner is telling his questioners
that they will find Faustus moving around among the things of nature.

20-21. *phlegmatic, slow to wrath*] Wagner is conforming to two of the injunctions of *James*

---

to wrath and prone to lechery (to love I would say), it were
not for you to come within forty foot of the place of execution—although I do not doubt but to see you both hanged
the next sessions. Thus having triumphed over you, I will set
my countenance like a precisian, and begin to speak thus: 25
Truly, my dear brethren, my master is within at dinner with
Valdes and Cornelius, as this wine if it could speak would
inform your worships; and so the Lord bless you, preserve
you, and keep you, my dear brethren, my dear brethren.

Exit.

I SCH.

Nay then, I fear he is fallen into that damned art, for which   30
they two are infamous through the world.

2 SCH.

Were he a stranger, and not allied to me, yet should I grieve
for him. But come, let us go and inform the Rector, and
see if he by his grave counsel can reclaim him.

I SCH.

O, but I fear me nothing can reclaim him.   35

2 SCH.

Yet let us try what we can do.

Exeunt.

1:19: "Wherefore my dear brethren, let every man be ... slow to speak, and slow to
wrath" (see Cornelius 240). In the following phrase, however, he lets the mask of
piety slip.

22-23. *come within forty foot ... execution*] Tilley lists the phrase as proverbial (Tilley F581).
"To do execution" could mean to eat heartily; the "place of execution" is in this sense
the dining-room where Faustus is conferring with Valdes and Cornelius. Wagner at
once reverts to the more obvious meaning, alluding, as Bevington and Rasmussen
note, to a legal prohibition of public access to the space surrounding the gallows.

25. *precisian*] a puritan, one who is scrupulous about religious observances.

28-29. *the Lord bless you ... and keep you*] See *Numbers* 6: 24. This is the first verse of the
priestly benediction delivered by God to Moses for Aaron and his sons to bless the
Israelites with. Wagner is mocking the language with which Christian services were
(and are) commonly brought to a close.

32. *allied to me*] bound to me in friendship (Bevington and Rasmussen).

33. *the Rector*] the academic head of the university.

— ACT I SCENE III —

Enter Faustus to conjure.

FAUSTUS.

    Now that the gloomy shadow of the earth,
    Longing to view Orion's drizzling look,
    Leaps from th'antarctic world unto the sky
    And dims the welkin with her pitchy breath,
5   Faustus, begin thine incantations,
    And try if devils will obey thy hest,

1-4.] Gill notes that "Marlowe invents a new myth ... when he hints at the love of the earth's shadow for the watery star, *nimbosus* Orion" (Gill 1990: 63). This myth may have resonances derived from the Hermetic creation myth, in which a shadow emerging from the primal light became a watery female Nature which, stirred by desire at the sight of the Son of God descending through the planetary spheres, enticed him by the reflection of his own beauty into sexual union (*Pymander* sig. A6v-8v, *Hermetica* 1-3). Marlowe may also be remembering the Hermetist Giordano Bruno's *Spaccio de la bestia trionfante* (*The Expulsion of the Triumphant Beast,* 1584), in which Christ is mocked under the name of Orion as an impostor (Bruno 1964: 256). Bevington and Rasmussen note that lines 1-4 also echo Spenser's *Faerie Queene* III. x. 46: "Now gan the humid vapour shed the ground / With pearly dew, and th'Earthes gloomy shade / Did dim the brightness of the welkin round."

1. *shadow of the earth*] As Norton-Smith observes, Macrobius in his *Commentum* I. xx. 18 writes of "the shadow of the earth which the sun, after setting and progressing into the lower hemisphere, sends out upwards, creating on earth the darkness which is called night...."

2. *Orion's drizzling look*] The constellation of Orion was associated in classical poetry with winter storms; cf. Virgil's *Aeneid* I. 535 (*nimbosus Orion*), and IV. 52 (*aquosus Orion*).

3. *th'antarctic world*] The thought that Marlowe held "the astonishing view that night comes not from the east but from the southern hemisphere" (Greg 310) has troubled commentators. But for observers in the northern latitudes of a geocentric world it is a matter of simple observation that the winter sun especially sinks into the western side of the lower hemisphere or *regio antarctica,* from which the shadow of the earth is therefore projected. For parallels to the Macrobius passage noted by Norton-Smith, see Virgil, *Georgics* I. 247-51; also Manilius, *Astronomica* I. 242-45.

4. *welkin*] sky.

pitchy breath] Norton-Smith points to a passage in Lucretius, *De rerum natura* VI. 476-79: "... from all rivers and from the earth itself we see clouds and steam rising up, which exhaled hence like breath are carried up in this way, and fill up the sky with their blackness...." In the Hermetic creation myth the desire of the shadowy, moist Nature for the Son of God is initially imaged in terms of "an unspeakable uproar, with a kind of great smoke erupting in the din" [*Pymander* sig. A6v]).

6. *hest*] behest.

Seeing thou hast pray'd and sacrific'd to them.
Within this circle is Jehovah's name,
Forward and backward anagrammatiz'd,
The breviated names of holy saints,   10
Figures of every adjunct to the heavens,
And characters of signs and erring stars
By which the spirits are enforc'd to rise;
Then fear not, Faustus, but be resolute,
And try the uttermost magic can perform.   15
Sint mihi dei Acherontis propitii! Valeat numen triplex
Iehovae! Ignei, aerii, aquatici spiritus salvete! Orientis prin-

---

9. *anagrammatiz'd*] Cabalist mystics saw hidden meanings in every possible recombina-
tion of letters in the Hebrew scriptures, though the names of God in particular were
thought to contain occult secrets of divine power and knowledge.

10. *breviated*] abbreviated. Roberts (1996: 155) identifies this as a reference to Agrippa's
explanation in *De occulta philosophia* III. xxx of a Cabalistic means of producing magical characters by rewriting the Hebrew name of an angel in a script whose figures are
contracted into a single composite shape.

11. *adjunct to*] "heavenly body fixed to" (Barnet).

12. *characters of signs and erring stars*] diagrams representing the constellations of the zodiac
(one Latin term for which was *signa*) and the planets.

16-22. Sint ... Mephastophilis] "May the gods of Acheron be propitious to me. Away with
the threefold divinity of Jehovah! Hail, spirits of fire, air, and water! Belzebub, Prince
of the East, monarch of burning hell, and Demogorgon, we invoke your favor that
Mephastophilis may appear and ascend. Why do you delay? By Jehovah, Gehenna, and
the holy water which I now sprinkle, by the sign of the cross which I now make, and by
our vows, may Mephastophilis himself now rise to serve us!" No known invocation by
a Renaissance magician includes anything resembling Faustus's abjuration of God.

16. Acherontis] Gill notes that Acheron, one of the rivers of the Greek underworld, is
here used as a metonymy for the whole.

16-17. Valeat numen triplex Iehouae!] Most scholars have understood *valeat* to be a force-
ful gesture of dismissal, and *numen triplex Iehouae* to refer to the Trinity. Faustus
is thus doing what at I. iii. 55 he claims to have done: abjuring the Trinity. This
dismissive sense of *valeat* occurs in Cicero's rejection of the gods of Epicurus in *De
natura deorum*, I. 124: "Deinde si maxime talis est deus ut nulla gratia, nulla hominum
caritate teneatur, valeat..." (Cicero i. 536: "If this is then indeed what God is, a being
who feels no love or care for humanity, away with him!"). The loveless God granted
by Cicero for the sake of argument is for Faustus a matter of subjective certainty: "Ay,
and Faustus will turn to God again. / To God? He loves thee not" (II. i. 9-10).

17. Ignei, aerii, aquatici] Greg and most subsequent editors have added "*terreni*," so that
Faustus addresses spirits of the earth, as well as of the other three elements. But
the omission may have been deliberate: according to Nashe, in *Pierce Penilesse his
Supplication to the Divell* (1592), the chief spirits of the earth "have no power to do any
great harm" (Nashe i. 231).

17-18. Orientis princeps Belzebub, inferni ardentis monarcha] Baal-zebub, god of

ceps Belzebub, inferni ardentis monarcha, et Demogorgon,
propitiamus vos ut appareat et surgat Mephastophilis. Quid
20   *tu moraris? Per Iehovam, Gehennam et consecratam aquam*
quam nunc spargo, signumque crucis quod nunc facio, et per
vota nostra, ipse nunc surgat nobis dicatus Mephastophilis.

Enter a devil.

Ekron, is mentioned in *2 Kings* 1: 2; the name means "Lord of the flies," and appears
to be a derisive modification of the name of a Canaanite god, "Baal, the Prince," or
"Baal of the Exalted Abode" (Fitzmyer 920). The New Testament name Beelzeboul
may mean in Hebrew "Lord of the house" (cf. *Matthew* 10: 25) or "Lord of the dung"
(Forsyth 295). In the *Vulgate*, and in most English translations, both names appear
as Beelzebub. In *Mark* 3: 22-26, *Matthew* 12: 24-28, and *Luke* 11: 15-20 the names of
Beelzebub, the ruler of the demons, and of Satan seem interchangeable. *Luke* 10: 18
("I saw Satan like lightning, fall down from heaven") has traditionally been understood as referring to *Isaiah* 14: 12 ("How art thou fallen from heaven, O Lucifer, son
of the morning?").

18.   Demogorgon] a god of the underworld; medieval writers understood the name
to mean either "terrible demon" or "terror to demons" (*OED*). Spenser's Duessa
says that Night (mythologized as an ancestral power of darkness) was "begot in
Daemogorgon's hall" (*Faerie Queene* I. v. 22).

19.   Mephastophilis] In the *Historia von D. Johann Fausten* (1587), and also in *EFB*,
this name appears as "Mephostophiles." The most frequent form in the A-text is
"Mephastophilis"; the usual form in B is "Mephostophilis." In all of its forms the
name reflects a thoroughly demonic contempt for the conventions of grammar. As
Russell (61) notes, it is a compound of three Greek words indicating negation (*me*),
light (*phos*), and loving (*philis*); its inventor made naive use of the fact that in Greek
dictionaries the gender of a substantive is indicated by the definite article which is
printed after it (e.g., *phos, to*). Thus we get "Me-phos-to-philis," "Not-light-lov-
ing"—perhaps parodying the Latin Lucifer, "Light-bearer." The A-text name might
possibly reflect the Homeric word for "light" (*phaos*) rather than the contracted Attic
form (*phos*); or it might be derived from a participial form (*phas*) of the verb *phimi*,
"to declare, affirm," thus (at a stretch) yielding the meaning "Not-affirming-loving."
As Butler writes, "A sinister ambiguity haunts the syllables and seems to mock such
conjectures" (Butler 1948: 132).

19-20.   Quid tu moraris?] Why do you delay? Peter of Abano advises in his *Heptameron*
that when the magician, after summoning spirits, perceives a great commotion, he
should then say: "Quid tardatis? quid moramini? quid facitis?" ("Why do you [pl.]
loiter? why do you delay? what are you doing?"), followed by further words of power
(Agrippa 1970: i. 572-73).

20.   Gehenna] hell, or, more precisely, "the type of hell" (Milton, *Paradise Lost* I. 405).
The name is derived from a site near Jerusalem where, according to *Jeremiah* 19: 2-6,
children had been slaughtered as burnt offerings to Baal.

I charge thee to return and change thy shape.
Thou art too ugly to attend on me;
Go, and return an old Franciscan friar: 25
That holy shape becomes a devil best.

Exit devil.

I see there's virtue in my heavenly words,
Who would not be proficient in this art?
How pliant is this Mephastophilis,
Full of obedience and humility: 30
Such is the force of magic and my spells!
Now, Faustus, thou art conjurer laureate
That canst command great Mephastophilis!
Quin redis, Mephastophilis, fratris imagine!

Enter Mephastophilis.

MEPH.
Now, Faustus, what wouldst thou have me do?   35
FAUSTUS.
I charge thee wait upon me whilst I live
To do whatever Faustus shall command,
Be it to make the moon drop from her sphere
Or the ocean to overwhelm the world.
MEPH.
I am a servant to great Lucifer,   40

---

27. *virtue*] power; also, ironically, moral virtue.
32. *laureate*] crowned with laurel; of proved distinction.
34. Quin ... imagine] "Why do you not return, Mephastophilis, in the shape of a
friar!"
38. *to make the moon drop from her sphere*] This and similar feats were ascribed to sorceresses
and magicians in various ancient texts: Virgil, *Eclogues* VIII. 69; Horace, *Epodes* V.
45-46 and XVII. 78; Ovid, *Metamorphoses* VII. 207; and Apuleius, *Metamorphoseon*
(*The Golden Ass*) I. iii. Greene's Friar Bacon claims to be able to "dim fair Luna to a
dark eclipse" (*Friar Bacon and Friar Bungay* ii. 48).
40. *Lucifer*] The name appears in *Isaiah* 14: 12 (see note to lines 17-18 above); the Hebrew
Helel ben Shahar ("Shining One, son of Dawn") of this verse was translated into
Greek as *Heosphoros* ("Dawn-bringing," the planet Venus as morning star), and into
the Latin of the *Vulgate* as Lucifer ("Light-bearer"). See Forsyth 134-36.

And may not follow thee without his leave;
No more than he commands must we perform.

FAUSTUS.

Did not he charge thee to appear to me?

MEPH.

No, I came now hither of my own accord.

FAUSTUS.

45 Did not my conjuring speeches raise thee? Speak.

MEPH.

That was the cause, but yet *per accidens*,
For when we hear one rack the name of God,
Abjure the Scriptures and his saviour Christ,
We fly, in hope to get his glorious soul;
50 Nor will we come unless he use such means
Whereby he is in danger to be damn'd.
Therefore the shortest cut for conjuring
Is stoutly to abjure the Trinity,
And pray devoutly to the prince of hell.

FAUSTUS.

55 So Faustus hath already done,
And holds this principle:
There is no chief but only Belzebub,
To whom Faustus doth dedicate himself.
This word "damnation" terrifies not him,
60 For he confounds hell in Elysium:

---

46. per accidens] The scholastics distinguished between an efficient cause, i.e., an agent
which itself produced an effect, and a cause *per accidens*, which was related to the final
effect only in the sense of having provided an occasion for the intervention of some
external agent.

47. *rack*] torture (i.e., "anagrammatize": cf. I. iii. 8-9).

49. *glorious*] splendid; possibly also boastful (the root meaning of *gloriosus*).

53. *stoutly*] courageously, resolutely.

the Trinity] B1 substitutes "all godlinesse" (one mark of censorship undertaken in response, presumably, to the 1606 Act of Abuses).

60. *confounds hell in Elysium*] identifies hell with Elysium; confuses the two; undoes
hell through belief in Elysium. C. L. Barber remarks that the "extraordinary
pun" in this phrase "suggests that Faustus is able to change the world by the way
he names it, to *destroy* or *baffle* hell by *equating* or *mixing* it with Elysium" (Barber
116). For Homer, Elysium is a place of comfort and perfect happiness reserved for
well-connected heroes like Menelaus, the son-in-law of Zeus (*Odyssey* IV. 563-69);

His ghost be with the old philosophers!
But leaving these vain trifles of men's souls,
Tell me, what is that Lucifer, thy lord?

MEPH.

Arch-regent and commander of all spirits.

FAUSTUS.

Was not that Lucifer an angel once?   65

MEPH.

Yes Faustus, and most dearly lov'd of God.

FAUSTUS.

How comes it then that he is prince of devils?

MEPH.

O, by aspiring pride and insolence,
For which God threw him from the face of heaven.

FAUSTUS.

And what are you that live with Lucifer?   70

MEPH.

Unhappy spirits that fell with Lucifer,
Conspir'd against our God with Lucifer,
And are for ever damn'd with Lucifer.

FAUSTUS.

Where are you damn'd?

MEPH.

                                        In hell.

FAUSTUS.

How comes it then that thou art out of hell?   75

MEPH.

Why this is hell, nor am I out of it:

Virgil identifies it as the home of the righteous dead in the underworld (*Aeneid* VI.
541-42). Hell and Elysium are linked in *1 Tamburlaine* V. i. 466, and in the Induction
to *The Spanish Tragedy* Kyd's Virgilian underworld includes "the fair Elysian green"
(I. i. 73); this may have prompted Nashe's scoffing remark in his Preface to Greene's
Menaphon (1589) about the "home-born mediocrity" of "those that thrust Elysium
into hell" (Nashe iii. 316).

61.] This line translates a saying, "Sit anima mea cum philosophis," that was attributed
to the 12th-century Islamic philosopher and Aristotelian commentator Averroes; see
Gill 1990: 66 .

76.] Compare Milton's Satan: "Which way I fly is hell; my self am hell" (*Paradise Lost*
IV. 75).

Think'st thou that I who saw the face of God
And tasted the eternal joys of heaven
Am not tormented with ten thousand hells
80   In being depriv'd of everlasting bliss?
O Faustus, leave these frivolous demands,
Which strike a terror to my fainting soul.

FAUSTUS.

What, is great Mephastophilis so passionate
For being deprived of the joys of heaven?
85   Learn thou of Faustus manly fortitude
And scorn those joys thou never shalt possess.
Go, bear these tidings to great Lucifer:
Seeing Faustus hath incurr'd eternal death
By desperate thoughts against Jove's deity,
90   Say he surrenders up to him his soul,
So he will spare him four and twenty years,
Letting him live in all voluptuousness,
Having thee ever to attend on me
To give me whatsoever I shall ask,
95   To tell me whatsoever I demand,
To slay mine enemies and aid my friends,
And always be obedient to my will.
Go, and return to mighty Lucifer,
And meet me in my study at midnight,
100   And then resolve me of thy master's mind.

MEPH.

I will, Faustus.

Exit.

FAUSTUS.

Had I as many souls as there be stars

79-80. *ten thousand ... bliss*] John Searle (cited by Jump 21-22) noted that Marlowe is here
echoing the words of St John Chrysostom, the fourth-century Greek Father who
declared that ten thousand hells are as nothing in comparison with being cut off from
the beatific vision (*Hom. in St Matt.*, xxiii. 9).

83. *passionate*] subject to strong emotion.

91. *So*] on condition that.

I'd give them all for Mephastophilis!
By him I'll be great emperor of the world,
And make a bridge through the moving air   105
To pass the ocean with a band of men;
I'll join the hills that bind the Afric shore,
And make that country continent to Spain,
And both contributory to my crown;
The Emperor shall not live but by my leave,   110
Nor any potentate of Germany.
Now that I have obtain'd what I desire,
I'll live in speculation of this art
Till Mephastophilis return again.

Exit.

— ACT I SCENE IV —

Enter Wagner and the Clown.

WAGNER.
Sirrah boy, come hither.
CLOWN.
How, "boy"? Swowns boy, I hope you have seen many
boys with such pickadevaunts as I have. "Boy," quotha?

104-09.] These lines appear to parody the quasi-divine powers of Fidelia in Spenser's
Faerie Queene I. x. 20: "Sometimes great hosts of men she could dismay, / Dry-shod
to pass, she parts the floods in tway; / And eke huge mountains from their native seat
/ She would command, themselves to bear away...." See Hattaway 77, and Cheney
1997: 207-08.

105. *through*] This is probably to be pronounced as though spelled "thorough." The
distinction between "through" and "thorough," like that between "travail" and
"travel," is a modern one; at II. iii. 165, "thoroughly" is spelled "throwly" in A1 and
"throughly" in B1.

108. *country*] A1's reading, "land," which upsets the verse rhythm, may be a compositorial repetition error influenced by "band" two lines previously. I suspect that B1's
"Country" preserves the reading of the underlying manuscript.
continent to] continuous with. Compare *1 Tamburlaine* I. i. 127-28.

0.1. Clown] a boorish rustic, a fool. This character is presumably to be identified with
the Robin of II. ii and III. ii.

2. *Swowns*] a contraction of "God's wounds."

WAGNER.

Tell me sirrah, hast thou any comings in?

CLOWN.

5   Ay, and goings out too, you may see else.

WAGNER.

Alas, poor slave: see how poverty jesteth in his nakedness.
The villain is bare, and out of service, and so hungry that I
know he would give his soul to the devil for a shoulder of
mutton, though it were blood raw.

CLOWN.

10   How, my soul to the devil for a shoulder of mutton though
'twere blood raw? Not so, good friend: b'urlady I had need
have it well roasted, and good sauce to it, if I pay so dear.

WAGNER.

Well, wilt thou serve me, and I'll make thee go like *Qui*
mihi discipulus?

CLOWN.

15   How, in verse?

WAGNER.

No sirrah, in beaten silk and stavesacre.

---

3. *pickadevaunt*] a short beard trimmed to a point; apparently from the French words *pique
devant*, "peak in front." In this passage one may suspect an obscene *double entendre*.
Nashe, in *Strange News* (1592), attributes "a good handsome pickerdevant" to the
hapless Gabriel Harvey (Nashe i. 257), who in *Have With You to Saffron Walden* (1596)
he says has spent "twice double his patrimony ... in careful cherishing and preserving
his pickerdevant" (Nashe iii. 7; see also iii. 54).

4. *comings in*] earnings.

5. *goings out*] expenses; a punning reference to the fact that the Clown is bursting out of
his tattered clothes.

7. *out of service*] unemployed, a masterless man.

11. *b'urlady*] a contraction of "by Our Lady."

13-14. Qui mihi discipulus] "You who are my pupil." The opening words of *Ad suos
discipulos monita paedagogica, seu carmen de moribus* ("Teacherly admonition to his pu-
pils, or poem of conduct"), a didactic poem by William Lily (c.1466-1522) which
appears in all of the many editions of *A Shorte Introduction of Grammar*, the standard
elementary Latin textbook used in Elizabethan schools (see Lily and Colet sig. D6v).
See the note to lines 70-71 below.

16. *beaten silk*] embroidered silk; with a punning suggestion that Wagner will thrash his
servant.

stavesacre] a preparation against lice made from the seeds of a plant related to the del-
phinium.

CLOWN.

How, how, knave's acre? Ay, I thought that was all the land
his father left him. Do ye hear, I would be sorry to rob you
of your living.

WAGNER.

Sirrah, I say in stavesacre!   20

CLOWN.

Oho, oho, stavesacre! Why then belike, if I were your man
I should be full of vermin.

WAGNER.

So thou shalt, whether thou beest with me or no. But sirrah,
leave your jesting, and bind yourself presently unto me for
seven years, or I'll turn all the lice about thee into familiars,   25
and they shall tear thee in pieces.

CLOWN.

Do you hear, sir? You may save that labor: they are too familiar with me already, swowns they are as bold with my flesh
as if they had paid for my meat and drink.

WAGNER.

Well, do you hear, sirrah? Hold, take these guilders.   30

---

17. *knave's acre*] slang name for Poultney Street in London, which ran into Glasshouse
Street, and was chiefly inhabited by dealers in glass bottles and old goods (Ward).
Bevington and Rasmussen (133) note that the Clown, in pretending to mishear
Wagner's words, "resembles the *zanni* in the Italian *commedia dell'arte.*"

21-29.] Gill suggests that this sequence may have been contributed by the comic actor
John Adams, who is known to have played with Sussex's Men in 1576 and the
Queen's Men in 1583 and 1588, and who may by the early 1590s have belonged to
the Admiral's Men. In the Induction to Jonson's *Bartholmew Fair* (1614), Adams is remembered, along with the clown Richard Tarleton, for just such a slapstick routine:
"And Adams, the rogue, ha' leaped and capered upon him [Tarleton], and ha' dealt
his vermin about, as though they had cost him nothing" (Jonson vi. 14). See Gill
1990: xix-xxi, and the note to lines 45-49 below.

21. *belike*] in all likelihood.

25. *seven years*] the standard time-period for an apprenticeship or a contract of indentured
labor.

familiars] Witches and sorcerers were commonly believed to have attendant spirits who
took the form of animals.

30-34. *guilders, French crowns, English counters*] The joke arises from the rapidly deflating
value of what Wagner is offering. He professes to give the Clown Dutch guilders;
these coins, minted after 1543 in silver, circulated internationally. Observing, it would
seem, that the coins he has been given have holes punched in them, the Clown affects
to mis-hear "guilders" as "gridirons"—whereupon Wagner re-identifies the coins as

CLOWN.

Gridirons, what be they?

WAGNER.

Why, French crowns.

CLOWN.

Mass, but for the name of French crowns, a man were as
good have as many English counters. And what should I do
35   with these?

WAGNER.

Why now, sirrah, thou art at an hour's warning whensoever
or wheresoever the devil shall fetch thee.

CLOWN.

No, no; here, take your gridirons again.

WAGNER.

Truly, I'll none of them.

CLOWN.

40   Truly, but you shall.

WAGNER.

Bear witness I gave them him!

CLOWN.

Bear witness I give them you again!

WAGNER.

Well, I will cause two devils presently to fetch thee away.
Baliol, and Belcher!

French crowns (which were widely counterfeited: in 1587 the government issued
a proclamation urging members of the public to strike holes in counterfeit French
crowns). The name carries the obscene secondary meaning of heads made bald by
venereal disease (see *A Midsummer Night's Dream* I. ii. 79, *All's Well That Ends Well* II.
ii. 19, and *Measure for Measure* I. ii. 46). "English counters," privately minted out of
brass or other cheap metals, were used by sixteenth-century English tradesmen and
merchants to assist in arithmetical calculations (cf. *The Winter's Tale* IV. iii. 30-34),
and also circulated as a substitute for small-denomination coinage. To be offered "a
counter instead of a penny" is to be taken for a fool (Skelton, *Magnyfycence*, l. 1172,
Happé 1979: 259).

33. *Mass*] by the Mass.

44. *Baliol*] a deformation of "Belial" (Ward), a name which occurs in *2 Corinthians* 6:
    15; it is derived from the Hebrew *beli ya'al*, "worthless," or alternatively from *beli'ol*,
    "unrestrained" (Forsyth 200). In *Pierce Penniless his Supplication to the Devil* (1592),
    Nashe puns on Belial and Belly-all (Nashe i. 201). If the name of Belcher helps to
    activate the same pun, then the demons' names in this scene resonate with the motif
    of surfeiting that appears elsewhere in the play.

CLOWN.

Let your Balio and Belcher come here, and I'll knock them,   45
they were never so knocked since they were devils! Say I
should kill one of them, what would folks say? "Do ye see
yonder tall fellow in the round slop, he has killed the devil":
so I should be called "kill-devil" all the parish over.

Enter two devils, and the clown runs up and down crying.

WAGNER.

Baliol and Belcher, spirits away!   50

Exeunt.

CLOWN.

What, are they gone? A vengeance on them, they have vile
long nails. There was a he-devil and a she-devil. I'll tell
you how you shall know them: all he-devils has horns, and
all she-devils has clefts and cloven feet.

WAGNER.

Well sirrah, follow me.   55

CLOWN.

But do you hear: If I should serve you, would you teach me
to raise up Banios and Belcheos?

45-49.] This jest is paralleled by a sequence in Thomas Lodge's and Robert Greene's
    A Looking-Glass for London and England (1594; first performed 1591-92), in which a
    man who has disguised himself as a devil in order to frighten Adam, the clown, is
    cudgelled by him. Gill, noting that the devil-beater in *Looking-Glass* is called both
    "Clown" and "Adam," and that play-scripts often attached the names of comic actors
    to their roles, suggests that John Adams (see note to lines 21-29 above) may have
    contributed the kill-devil jest to both plays. Adams would thus be the kind of clown
    of whom Hamlet said that he "keeps one suit of jests, as a man is known by one suit
    of apparel" (*Hamlet* Q1, III. ii. 33-35). See Gill 1990: xix-xx.
48. *tall*] valiant, handsome.
round slop] baggy breeches.
53. *horns*] standard demonic equipment, perhaps with an overtone of cuckoldry. The
    pairing of "horns" with "clefts" may also give the word phallic overtones.
54. *clefts*] vulvas.
57. *Banios*] If, as Kocher suggested, there is a pun here on "bagnio," a brothel, this
    would antedate by several decades the *OED*'s earliest citation of this word, in Philip
    Massinger's *Parliament of Love* (1624).

WAGNER.

I will teach thee to turn thyself to anything: to a dog, or a cat, or a mouse, or a rat, or any thing.

CLOWN.

60   How? A Christian fellow to a dog or a cat, a mouse or a rat? No, no, sir. If you turn me into anything, let it be in the likeness of a little pretty frisking flea, that I may be here and there

and everywhere: O, I'll tickle the pretty wenches' plackets, I'll be amongst them i'faith!

WAGNER.

65   Well sirrah, come.

CLOWN.

But do you hear, Wagner?

WAGNER.

How? Baliol and Belcher!

CLOWN.

O Lord! I pray sir, let Banio and Belcher go sleep.

WAGNER.

Villain, call me Master Wagner, and let thy left eye be diame-
70   tarily fix'd upon my right heel, with *quasi vestigiis nostris insistere*.

---

62. *pretty frisking flea*] The same jest resurfaces at II. iii. 110-13.

63. *placket*] pocket in a woman's skirt; metaphorically a woman's genitals.

69-70. *diametarily*] a variant form of "diametrally" (B1's reading). Compare Thomas Blundevil: "The moon [is] said to be diametrally opposite to the sun ... when a right line drawn from the center of the sun to the center of the moon passeth through the center of the earth" (*Exercise* [1594] III. I, cited in *OED*, "diametrally," 3.a.). If the Clown manages to keep his eye and Wagner's heel at opposite ends of the diameter of a circle, his own gait as he follows in his footsteps will be peculiar.

70-71. *quasi vestigiis nostris insistere*] "as if treading in our footsteps (or traces)." In his preface to Greene's *Menaphon*, Nashe praises Erasmus, "in whose traces ... many other reverent Germans insisting, have re-edified the ruins of our decayed libraries" (Nashe iii. 316, Greene 1996: 86). Wagner's words may be an ironic reminiscence of lines 71-72 of William Lily's poem *Ad suos discipulos..., seu carmen de moribus*: "How I wish you not to follow the perverse footsteps of a fool ("prava ... vestigia morum"), lest in the end through your deeds you suffer a worthy punishment" (Lily and Colet sig. D7v:). See the note to lines 13-14 above.

Exit.

CLOWN.

God forgive me, he speaks Dutch fustian. Well, I'll follow
him, I'll serve him, that's flat.

Exit.

---

72. *fustian*] bombast, nonsense. Fustian was a coarse cloth made of cotton and flax; the
word was metaphorically applied to inflated or inappropriately lofty language.

ACT II

ACT II SCENE I

Enter Faustus in his study.

FAUSTUS.

    Now Faustus, must thou needs be damn'd,
    And canst thou not be sav'd.
    What boots it then to think of God or heaven?
    Away with such vain fancies, and despair,
5   Despair in God, and trust in Belzebub.
    Now go not backward: no Faustus, be resolute.
    Why waverest thou? O, something soundeth in mine ears:
    "Abjure this magic, turn to God again."
    Ay, and Faustus will turn to God again.
10   To God? He loves thee not;
    The god thou serv'st is thine own appetite,
    Wherein is fix'd the love of Belzebub:
    To him I'll build an altar and a church,
    And offer lukewarm blood of new-born babes!

Enter Good Angel, and Evil.

GOOD ANGEL.

15   Sweet Faustus, leave that execrable art.

FAUSTUS.

    Contrition, prayer, repentance: what of them?

GOOD ANGEL.

    O, they are means to bring thee unto heaven.

EVIL ANGEL.

    Rather illusions, fruits of lunacy,

---

3. *boots*] avails.

7-8. *O ... again*] Compare *Isaiah* 30: 21: "And thine ears shall hear a word behind thee, saying, this is the way, walk ye in it."

9.] This line is omitted in B1, thereby erasing one of Faustus's swings towards penitence.

18-19. *illusions, fruits ... That makes*] A false concord of a plural subject with a singular verb form is common in the writings of Marlowe and his contemporaries.

104   CHRISTOPHER MARLOWE

That makes men foolish that do trust them most.

GOOD ANGEL.

Sweet Faustus, think of heaven and heavenly things. 20

EVIL ANGEL.

No Faustus, think of honor and of wealth.

Exeunt Angels.

FAUSTUS.

Of wealth?
Why, the signory of Emden shall be mine!
When Mephastophilis shall stand by me
What God can hurt thee, Faustus? Thou art safe, 25
Cast no more doubts. Come Mephastophilis,
And bring glad tidings from great Lucifer!
Is't not midnight? Come Mephastophilis,
Veni, veni, Mephastophilis!

Enter Mephastophilis.

Now tell: what says Lucifer thy lord? 30

MEPH.

That I shall wait on Faustus whilst he lives,

---

23. *signory*] lordship, rule.

Emden] a prosperous port in north-west Germany which conducted an extensive trade
with England.

24-25. *When ... Faustus?*] a blasphemous distortion of *Romans* 8: 31: "If God be on our
side, who can be against us?" B1 substitutes "power" for "God" in line 25, no doubt
to avoid charges of blasphemy under the 1606 Act of Abuses.

26. *Cast*] revolve in one's mind, ponder (*OED*, 42.b).

27. *glad tidings*] Compare *Luke* 2: 10: "I bring you tidings of great joy."

29. Veni, veni, Mephastophilis!] "Come, O come, Mephastophilis!" Bevington and
Rasmussen note that this is a blasphemous echo of the 12th-century Advent hymn
Veni, veni, Emmanuel (translated in 1851 by J. M. Neale as "O come, O come,
Emmanuel"). Faustus's words may also echo the opening words of the Whitsuntide
hymn *Veni Creator Spiritus*, which invokes the third person of the Trinity and was
used in the liturgy for the consecration of priests. See Barnes 263-64.

30.] This A1 line is metrically irregular—and more emphatic for that reason. B1's reading,
"Now tell me," may be the work of an editor who appears at several points (e.g. III. i. 49)
to have regularized not-quite-decasyllabic lines, probably when B1 was printed in 1616.

31.] A1's "whilst I live" is an obvious compositorial error.

So he will buy my service with his soul.

FAUSTUS.

Already Faustus hath hazarded that for thee.

MEPH.

But now thou must bequeath it solemnly,
35 And write a deed of gift with thine own blood,
For that security craves great Lucifer.
If thou deny it I will back to hell.

FAUSTUS.

Stay Mephastophilis, and tell me,
What good will my soul do thy lord?

MEPH.

40 Enlarge his kingdom.

FAUSTUS.

Is that the reason why he tempts us thus?

MEPH.

Solamen miseris socios habuisse doloris.

FAUST.

Why, have you any pain that tortures others?

MEPH.

As great as have the human souls of men.
45 But tell me, Faustus, shall I have thy soul?
And I will be thy slave and wait on thee,
And give thee more than thou hast wit to ask.

FAUSTUS.

Ay Mephastophilis, I give it thee.

---

32. *So*] on condition that.

34. *But now*] A1's reading, "But Faustus," is arguably a compositorial error involving the repetition of "Faustus" from the preceding line.

35, 60, 90. *deed of gift*] a legally binding promise to make a gift; the phrase does not occur in *EFB*.

40. *Enlarge his kingdom*] This may refer to the devil's contested rule as "the god of this world" (2 *Corinthians* 4: 4; see also *Romans* 16: 20, *Revelation* 12: 10-11), as well as to his rule over hell.

42. Solamen ... doloris] "It is a comfort to the wretched to have had companions in misfortune." This Latin hexameter appears also in Greene's *Menaphon* (Greene 1996: 103) and in Dekker's *The Seven Deadly Sins of London* (21); the same sentiment is voiced by the devil Astarotte in Luigi Pulci's *Il Morgante Maggiore* (1482), xxv. 209 (see Thomas and Tydeman 179-80), and has been traced back to Publilius Syrus and to Seneca's *De consolatione*.

MEPH.

Then stab thine arm courageously,
And bind thy soul, that at some certain day   50
Great Lucifer may claim it as his own:
And then be thou as great as Lucifer!

FAUSTUS.

Lo Mephastophilis, for love of thee
I cut mine arm, and with my proper blood
Assure my soul to be great Lucifer's,   55
Chief lord and regent of perpetual night.
View here the blood that trickles from mine arm,
And let it be propitious for my wish.

MEPH.

But Faustus, thou must
Write it in manner of a deed of gift.   60

FAUSTUS.

Ay, so I will. But Mephastophilis,
My blood congeals, and I can write no more.

MEPH.

I'll fetch thee fire to dissolve it straight.

Exit.

FAUSTUS.

What might the staying of my blood portend?
Is it unwilling I should write this bill?   65
Why streams it not, that I may write afresh?

---

54. *proper*] own.

58. *propitious*] of favorable import. As Gill 1990: 71 notes, Faustus's use of this word
emphasizes the blasphemy of his action: Christ's blood was shed as a sacrifice to make
God propitious to us despite our sins, as the language used by *The Book of Common
Prayer* in the preparation for holy communion makes clear: "If any man sin, we have
an advocate with the father, Jesus Christ the righteous, and he is the propitiation for
our sins [*1 John* 2: 1-2]" (*Prayer Book* 101). The minister is to say to communicants:
"The blood of our lord Jesu Christ, which was shed for thee, preserve thy body and
soul into everlasting life: and drink this in remembrance that Christ's blood was
shed for thee, and be thankful" (*Prayer Book* 103). By his inversion of Christ's act
of propitiation, Faustus seems to be symbolically excluding himself from those for
whom Christ's blood was shed—though at V. ii. 92 he will remember that Christ's
blood "hath ransom'd me."

65. *bill*] contract.

"Faustus gives to thee his soul": ah, there it stay'd.
Why should'st thou not? Is not thy soul thine own?
Then write again: "Faustus gives to thee his soul."

Enter Mephastophilis with a chafer of coals.

MEPH.

70   Here's fire: come Faustus, set it on.

FAUSTUS.

So: now the blood begins to clear again;
Now will I make an end immediately.

MEPH. *[aside]*

O, what will not I do to obtain his soul!

FAUSTUS.

Consummatum est: this bill is ended,

75   And Faustus hath bequeath'd his soul to Lucifer.
But what is this inscription on mine arm?
Homo fuge! Whither should I fly?
If unto God he'll throw thee down to hell.
My senses are deceiv'd: here's nothing writ.

80   I see it plain! Here in this place is writ
Homo fuge; yet shall not Faustus fly.

MEPH.

I'll fetch him somewhat to delight his mind.

69.1. chafer] a kind of saucepan or chafing-dish, in this case apparently with a grate over
    which other dishes could be heated.

71.] Greg remarks that this is "certainly no earthly fire, that will liquify coagulated
    blood."

74. Consummatum est] "It is finished." According to the *Gospel of John*, but not the
    synoptic gospels (*Mark, Matthew,* and *Luke*), these were the last words of Jesus on the
    cross (*John* 19: 30).

77. Homo fuge] "Man, flee!" The Latin words occur in the *Vulgate* text of *1 Timothy* 6: 11
    ("Tu autem o homo Dei haec fuge": "But thou, O man of God, flee these things").
    The line as a whole appears to allude more distinctly to *Psalm* 139: 7-8: "Whither
    shall I go from thy spirit? or whither shall I flee from thy presence? If I ascend into
    heaven, thou art there: if I lie down in hell, thou art there." There may also be an
    allusion to *Amos* 9: 1-2: "... he that fleeth of them shall not flee away, and he that
    escapeth of them shall not be delivered. Though they dig into hell, thence shall mine
    hand take them; though they climb up to heaven, thence will I bring them down."

78.] B1 substitutes "heaven" for A1's "God": another instance of censorship apparently
    prompted by the 1606 Act of Abuses.

Exit.

Enter with devils, giving crowns and rich apparel to Faustus, and dance,
and then [the devils] depart.

FAUSTUS.

Speak Mephastophilis: what means this show?

MEPH.

Nothing, Faustus, but to delight thy mind,
And let thee see what magic can perform.   85

FAUSTUS.

But may I raise such spirits when I please?

MEPH.

Ay Faustus, and do greater things than these.

FAUSTUS.

Then there's enough for a thousand souls!
Here Mephastophilis, receive this scroll,
A deed of gift, of body and of soul: 90
But yet conditionally, that thou perform
All articles prescrib'd between us both.

MEPH.

Faustus, I swear by hell and Lucifer
To effect all promises between us made.

FAUSTUS.

Then hear me read them.   95
On these conditions following:
First, that Faustus may be a spirit in form and substance;

84-85.] These lines in A1 ("Nothing Faustus, but to delight thy mind withall, / And to
show thee what magic can perform") deviate ineffectively from metrical norms in
ways suggestive of careless copying. Although the B1 readings I have preferred could
be editorial emendations, I think it more likely that they preserve readings derived
from the underlying manuscript.

86. *raise such*] A1's more obvious reading ("raise up"), which loses a nuance of meaning,
may be an error by a compositor who was working aurally.

88.] The absence of this line in B1 is strongly suggestive of censorship.

97. a spirit in form and substance] As noted by Greg (1946: 97-99), "spirit" at certain points
in the play clearly means "evil spirit" or "devil": Faustus understands it thus when
Mephastophilis tells him that Lucifer is "Arch-regent and commander of all spirits" (I. iii.
64), and the same meaning is implied when the Evil Angel (who in B1 at his first entrance
is called "Spirit") tells Faustus, "Thou art a spirit, God cannot pity thee" (II. iii. 13).

> Secondly, that Mephastophilis shall be his servant, and at his
> command;
100 Thirdly, that Mephastophilis shall do for him, and bring him
> whatsoever;
> Fourthly, that he shall be in his chamber or house invisible;
> Lastly, that he shall appear to the said John Faustus at all
> times, in what form or shape soever he please;
105 I, John Faustus of Wittenberg, Doctor, by these presents do
> give both body and soul to Lucifer, Prince of the East, and
> his minister Mephastophilis, and furthermore grant unto
> him that four and twenty years being expired, the articles
> above written inviolate, full power to fetch or carry the
110 said John Faustus, body and soul, flesh, blood, or goods,
> into their habitation wheresoever.
> By me, John Faustus.

MEPH.

Speak Faustus, do you deliver this as your deed?

FAUSTUS.

Ay, take it, and the devil give thee good on't.

MEPH.

115 So. Now, Faustus, ask me what thou wilt.

FAUSTUS.

First will I question with thee about hell.

Tell me, where is the place that men call hell?

MEPH.

Under the heavens.

FAUSTUS.

Ay, so are all things else; but whereabouts?

---

105. these presents] these legal articles in the present document.
106. Lucifer, Prince of the East] See notes to I. iii. 17-18, 40.
116. *question with thee*] This phrase in A1 carries overtones of academic disputation;
compare Richard Eden's translation of a sentence from Peter Martyr d'Anghiera's
De orbe novo decades (*The Decades of the Newe Worlde* [1555], 10): "I questioned with
him as concerning the elevation of the pole" (cited in *OED*, "question," v. 2). These
overtones are lost in the A3 and B1 reading "question thee."
119.] In A1, this and the preceding speech are half-lines making up a single decasyllabic
line; I suspect that the A1 compositor inadvertently omitted "so are all things else."

MEPH.

Within the bowels of these elements,   120
Where we are tortur'd and remain forever.
Hell hath no limits, nor is circumscrib'd
In one self place, for where we are is hell,
And where hell is there must we ever be;
And to conclude, when all the world dissolves   125
And every creature shall be purify'd,
All places shall be hell that is not heaven.

FAUSTUS.

Come, I think hell's a fable.

MEPH.

Ay, think so still, till experience change thy mind.

FAUSTUS.

Why, think'st thou then that Faustus shall be damn'd?   130

MEPH.

Ay, of necessity, for here's the scroll
Wherein thou hast given thy soul to Lucifer.

FAUSTUS.

Ay, and body too, but what of that?
Think'st thou that Faustus is so fond to imagine
That after this life there is any pain?   135
Tush, these are trifles and mere old wives' tales.

MEPH.

But I am an instance to prove the contrary,

---

120. *these elements*] earth, water, air and fire, which were held to constitute the world up
to the sphere of the moon.

122-24.] This description of hell, McAdam notes, seems to parody the definition of God as
"an infinite sphere whose centre is everywhere and whose circumference is nowhere"
(a definition best known from the pseudo-Hermetic *Liber XXIV philosophorum* 56).

123. *self*] single, particular.

124.] A1's omission of "there" in line 124 appears to be a compositorial error (which may
have been conditioned by the repeated "where" of lines 123-24).

125-26. *And to conclude ... purify'd*] Bevington and Rasmussen note that these lines draw
on *2 Peter* 3: 10-11 ("the elements shall melt with heat ... all these things must be
dissolved"), and on *Daniel* 12: 10 ("Many shall be purified...").

134. *fond*] foolish.

136. *Tush*] B1 substitutes "No" for this mild expletive (another sign of censorship in the
B text).

137-40.] These lines are from B1, where the whole passage is in verse until Faustus

For I tell thee I am damn'd, and now in hell.

FAUSTUS.

Nay, and this be hell, I'll willingly be damn'd!
140 What, sleeping, eating, walking and disputing?
But leaving this, let me have a wife, the fairest maid in Germany, for I am wanton and lascivious, and cannot live without
a wife.

MEPH.

How, a wife? I prithee Faustus, talk not of a wife.

FAUSTUS.

145 Nay, sweet Mephastophilis, fetch me one, for I will have one.

MEPH.

Well, thou wilt have one. Sit there till I come; I'll fetch thee
a wife in the devil's name.

Enter with a devil dressed like a woman, with fireworks.

MEPH.

Tell, Faustus: how dost thou like thy wife?

FAUSTUS.

A plague on her for a hot whore!

[*Exit devil.*]

MEPH.

150 Tut Faustus, marriage is but a ceremonial toy.
If thou lov'st me, think no more of it.

---

changes the subject from hell and damnation to his desire for a wife ("But leaving
this..." [141]). A1 shows signs of textual disturbance: A's prose equivalent of lines
139-40 ("How? now in hell? nay and this be hell, I'll willingly be damned here: what
walking, disputing, &c.") contains repetition and omissions that may be the result of
some kind of oral or memorial transmission.

140.] Bevington proposes that "at this moment Faustus's idea of hell is of a university
made up of congenial sceptics like himself" (Bevington 1991: 18).

147.2. fireworks] The devils and wild men who appear in the comic sequences of 16th-
century pageants and plays "regularly carried wild fire and squibs or breathed fire"
(Baskervill 315); the fireworks were often attached to the costumes of devils and
clowns in ways designed to make fun of sexual and excretory functions.

150. *toy*] trifle.

I'll cull thee out the fairest courtesans
And bring them every morning to thy bed.
She whom thine eye shall like, thy heart shall have,
Be she as chaste as was Penelope,   155
As wise as Saba, or as beautiful
As was bright Lucifer before his fall.
Hold, take this book: peruse it thoroughly.
The iterating of these lines brings gold;
The framing of this circle on the ground   160
Brings whirlwinds, tempests, thunder and lightening.
Pronounce this thrice devoutly to thyself,
And men in armor shall appear to thee,
Ready to execute what thou desir'st.

FAUSTUS.

Thanks, Mephastophilis; yet fain would I have a book   165
wherein I might behold all spells and incantations, that I
might raise up spirits when I please.

MEPH.

Here they are in this book.

---

155. *Penelope*] the faithful wife of Odysseus in Homer's *Odyssey*.

156. *Saba*] the Queen of Sheba, who in *1 Kings* 10: 1-13 (see also *2 Chronicles* 9: 1-12)
comes to Jerusalem to test King Solomon's knowledge of God with "hard questions."
In the *Vulgate* text, she is called "regina Saba"; as Greg notes, this spelling is reproduced in the *Bishops' Bible* and in the heading, but not the text, of the *Geneva Bible*.

165.] B1 ends the scene here with two lines: "Thanks Mephostophilis for this sweet
book. / This will I keep, as chary as my life." The second of these lines is lifted from
II. iii. 168 (where it occurs in both the A and B texts); this is clear evidence that B
has been revised.

165-78.] This sequence parodies the apocryphal *Wisdom of Solomon* 7: 17-21: "For [God]
hath given me the true knowledge of the things that are, so that I know how the
world was made, and the powers of the elements [the wording here—*virtutes elemen-
torum* in the Vulgate—could be understood as referring to elemental spirits], [18]
The beginning, and the end, and the midst of the times: how the times alter, and the
change of the seasons, [19] The course of the year, the situation of the stars, [20] The
nature of living things, and the furiousness of beasts, the power of the winds, and the
imaginations of men, the diversities of plants, and the virtues of roots, [21] And all
things both secret and known do I know: for wisdom the worker of all things hath
taught me it." If Faustus is perverse in seeking from a demonic source something like
the knowledge that Solomon claimed to have received from the divine Wisdom, he
is doubly foolish in failing here to recognize that the knowledge he desires is literally
in his grasp. His speech to Helen of Troy (V. i. 91-110) contains echoes of other verses
from this same passage of the *Wisdom of Solomon.*

FAUSTUS.

170 Now would I have a book where I might see all characters and planets of the heavens, that I might know their motions and dispositions.

MEPH.

Here they are too.

Turn to them.

FAUSTUS.

175 Nay, let me have one book more, and then I have done, wherein I might see all plants, herbs, and trees that grow upon the earth.

MEPH.

Here they be.

FAUSTUS.

O, thou art deceived.

MEPH.

Tut, I warrant thee.

Turn to them.
Exeunt.

— ACT II SCENE II —

Enter Robin the ostler with a book in his hand.

ROBIN.

O, this is admirable! Here I ha' stolen one of Doctor Faustus' conjuring books, and i'faith I mean to search some circles

---

169. *characters*] talismanic symbols of the planets and of the spiritual powers that govern them.

178. *I warrant thee*] I assure you (that the book contains all that I say it does).

0.1] Robin, who at I. iv. 8 was "out of service," appears to have escaped Wagner's tutelage and found work in the stables of an inn.

2. circles] magic circles, and also women's vaginas. As Bevington and Rasmussen observe, the same jest is developed at length in *Romeo and Juliet* II. i. 23-26: "'Twould

for my own use: now will I make all the maidens in our parish
dance at my pleasure stark naked before me, and so by that
means I shall see more than e'er I felt, or saw yet.   5

Enter Rafe, calling Robin.

RAFE.

Robin, prithee come away! There's a gentleman tarries to
have his horse, and he would have his things rubbed and
made clean: he keeps such a chafing with my mistress about
it, and she has sent me to look thee out; prithee come away!

ROBIN.

Keep out, keep out, or else you are blown up, you are dis-   10
membered, Rafe! Keep out, for I am about a roaring piece
of work.

RAFE.

Come, what dost thou with that same book? Thou canst not
read.

ROBIN.

Yes, my master and mistress shall find that I can read: he for   15
his forehead, she for her private study. She's born to bear
with me, or else my art fails.

RAFE.

Why Robin, what book is that?

ROBIN.

What book? Why, the most intolerable book for conjuring
that e'er was invented by any brimstone devil!   20

RAFE.

Canst thou conjure with it?

---

anger him / To raise a spirit in his mistress' circle / Of some strange nature, letting
it there stand / Till she had laid it and conjured it down."

3-4.] Ormerod and Wortham suggest that there may be a slanting allusion in these lines
to the orgiastic naked dancing imagined to take place at witches' sabbaths.

11. *roaring*] noisy, riotous. For an account of "the mathematical science of roaring" as it
came to be practised by Elizabethan and Jacobean bullies and gallants, see Middleton
and Rowley, *A Fair Quarrel* IV. i, iv.

16. *forehead*] A deceived husband or cuckold was said to wear horns on his forehead.

private study] with a quibble, Ormerod and Wortham suggest, on private parts.

16-17. *to bear with*] to put up with; also (another bawdy quibble) to lie under, to bear the
weight of his body.

ROBIN.

I can do all these things easily with it: first, I can make thee
drunk with hippocras at any tavern in Europe for nothing;
that's one of my conjuring works.

RAFE.

25 Our master parson says that's nothing.

ROBIN.

True, Rafe. And more, Rafe, if thou hast any mind to Nan
Spit our kitchen maid, then turn her and wind her to thine
own use, as often as thou wilt, and at midnight.

RAFE.

O brave Robin, shall I have Nan Spit, and to mine own use?
30 O   that condition I'll feed thy devil with horse-bread as long
as he lives, of free cost.

ROBIN.

No more, sweet Rafe: let's go and make clean our boots
which lie foul upon our hands; and then to our conjuring, in
the devil's name!

Exeunt.

---

23. *hippocras*] wine flavored with spices.

26-27. *Nan Spit ... turn her and wind her*] One of the humblest occupations in the kitchen
of a large household or inn was that of the turnspit, whose job was to stand by the
open fireplace and crank the horizontally-mounted spit on which roasting meat was
impaled. Robin tempts Rafe with the thought of sexually impaling and "turning"
this kitchen maid—of treating her, in effect, as she treats a roast of meat.

30. *horse-bread*] bread made of beans, bran, etc. for horses—but apparently sometimes eaten
also by the very poor. (See Jonson, *Every Man Out of His Humour* III. viii. 22: "You
threadbare, horse-bread-eating rascals....") Rafe assumes that Robin's devil will eat the
same fodder as the horses he tends—and, like them, will be mortal. All but this last as-
sumption would have seemed plausible to most 16th-century clergymen: in 1546 Paolo
Giovio announced that Cornelius Agrippa's black dog had really been a devil, and in 1548
the Lutheran Johannes Gast went one better by claiming that the necromancer Faustus's
dog, and his horse as well, had both been devils (Nauert 327, Palmer and More 98).

— ACT II SCENE III —

Enter Faustus in his study, and Mephastophilis.

FAUSTUS.
When I behold the heavens then I repent
And curse thee, wicked Mephastophilis,
Because thou hast depriv'd me of those joys.
MEPH.
Why Faustus,
Think'st thou heaven is such a glorious thing?   5
I tell thee 'tis not half so fair as thou
Or any man that breathes on earth.
FAUST.
How prov'st thou that?
MEPH.
                                    It was made for man,
Therefore is man more excellent.
FAUSTUS.
If it were made for man, 'twas made for me: 10
I will renounce this magic and repent.

Enter Good Angel and Evil Angel.

GOOD ANGEL.
Faustus, repent yet, God will pity thee.

1-10.] These exchanges between Faustus and Mephastophilis reflect the movement of
Psalm 8: 3-6, in which a contemplation of the creation leads first to a recognition
of divine majesty ("When I behold thine heavens, even the works of thy fingers ...
What is man, say I, that thou art mindful of him?"), and then to a contrasting emphasis upon human dignity ("Thou hast made him a little lower than God ... Thou
hast made him to have dominion in the works of thy hands"). If Mephastophilis
makes sophistical use of this pattern, Faustus seems inclined rather to recognize that
"The heavens declare the glory of God, and the firmament showeth the work of his
hands" (*Psalm* 19: 1). He may read written texts perversely, but he is for once reading
nature in an orthodox manner.

4.] B1 substitutes for these words, in one of its more open revisions of the play's meanings, a direct statement of Faustus's apparently autonomous wilfulness: "'Twas thine
own seeking Faustus, thank thy self."

12.] A1's punctuation, followed here, suggests the meaning that if Faustus does repent,

EVIL ANGEL.

Thou art a spirit, God cannot pity thee.

FAUSTUS.

Who buzzeth in mine ears I am a spirit?

15   Be I a devil, yet God may pity me.

Ay, God will pity me if I repent.

EVIL ANGEL.

Ay, but Faustus never shall repent.

Exeunt Angels.

FAUSTUS.

My heart's so harden'd I cannot repent.

Scarce can I name salvation, faith, or heaven,

20   But fearful echoes thunders in mine ears,

"Faustus, thou art damn'd!" Then swords and knives,

Poison, guns, halters, and envenom'd steel

Are laid before me to dispatch myself,

And long ere this I should have slain myself

25   Had not sweet pleasure conquer'd deep despair.

Have I not made blind Homer sing to me

---

even now, then God will pity him (with the implication that even now penitence
is not out of the question). B1's punctuation ("Faustus repent, yet God will pity
thee") shifts the emphasis to the continued availability of God's pity once Faustus has
repented. Underlying both meanings is the question, brought to the surface at II. iii.
18, and again at II. iii. 81, of whether Faustus is able to repent.

14. *buzzeth*] murmurs or whispers, speaks indistinctly. Compare Shakespeare's *Titus
Andronicus* IV. iv. 6-7: "these disturbers of our peace / Buzz in the people's ears"; and
Philip Stubbes' *Anatomy of Abuses* (1583): "Having buzzed his venomous suggestions
into their ears" (cited in *OED*, "buzz," v.¹ 4).

18. *My heart's so harden'd*] Taking their cue from God's hardening of Pharaoh's heart in
Exodus 4: 21, 7: 3, 7: 13, and 10: 1, 20, 27, Calvinists understood an impenitent hard-
ness, whether wavering or obdurate, as a condition determined by the will of God.
Calvin himself wrote, in commenting on St. Paul's *Letter to the Romans*, that "the
hidden counsel of God is the cause of hardening" (*Institutes* III. xxiii. 1; Calvin 1587:
fol. 315; see Calvin 1960: ii. 948-49).

19-20.] These lines are omitted in B1, no doubt because the revisers noticed that they
tend to contradict the view of Faustus as a largely autonomous agent responsible for
his own miserable fate.

22. *halters*] hangman's nooses.

Of Alexander's love and Oenon's death?
And hath not he that built the walls of Thebes
With ravishing sound of his melodious harp
Made music with my Mephastophilis?   30
Why should I die, then, or basely despair?
I am resolv'd: Faustus shall ne'er repent.
Come Mephastophilis, let us dispute again,
And reason of divine astrology.
Speak, are there many spheres above the moon?   35

---

27. *Alexander's love and Oenon's death*] These are matters which Homer left unsung; Faustus would have been the first to hear them from his lips. In *Iliad* XXIV. 25-30, Homer alludes to the Judgment of Paris (also named Alexandros, as in *Iliad* III. 15 ff.), but he does not mention Oenone. The tale of Troy, up to the point at which the *Iliad* begins, was filled in by the post-Homeric *Cypria* (of which only fragments now survive). This epic told how Alexandros, a son of King Priam and Queen Hecuba of Troy, was cast out by his parents (for it was prophesied that he should cause the destruction of Troy) and brought up among the shepherds of Mount Ida, where he won the love of Oenone. Asked by Hera, Athena, and Aphrodite to award a golden apple to the most beautiful goddess, he succumbed to Aphrodite's bribe of the love of the fairest woman alive, abandoned Oenone and abducted Helen from Sparta, thus provoking the Trojan War. (See Ovid, *Heroides*, Ep. v, and also George Peele's play *The Arraignment of Paris* [1584].) Quintus Smyrnaeus, whose epic *The Fall of Troy* is a belated (4th c. A.D.) embellishment of Homeric traditions, tells in Book X how Paris, wounded by a poisoned arrow, could have been healed only by Oenone; after jealously refusing to cure him, she was overwhelmed by remorse, and threw herself onto his funeral pyre. Ormerod and Wortham suggest that Marlowe probably knew the story through such subsequent adaptations as the *Ilias Latina* of Pindarus Thebanus, which "was widely used as a school text in the sixteenth century" (66).

28-29.] Amphion and his brother built the walls of Thebes (*Odyssey* XI. 260-65); the music of Amphion's lyre magically moved huge stones into place (Apollonius Rhodius, *Argonautica* I. 735-41).

34. *reason of*] The evidence that in the immediately following lines B1 offers readings that are earlier and more authentic than A1's leads me to think that here too B1's—in my opinion—better reading (A1 has "argue of") may also be the earlier one.

astrology] not clearly distinguished from astronomy until the seventeenth century.

35-40.] I have followed the readings of B1 in these lines. The rotation of variants in this passage, and the absence of line 39 in A1, indicate that the compositor of B1 had access to a manuscript that contained readings lost in A1 as a result, most likely, of compositorial fatigue or carelessness. (See Keefer 2006.)

35-62.] The elements (earth, water, air, fire) which make up "the substance of this centric earth" were thought to be concentrically disposed; so also, in the old geocentric cosmology, were the spheres which governed the motions of those wandering or "erring" stars, the planets. Mephastophilis says there are nine spheres: those of the planets, including the moon and the sun; the firmament, to which the fixed stars are attached; and the empyrean, the outermost and motionless sphere of the

Are all celestial bodies but one globe,
As is the substance of this centric earth?

MEPH.
As are the elements, such are the heavens,
Even from the moon unto the empyreal orb,
40   Mutually folded in each other's spheres,
And jointly move upon one axle-tree
Whose termine is term'd the world's wide pole.
Nor are the names of Saturn, Mars, or Jupiter
Feign'd, but are erring stars.

FAUSTUS.
45   But tell me, have they all one motion, both *situ et tempore?*

MEPH.
All jointly move from east to west in four and twenty hours
upon the poles of the world, but differ in their motions upon
the poles of the zodiac.

---

universe. (He apparently conflates the *primum mobile,* thought of by some astronomers as a distinct sphere which imparts motion to the heavens, with the firmament.)
All of this is utterly commonplace.

41. *And jointly*] This is B1's reading; A1's "And Faustus all jointly" is hypermetrical.

axle-tree] Renaissance science hypothesized "a right [i.e., vertical] imaginative line,
called of the Astronomers the Axletree of the world, about the which the world
continually turneth like a Cart-wheel" (Thomas Blundevil, *Exercises* [1594]; cited
in *OED*, "axle-tree," 4.a). The metaphor of a celestial axle occurs in classical texts,
e.g., Virgil's *Aeneid* vi. 535-36. Bevington and Rasmussen note that Marlowe writes
of "the axle-tree of heaven" in *1 Tamburlaine* IV. ii. 50 and *2 Tamburlaine* I. i. 90; see
also Shakespeare's *Troilus and Cressida* I. iii. 65-66, and Chapman's *Bussy d'Ambois* V.
iii. 152.

42. *termine*] B1's reading; A1's "terminine" is an obvious compositorial error.

44. *erring stars*] planets, which if observed over periods of weeks and months, appear to
wander among the other apparently fixed stars.

45-46. situ et tempore] "in position and time"; i.e., in the direction of their revolutions
around the earth and in the time these take.

48-49, 51. *poles of the world ... poles of the zodiac; the double motion of the planets*] The apparent diurnal motion of the planetary spheres "upon one axle-tree" (the northern
"termine" of which nearly coincides with the star Polaris) is of course due, in post-
Copernican terms, to the earth's rotation upon its axis. The second component of the
planets' apparent "double motion" is an effect of the differences between the earth's
period of revolution around the sun, and theirs. The periods of planetary revolution
given by Faustus correspond for the most part to the then-accepted figures: "Robert
Recorde's *Castle of Knowledge* (1556, pp. 572-9), gives them as Saturn 28 years,
Jupiter 12 years, Mars 2 years, Venus, Mercury, and, of course, the sun 1 year, and

FAUSTUS.

Tush, these slender trifles Wagner can decide: ·

Hath Mephastophilis no greater skill? 50

Who knows not the double notion of the planets?

The first is finish'd in a natural day,

The second thus, as Saturn in thirty years,

Jupiter in twelve, Mars in four, the Sun, Venus, and Mercury

in a year, the Moon in twenty-eight days. Tush, these are 55

freshmen's suppositions! But tell me, hath every sphere a

dominion or *intelligentia?*

MEPH.

Ay.

FAUSTUS.

How many heavens or spheres are there?

MEPH.

Nine: the seven planets, the firmament, and the empyreal 60

heaven.

FAUSTUS.

But is there not *coelum igneum, et crystallinum?*

---

the moon 1 month" (Greg). The actual—as opposed to apparent—periods for the
inner planets are of course much less: 7½ and 3 months respectively. The zodiac is
a belt of the celestial sphere which contains the paths traced out by the sun, moon,
and planets. Extending some eight or nine degrees north and south of the ecliptic
(the apparent path described by the sun around the celestial sphere), the zodiac is
conventionally divided into twelve equal segments named according to the constellations which occupy these spaces. The inclination of the earth's axis of rotation from
the perpendicular in relation to the plane of its revolutions around the sun means that
the "poles of the zodiac" differ from those of the world.

49. Tush] Here, as line 55 below and at II. i. 136, a mild expletive which appears in A1 is
censored out of B1.

57. *dominion or* intelligentia] It was widely believed that the planets were moved or
guided by angels or intelligences; see Agrippa, *De occulta philosophia* III. xvi-xvii; also
I. xxii for the divine names and signs of the planetary *intelligentiae.* In stating that the
planets' names are not feigned (lines 43-44), Mephastophilis has already implied that
the planets are spiritual agents.

62. coelum igneum, et crystallinum] "a fiery, and a crystalline heaven." The latter was
supposed to "account for the 'trepidation of the spheres' (Donne, 'A Valediction: for-
bidding mourning'), i.e., the supposed variation in the rate of precession of the equi-
noxes" (Jump 38). F.R. Johnson (1946) argues that Mephastophilis's refusal to allow
moving spheres other than those carrying observable bodies is evidence of Marlowe's
alignment with sceptical and empiricist tendencies in Renaissance astronomy.

MEPH.

No Faustus, they be but fables.

FAUSTUS.

Resolve me then in this one question: Why are not conjunc-
65   tions, oppositions, aspects, eclipses all at one time, but in
some years we have more, in some less?

MEPH.

Per inaequalem motum respectu totius.

FAUSTUS.

Well, I am answer'd. Now tell me who made the world.

MEPH.

I will not.

FAUSTUS.

70   Sweet Mephastophilis, tell me.

MEPH.

Move me not, Faustus.

FAUSTUS.

Villain, have I not bound thee to tell me any thing?

62–64.] The first two of these lines are missing in A1: actors may have thought them
superfluous, or a compositor who was not thrilled with astronomy may have thought
they could safely be omitted. In line 64 I have followed B1, which preserves a suggestion of growing irritation, a nuance that is lost in A1's looser wording ("Well,
resolve me in this question").

64–65. *conjunctions, oppositions, aspects*] astrological terms referring respectively to the apparent proximity of two planets, to their positioning on opposite sides of the sky, and
to any other angular relation between their positions.

67. *Per inaequalem motum respectu totius*] "through an unequal motion with respect
to the whole."

68. *Well, I am answer'd*] These words seem to express resentment (rather than despon-
dency, as Bevington 1991: 21 would have it); Faustus follows them with a deliberately
provocative demand.

71. *move*] anger. A1's version of this line includes a repetition that could stem either from
a copyist's error or from theatrical corruption. (Where B1 has "Faustus," A1 prints
"for I will not tell thee," which disperses the menace of B's version of this line, and
is arguably influenced by "Tell me" in lines 68, 70, and 72.)

72. *Villain*] a term of opprobrious address (*OED*, 1.a), signifiying the addressee's low
social (and, by extension, moral and mental) status. Under the feudal system, a villain
or villein was a serf or bondsman attached to a manor and wholly subject to its lord;
although the institution of villenage disappeared during the 15th century with the
rise of copyhold tenancy, the word continued to carry connotations of baseness and
rusticity, as well as of malicious hostility to social superiors.

have I not] A1; B1's "have not I" is derived from A3, and has no manuscript authority.

MEPH.

Ay, that is not against our kingdom.

This is. Thou are damn'd, think thou of hell.

FAUSTUS.

Think, Faustus, upon God that made the world!   75

MEPH.

Remember this.

Exit.

FAUSTUS.

Ay, go accursed spirit to ugly hell:

'Tis thou hast damn'd distressed Faustus' soul.

Is't not too late?

Enter Good Angel and Evil Angel.

EVIL ANG.

            Too late.

GOOD ANG.

Never too late, if Faustus can repent.   80

EVIL ANG.

If thou repent, devils shall tear thee in pieces.

GOOD ANG.

Repent, and they shall never raze thy skin.

Exeunt Angels.

73-74.] I have followed B1 here. A1's lines—"Ay, that is not against our kingdom, but
    this is, / Think thou on hell Faustus, for thou art damn'd"—contain two additional
    words, and are significantly less emphatic. As at lines II. iii. 62-64, 68, and 71, A1's
    readings are suggestive either of theatrical alteration or corruption by a copyist.

80. *if Faustus can repent*] This condition raises the issue of Calvinist double predestination:
    if Faustus *is able to* repent, i.e., if he is one of the elect, then it is never too late to
    do so—but if he is one of the reprobate, and cannot repent, then it will always have
    been too late. B1's "will repent" appears to be a theologically motivated revision: to
    say that it is never too late if Faustus *will* repent is to superimpose upon the question
    of fact (will he repent?) the suggestion that he can choose to do so. The notion of a
    will that is anything other than autonomous may seem paradoxical; but so also, to
    Calvinists, was any notion of human autonomy.

82. *raze*] graze.

FAUSTUS.

> Ah Christ, my Saviour,
> Seek to save distressed Faustus' soul!

Enter Lucifer, Belzebub, and Mephastophilis.

LUCIFER.

85
> Christ cannot save thy soul, for he is just;
> There's none but I have interest in the same.

FAUSTUS.

> O, what art thou that look'st so terribly?

LUCIFER.

> I am Lucifer, and this is my companion prince in hell.

FAUSTUS.

> O Faustus, they are come to fetch away thy soul!

BELZEBUB.

90
> We come to tell thee thou dost injure us.

LUCIFER.

> Thou talk'st of Christ, contrary to thy promise.

---

84. *Seek*] According to the Calvinist orthodoxy of Elizabethan England, the process of salvation had to be initiated by God. Faustus's "seek" suggests that he lacks faith in Christ's ability to save him; the word may also imply that it is primarily up to Christ to save Faustus's soul, and that he has not previously been trying to. B1's theologically motivated substitution of "help" removes these implications.

86. *interest in*] a legal claim upon.

87.] B1, which I follow here, has two distinctly superior readings which are normalized in A1, arguably by a copyist or by the compositor. B1's "what art thou" suggests that Faustus does not initially recognize the terrifying object as belonging to any familiar category (A1's "who art thou" normalizes this more difficult reading); B1's "terribly" conveys the fear projected by Lucifer's gaze (A1's "terrible" reduces this to a fear imparted by his bearing and appearance).

89. *fetch away*] A1; it is possible that an editorial hand in B1 deleted "away" out of a concern to regularize decasyllabic lines.

90-93.] B1's alternation of demonic speakers, which is followed here, produces a grimly comic effect that is absent in A1, where all of these lines are spoken by Lucifer. With B1's speech assignations, line 93 is a joke about transgressive sexuality that seems thoroughly Marlovian.

90. *We come*] A1; B1's "We are come," which makes the line hypermetrical, is arguably a compositorial error influenced by "are come" in the preceding line.

91. *thou talk'st of Christ*] These words in A1 demean Faustus's appeal to Christ in what seems an appropriately demonic manner; B1's "Thou call'st on Christ," which sacrifices that nuance for greater literal accuracy, may be an editorial emendation.

BELZEBUB.

Thou should'st not think of God.

LUCIFER.

Think of the devil.

BELZEBUB.

And of his dam too.

FAUSTUS.

Nor will I henceforth: pardon me in this,
And Faustus vows never to look to heaven,   95
Never to name God or to pray to him,
To burn his Scriptures, slay his ministers,
And make my spirits pull his churches down.

LUCIFER.

Do so, and we will highly gratify thee.

BELZEBUB.

Faustus, we are come from hell to show thee some pastime.   100
Sit down, and thou shalt see all the Seven Deadly Sins
appear in their proper shapes.

FAUSTUS.

That sight will be as pleasing unto me as Paradise was to
Adam, the first day of his creation.

LUCIFER.

Talk not of Paradise, nor creation, but mark this show.   105
Talk of the devil and nothing else: come away!

Enter the Seven Deadly Sins.

BELZEBUB.

Now Faustus, examine them of their several names and dispositions.

FAUSTUS.

What art thou, the first?

---

94. *Nor will I henceforth*] i.e. think of God.

96-98.] The deletion of these lines from B1 is an obvious instance of censorship.

97-98.] Compare *The Jew of Malta* V. i. 64-65: "I'll help to slay their children and their
    wives, / To fire the churches, pull their houses down"; Bevington and Rasmussen
    also note *Edward II* I. iv. 100-1: "I'll fire thy crazed buildings, and enforce / The papal
    towers to kiss the lowly ground."

PRIDE.

110   I am Pride. I disdain to have any parents. I am like to Ovid's
flea, I can creep into every corner of a wench: sometimes
like a periwig I sit upon her brow, or like a fan of feathers, I
kiss her lips; indeed I do, what do I not? But fie, what a
scent is here? I'll not speak another word, except the ground

115   were perfumed and covered with cloth of arras.

FAUSTUS.
What art thou, the second?

COVETOUSNESS.

I am Covetousness, begotten of an old churl in an old
leathern bag; and might I have my wish, I would desire that
this house and all the people in it were turned to gold, that

120   I might lock you up in my good chest. O, my sweet gold!

FAUSTUS.
What art thou, the third?

WRATH.

I am Wrath. I had neither father nor mother; I leapt out of a
lion's mouth when I was scarce half an hour old, and ever
since I have run up and down the world with this case of

125   rapiers, wounding myself when I had nobody to fight withal.
I was born in hell, and look to it: for some of you shall be
my father.

FAUSTUS.
What art thou, the fourth?

ENVY.

I am Envy, begotten of a chimney-sweeper and an oyster

130   wife. I cannot read, and therefore wish all books were
burned; I am lean with seeing others eat. O, that there would
come a famine through all the world, that all might die, and

112-113. *Ovid's flea*] The *Elegia de pulice*, a poem written in imitation of Ovid's amatory elegies, was wrongly ascribed to him. Jump quotes from it a line addressed to the flea: "Is
quocumque placet; nil tibi, saeve, latet": "You go wherever you wish; nothing, savage,
is hidden from you." See *Poetae latini minores*, ed. N.E. Lemaire (Paris, 1826), vii. 275-
78, qtd. by Jump 41. (At I. iv. 61-64, the Clown's speech alludes to this same poem.)
115. *cloth of arras*] tapestry fabric of the kind woven at Arras in Flanders; to use it as a floor
covering would be grossly ostentatious.
124. *case*] pair.
129-30. *begotten ... wife*] and therefore filthy and foul-smelling.

I live alone: then thou should'st see how fat I would be. But
must thou sit and I stand? Come down, with a vengeance!

FAUSTUS.

Away, envious rascal! What art thou, the fifth?   135

GLUTTONY.

Who I, sir? I am Gluttony. My parents are all dead, and the
devil a penny they have left me, but a bare pension, and that
is thirty meals a day and ten bevers: a small trifle to suffice
nature. O, I come of a royal parentage: my grandfather was
a gammon of bacon, my grandmother a hogshead of claret   140
wine. My godfathers were these: Peter Pickle-herring and
Martin Martlemas-beef. O, but my godmother she was a
jolly gentlewoman, and well-beloved in every good town
and city: her name was Mistress Margery March-beer.
Now, Faustus, thou hast heard all my progeny, wilt thou bid   145
me to supper?

FAUSTUS.

No, I'll see thee hanged: thou wilt eat up all my victuals.

GLUTTONY.

Then the devil choke thee.

FAUSTUS.

Choke thyself, glutton! What art thou, the sixth?

SLOTH.

I am Sloth. I was begotten on a sunny bank, where I have   150

---

134. *with a vengeance*] with a curse on you. The phrase was used as a vehement intensifier.

138. *bevers*] drinks; also light meals or snacks.

140. *hogshead*] a wine-barrel of a standard size, holding (in modern terms) 225 litres or 63
American gallons—the equivalent of 25 cases of a dozen bottles of wine.

claret] light red wine from the Bordeaux region (in the 16th century claret was made in
the manner of a modern rosé). The term was also more widely used until the early
seventeenth century to distinguish wines of a deep yellow or light reddish color from
red and white wines.

141. *Pickle-herring*] a clown figure associated (like Jack a Lent and Steven Stockfish) with
carnival festivities and popular farces. See Baskervill 47-48, 93, 126-32.

142. *Martlemas-beef*] Martinmas, or St. Martin's day (November 11), was the traditional
time to slaughter cattle that could not be fed over the winter and to commence the
production of salt beef; it was therefore also a time for feasting on "green" or unsalted
beef.

144. *March-beer*] a strong beer brewed in March.

145. *progeny*] lineage.

lain ever since, and you have done me great injury to bring
me from thence. Let me be carried thither again by Gluttony
and Lechery. I'll not speak another word for a king's
ransom.

FAUSTUS.

155   What are you, mistress minx, the seventh and last?

LECHERY.

Who I, sir? I am one that loves an inch of raw mutton better
than an ell of fried stock-fish, and the first letter of my name
begins with Lechery.

LUCIFER.

Away, to hell, to hell.

Exeunt the Sins.

160   Now Faustus, how dost thou like this?

FAUSTUS.

O, this feeds my soul.

LUCIFER.

Tut, Faustus, in hell is all manner of delight.

FAUSTUS.

O, might I see hell, and return again, how happy were I then!

LUCIFER.

Thou shalt. I will send for thee at midnight. In mean time,
165   take this book, peruse it thoroughly, and thou shalt turn thyself into what shape thou wilt.

---

155. *minx*] hussy, wanton woman.

156. *raw mutton*] a metaphor for prostitutes in Skelton's *Magnyfycence* (1518, printed 1533),
lines 2263-75 (Happé 1979: 299); the expression here takes on a phallic meaning.

157. *ell*] a measure of length (equal in England to some forty-five inches), commonly
contrasted to an inch, as in "Ye liked ... better an inch of your will, than an ell of
your thrift" (J. Heywood [1562], qtd. in *OED*, "ell," I.b).

stock-fish] unsalted dried fish, sometimes derisively associated with the male organ, as in
1 Henry IV II. v. 227: "you bull's pizzle, you stock-fish," and more generally with
sexual coldness or impotence, as in *Measure for Measure* III. i. 353-54: "he was begot
between two stockfishes." Compare the words of the female character in a jig (or
farcical song and dance routine) dating from c.1570: "I love very well the things that
be lickerish / marchpain and quince pie I care for no stockfish" (Baskervill 416).
As Gill remarks, "Lechery prefers a small quantity of virility to a large extent of
impotence" (Gill 1990: 77).

FAUSTUS.

    Great thanks, mighty Lucifer:

    This will I keep as chary as my life.

LUCIFER.

    Farewell, Faustus, and think on the devil.

FAUSTUS.

    Farewell, great Lucifer. Come, Mephastophilis.   170

Exeunt omnes.

---

168. *chary*] carefully.

ACT III

— ACT III CHORUS —

Enter the Chorus [Wagner].

WAGNER.

Learned Faustus,
To know the secrets of astronomy
Graven in the book of Jove's high firmament,
5   Did mount him up to scale Olympus' top,
Where sitting in a chariot burning bright,
Drawn by the strength of yoked dragons' necks,
He views the clouds, the planets and the stars,
The tropics, zones, and quarters of the sky,
10   From the bright circle of the horned moon
Even to the height of *primum mobile*;
And whirling round with this circumference

---

4. *to scale Olympus' top*] i.e., to ascend to the dwelling-place of the gods.

5. *a chariot burning bright*] This fiery chariot is derived from the *English Faust Book*, ch. 21 (*EFB* 123), a passage which appears to contain parodic echoes of the vision of the divine chariot-throne in *Ezekiel* I: 13-28. Mystical (and magical) expositions of this vision were an important component of the Kabbalah, Christian appropriations of which gave added authority to the magical doctrines espoused by figures like Agrippa and the historical Doctor Faustus. See Scholem 13-16, 30, and (on the Christian "Cabala"), 196-201.

8. *tropics, zones*] The tropics of Cancer and Capricorn, the arctic and antarctic circles and the equator divided the celestial sphere into five belts or zones. See Manilius, *Astronomica* I. 561-602.

quarters] Traditional astronomy also quartered the celestial sphere with two other circles which passed through its north and south poles: the solstitial colure, which intersects the two tropics at the solstitial points (those at which the ecliptic meets the tropics); and the equinoctial colure, which intersects the equator at the equinoctial points (those at which the ecliptic crosses the equator). See Manilius, *Astronomica* I. 603-32.

9-10.] "from the lowest to the highest of the moving spheres" (Jump 46).

11. *whirling round with this circumference*] The image of the astronomer or astrologer borne in a flying chariot around the circuit of the heavens may be derived from Manilius, *Astronomica* II. 58-59: "in a lone chariot I soar to heaven," and II. 138-40: "Neither in nor for the crowd shall I construct my song, but alone, as though carried round a vacant circuit I were freely driving my chariot, with none to forestall me...."

12. *compass*] circle, circuit, circular arc.

Within the concave compass of the pole,
From east to west his dragons swiftly glide,
And in eight days did bring him home again.
Not long he stay'd within his quiet house   15
To rest his bones after his weary toil,
But new exploits do hale him out again,
And mounted then upon a dragon's back
That with his wings did part the subtle air,
He now is gone to prove cosmography,   20
That measures coasts and kingdoms of the earth,
And as I guess, will first arrive at Rome
To see the Pope, and manner of his court,
And take some part of holy Peter's feast,
The which this day is highly solemniz'd.   25

Exit.

— ACT III SCENE I —

Enter Faustus and Mephastophilis.

FAUSTUS.

Having now, my good Mephastophilis,

18-19. *And mounted then … the subtle air*] Cheney suggests that this may derive from words
  spoken of another demonic magician, Archimago, in Spenser's *Faerie Queene* I. ii. 3:
  2-3 ("spread / A seeming body of the subtile aire").

19. *subtle*] rarified.

20. *to prove*] to put to the test.

cosmography] The relationship between cosmography and geography as sister sciences
  of world measurement is explained by Agrippa in *De vanitate*, ch. 27. Geography,
  without "consideration of the celestial bodies," measures the world in terms of its
  land forms and political divisions, and describes the inhabitants and their cities "and
  other things worthy of memory." Cosmography, in contrast, "according to the order
  of the heavenly bodies and their division showeth the situation of countries … by the
  measures of degrees and minutes, and with mathematical rules teacheth the order of
  the climates, the difference of the day and night, the quarters from whence the winds
  do blow, the divers risings of the stars, the elevations of the poles, the parallels, and
  noon tides…" (Agrippa 1974: 85).

24-25.] The feast day of St. Peter the apostle is June 29.

Pass'd with delight the stately town of Trier,
Environ'd round with airy mountain tops,
With walls of flint, and deep entrenched lakes,
5   Not to be won by any conquering prince;
From Paris next, coasting the realm of France,
We saw the river Main fall into Rhine,
Whose banks are set with groves of fruitful vines;
Then up to Naples, rich Campania,
10   Whose buildings, fair and gorgeous to the eye
(The streets straight forth and pav'd with finest brick),
Quarters the town in four equivalents.
There saw we learned Maro's golden tomb,
The way he cut, an English mile in length,
15   Through a rock of stone in one night's space.
From thence to Venice, Padua, and the rest,
In midst of which a sumptuous temple stands,
That threats the stars with her aspiring top.
Thus hitherto hath Faustus spent his time.
20   But tell me now, what resting place is this?

---

2. *Trier*] a city on the Moselle river, capital of an electoral state of the Holy Roman
Empire which under the rule of Elector-Archbishop Johann von Schönenburg was
subjected during the 1580s and 1590s to a violent wave of witch-hunts (see Robbins
514-16).

9. *Campania*] in ancient usage, the plain surrounding the city of Capua; since medieval
times, Naples has been the principal city of this region. (In modern Italy the name
Campania is applied to a much larger area.)

12.] The versifying of *EFB*'s narrative is at this point very careless. This line, missing in
B1, may have been deleted by Samuel Rowley and William Birde (who in their work
of revision seem to have altered other lines in this speech). They evidently had a copy
of *EFB* at hand, and may have noticed both the syntactical oddity of lines 11-12, and
the fact that line 12 is not based on anything in *EFB*.

13. *Maro*] Virgil, or Publius Vergilius Maro, died at Naples in 19 B.C. In part because his
Fourth Eclogue was interpreted as a prophecy of the coming of Christ, he acquired a
reputation during the medieval period as a necromancer. His supposed tomb stands
on the promontory of Posilipo on the Bay of Naples, at the Naples end of a tunnel, nearly half a mile in length, which cuts through the promontory—and which,
as Petrarch wrote, "the insipid masses conclude was made by Virgil with magical
incantations" (qtd. from *Itinerarium syriacum* by Dyce 91).

14. *way*] road. The tunnel is some seven yards wide.

17-18. *sumptuous temple ... That threats the stars*] identified in *EFB* as Saint Mark's in
Venice. Line 18 is not derived from *EFB*; the "aspiring top" is presumably that of the
campanile, which stands at some distance from the church.

Hast thou, as erst I did command,
Conducted me within the walls of Rome?

MEPH.

Faustus, I have, and because we will not be unprovided, I
have taken up his Holiness' privy chamber for our use.

FAUSTUS.

I hope his Holiness will bid us welcome.   25

MEPH.

Tut, 'tis no matter, man, we'll be bold with his good cheer.
And now my Faustus, that thou may'st perceive
What Rome containeth to delight thee with,
Know that this city stands upon seven hills
That underprop the groundwork of the same;   30
Just through the midst runs flowing Tiber's stream,
With winding banks that cut it in two parts,
Over the which four stately bridges lean,
That make safe passage to each part of Rome.
Upon the bridge call'd Ponte Angelo   35
Erected is a castle passing strong,

22.] Gill 1990 notes that the stage properties belonging to the Admiral's Men in 1598
included "The sittie of Rome"—perhaps a backcloth for this scene.

24. *privy chamber*] a synonym in the late Middle Ages for a privy, jakes, or latrine in
the private suite of rooms of the master or mistress of a great house; the term was
subsequently applied to a bed chamber adjoining the privy. In the late 16th century
the privy chamber in English palaces and great houses "became a private dining and
reception room, with a suite of private chambers behind it" (Girouard 57); only the
most privileged guests would pass beyond the more public reception rooms into this
room. The term may retain overtones of scatological intimacy, since prior to the
development of the flush toilet (an invention publicized by Sir John Harington in
1594), the lord of a great house might use a portable privy stool or close stool in the
privy chamber.

31-32.] These lines, missing in A, are clearly essential to the meaning of this passage. Gill
(1990: 79) suggests that "B's editor noticed a surprising deficiency in A" and provided
two lines which versify the appropriate material from *EFB*. It is much more likely
that the manuscript which (along with a copy of A3) was used in the printing of B1
contained these lines. Their omission from A1 is presumably due to compositorial
fatigue or carelessness.

35-36.] The papal fortress of Castel San Angelo, which incorporates the ancient mausoleum of the emperor Hadrian, stands a short distance from the north end of the Ponte
San Angelo; this bridge, originally named the Pons Aelius, was built by Hadrian
in 134 to provide a connection between his circular mausoleum and the Campus
Martius.

Within whose walls such stores of ordnance are,
And double cannons, fram'd of carved brass,
As match the days within one complete year—
40   Besides the gates and high pyramides
Which Julius Caesar brought from Africa.

FAUSTUS.

Now, by the kingdoms of infernal rule,
Of Styx, Acheron, and the fiery lake
Of ever-burning Phlegethon, I swear
45   That I do long to see the monuments
And situation of bright splendent Rome.
Come therefore, let's away.

MEPH.

Nay Faustus, stay: I know you'd fain see the Pope,
And take some part of holy Peter's feast,
50   Where thou shalt see a troop of bald-pate friars
Whose *summum bonum* is in belly-cheer.

FAUSTUS.

Well, I am content to compass then some sport,
And by their folly make us merriment.

---

37. *ordnance*] military materials, especially artillery.

37-39.] In B1 these lines are expanded into four lines; the revision is presumably the work of Rowley or Birde.

38. *double cannons*] Jump, identifying these as "probably cannons of very large calibre," cites from C. ffoulkes, *The Gun-Founders of England* (Cambridge, 1937), an account of a "fair double cannon" cast at Calais (then still held by England) in 1536.

40. *pyramides*] an obelisk, in this case the one brought to Rome from Egypt by the emperor Caligula (not Julius Caesar), and moved to its present site in the Piazza San Pietro in 1586. The word is pronounced with four syllables, with the stress on the second syllable, as in *The Massacre at Paris* ii. 43-46 ("Set me to scale the high pyramides..."). As that passage makes clear, the word is singular, not plural.

42-46.] Greg remarks that it is "an extraordinary piece of rhodomontade" for Faustus to swear by three of the four rivers of Hades "that he wants to see the sights!" (Greg 113).

46. *situation*] the location of something in relation to its surroundings; here, as Gill suggests, the word seems to mean "lay-out." Greg notes a similar usage in Samuel Rowley's *When You See Me You Know Me* (1605): "Mean while, your Majesty may here behold / This warlike kingdom['s] fair metropolis, / The city London, and the river Thames, / And note the situation of the place."

49. *of*] in.

51. summum bonum] highest good.

52. *compass*] contrive.

Then charm me, that I may be invi[sible, ...]
To do what I please
Unseen of any whilst I stay in Rome.

[*Mephastophilis charms him.*]

MEPH.

So, Faustus: now
Do what thou wilt, thou shalt not be discern'd.

*Sound a sennet. Enter the Pope and the Cardinal of Lorraine to the
banquet, with Friars attending.*

POPE.

My lord of Lorraine, will't please you draw near?

FAUSTUS.

Fall to, and the devil choke you and you spare.   60

POPE.

How now, who's that which spake? Friars, look about!

FRIAR.

Here's nobody, if it like your Holiness.

56.1. Mephastophilis charms him] Bevington and Rasmussen (164) note that Henslowe's
    Diary lists among the Admiral's Men's props a "robe for to go invisible."
58.1. sennet] a flourish on the trumpet to announce a ceremonial entrance.
Cardinal of Lorraine] This position was held during the sixteenth century by members
    of the powerful Guise family, notably Charles de Guise (1524-1574), who helped fo-
    ment the wars of religion that convulsed France for decades after 1562 and acquired a
    reputation for dissimulation and cruelty; and Louis de Guise (1555-1588), who along
    with his brother, Henri, third Duc de Guise (1550-1588), was assassinated by King
    Henri III. As leaders of the pro-Spanish and ultra-Catholic Ligue, and thus major
    figures in the Spanish-led campaign against Protestantism, Louis and Henri de Guise
    were feared and detested in England. In *EFB* the Pope's dinner guest is the Cardinal
    of Pavia (*EFB* 131); in the B text, it is the Archbishop of Reames (or Rheims), a
    French city well-known in England as the site of a seminary where Roman Catholic
    priests were trained for undercover missionary work in England.
60. the devil choke you] The same phrase is used by Gluttony at II. iii. 148; Greg thought
    this might be a sign of common authorship of this sequence and the pageant of the
    Seven Deadly Sins.
 and you spare] if you eat sparingly.
62. like] please.

POPE.

My lord, here is a dainty dish was sent me from the Bishop
of Milan.

FAUSTUS.

Snatch it.

POPE.

How now, who's that which snatch'd the meat from me?
Will no man look? My lord, this dish was sent me from the
Cardinal of Florence.

FAUSTUS.

You say true, I'll ha'it.

[Snatch it.]

POPE.

70 What, again! My lord, I'll drink to your grace.

FAUSTUS.

I'll pledge your grace.

[Snatch it.]

LORRAINE.

My lord, it may be some ghost newly crept out of purgatory
come to beg a pardon of your Holiness.

POPE.

It may be so. Friars, prepare a dirge to lay the fury of this
75 ghost. Once again, my lord, fall to.

The Pope crosseth himself.

---

74. *dirge*] originally "dirige," the first word of the antiphon at matins in the Office of
the Dead ("Dirige, Domine, Deus meus, in conspectu tuo viam meam": "Direct, O
Lord, my God, my way in thy sight"; these words echo *Psalm* 5: 8 [*Psalm* 5: 9 in the
Vulgate text]). Hence, as Greg remarks, "dirge" is used correctly here, but incor-
rectly at line 94 below.

FAUSTUS.

What, are you crossing of your self? Well, use that trick no
more, I would advise you.

Cross again.

FAUSTUS.

Well, there's the second time. Aware the third, I give you
fair warning.

Cross again, and Faustus hits him a box of the ear,
and they all run away.

Come on, Mephastophilis, what shall we do?   80

MEPH.

Nay, I know not; we shall be cursed with bell, book and
candle.

FAUSTUS.

How? Bell, book and candle, candle, book and bell,
Forward and backward, to curse Faustus to hell.
Anon you shall hear a hog grunt, a calf bleat, and an ass bray,   85
Because it is Saint Peter's holy day!

Enter all the Friars to sing the dirge.

FRIAR.

Come brethren, let's about our business with good devotion.

[They] sing this:
Cursed be he that stole away his Holiness' meat from the table.
Maledicat dominus!
Cursed be he that struck his Holiness a blow on the face.   90
Maledicat dominus!

81-82. *bell, book and candle*] At the end of the ritual of excommunication, the bell is tolled,
the book closed, and the candle extinguished. As Ward noted, this ritual is confused,
both here and in *EFB*, with the office of exorcism.

89. Maledicat dominus] "May the Lord curse him."

Cursed be he that took Friar Sandelo a blow on the pate.
    Maledicat dominus!
Cursed be he that disturbeth our holy dirge.
95   *Maledicat dominus!*
Cursed be he that took away his Holiness' wine.
    Maledicat dominus! Et omnes sancti! Amen.

*[Faustus and Mephastophilis] beat the Friars
and fling fireworks among them, and so exeunt.*

— ACT III SCENE II —

Enter Robin and Rafe with a silver goblet.

ROBIN.

Come Rafe, did I not tell thee we were for ever made by this
Doctor Faustus' book? *Ecce signum*, here's a simple purchase
for horse-keepers! Our horses shall eat no hay as long
as this lasts.

Enter the Vintner.

RAFE.

5   But Robin, here comes the Vintner.

ROBIN.

Hush, I'll gull him supernaturally. Drawer, I hope all is
paid. God be with you; come Rafe.

VINTNER.

Soft, sir; a word with you. I must yet have a goblet paid
from you ere you go.

---

97. Et omnes sancti] and (may) all the saints (curse him).

2. Ecce signum] "Behold the sign." Gill notes that Falstaff uses the same phrase in *1
Henry IV* II. v. 153-54 when he shows his "sword hacked like a handsaw. *Ecce signum*."
Applied to a silver goblet, the expression has blasphemous overtones as a reminiscence of the sacrament of communion, which the Anglican church interpreted as an
effectual sign of grace (*Thirty-Nine Articles*, 25 [Kastan 246]).

6. Drawer] an insult: Robin pretends to mistake the Vintner or innkeeper for his em-
ployee the tapster or drawer who serves the customers.

8. Soft] softly, slowly; here carrying an imperative force, as in "not so fast!"

ROBIN.

I a goblet? Rafe, I a goblet? I scorn you, and you are   10
but a etc. I a goblet? Search me!

VINTNER.

I mean so, sir, with your favor.

[*Searches Robin.*]

ROBIN.

How say you now?

VINTNER.

I must say somewhat to your fellow. You, sir.

RAFE.

Me, sir? Me, sir! Search your fill! Now, sir, you may be   15
ashamed to burden honest men with a matter of truth.

VINTNER.

Well, t'one of you hath this goblet about you.

ROBIN.

You lie, drawer, 'tis afore me. Sirrah you, I'll teach ye to
impeach honest men: stand by, I'll scour you for a goblet.
Stand aside, you had best, I charge you in the name of Bel-   20
zebub! Look to the goblet, Rafe.

VINTNER.

What mean you, sirrah?

10-19. *I a goblet?.... I'll scour you for a goblet.*] Tucker Brooke noted that this sequence is
imitated in a pot-stealing sequence in the anonymous play *Mucedorus* (c. 1588-98); the
parallel suggests that B's loosely parallel version of the episode is a later revision.

11. *etc.*] an invitation to the actor to improvise (Boas); or alternatively, a substitute for a
scatological or obscene expression. In *Romeo and Juliet*, the key expression in a clause
emended by modern editors to read "O that she were / An open-arse" (II. i. 37-38;
"open, or" in Q2) appears in the First Quarto (1597) as "open *Et caetera*"; and when in
2 Henry IV Pistol asks, "And are etceteras nothings?" (II. iv. 160), the last two words
both refer to women's genitalia.

16. *a matter of truth*] "charge affecting their reputation for honesty" (Jump 113).

19. *impeach*] accuse.

scour] "beat, scourge, punish, with some play on the primary meaning of *scour*, 'to cleanse
or polish', which would apply to the goblet" (Bevington and Rasmussen 168).

21, 25. *Look to the goblet, Rafe*] Robin and Rafe are apparently passing the goblet back
and forth between them.

ROBIN.

I'll tell you what I mean.

He reads.

Sanctabulorum periphrasticon—Nay, I'll tickle you, Vint-
25   ner! Look to the goblet, Rafe. *Polypragmos Belseborams
      framanto pacostiphos tostu Mephastophilis*, etc.

Enter Mephastophilis; sets squibs at their backs; they run about.

VINTNER.

O nomine Domini! What mean'st thou, Robin? Thou hast
no goblet!

RAFE.

Peccatum peccatorum! Here's thy goblet, good Vintner!

ROBIN.

30   *Misericordia pro nobis!* What shall I do? Good devil,
      forgive me now, and I'll never rob thy library more!

MEPH.

Monarch of hell, under whose black survey
Great potentates do kneel with awful fear,

24-26.] Robin's incantation is gibberish, though some of it comes close to deviating into
sense. The Greek *periphrastikos* means "circumlocutory" (*periphrasticon* could be a
genitive plural, like the Latinate nonsense-word *sanctabulorum*). In Greek *polyprag-
mosyne* means "curiosity" or "meddlesomeness," and a *polypragmon* is a "busybody."
(Dekker addresses the gulls who will use the leaves of *The Guls Horn-Booke* [1609] to
dry tobacco as "good dry brained *polypragmonists*" [Dekker 1904: 9].) The invocation's
opening words might then be understood as addressed to "Busy-bod Belseborams
... of the circumlocutory holy-molydoms ...!" The "etc." at the end of the speech is
clearly an invitation to improvise further portentous nonsense.

26.1. squibs] fireworks. The action indicated here was a popular element in low comedy.
Baskervill notes the imprecation uttered by Ignorance in Redford's *Wit and Science*
(c. 1540): "The devil set fire on thee!" (line 361, Happé 1972: 196).

27-30.] garbled scraps of liturgical Latin. The Vintner is dimly remembering *Psalm* 118:
26 (117: 26 in the *Vulgate*): "Benedictus qui venit in nomine Domini" ("Blessed be
he, that cometh in the name of the Lord"). Rafe's "Sin of sins!" is perhaps more
appropriate to the situation. Bevington and Rasmussen (169) suggest that Robin
may be misremembering "miserere nobis" ("have mercy on us") from the Mass; or
he may have meant to say "Ora pro nobis" ("Pray for us"), but substituted the noun
"misericordia" ("mercy") for the imperative "ora" ("pray").

Upon whose altars thousand souls do lie,
How am I vexed with these villains' charms!   35
From Constantinople am I hither come
Only for pleasure of these damned slaves.

ROBIN.

How, from Constantinople? You have had a great journey,
will you take sixpence in your purse to pay for your supper,
and be gone?   40

MEPH.

Well villains, for your presumption, I transform thee into an
ape, and thee into a dog, and so be gone!

Exit.

ROBIN.

How, into an ape? That's brave, I'll have fine sport with the
boys; I'll get nuts and apples enow.

RAFE.

And I must be a dog.   45

ROBIN.

I'faith, thy head will never be out of the pottage pot.

Exeunt.

---

35. *How am I vexed with these villains' charms*] If Mephastophilis has appeared under compulsion, then he is contradicting what he said at I. iii. 46-51. Being "vexed with"
some action means being "troubled, afflicted or harassed" (*OED*, "vex," v. I. 1.b).
Mephastophilis's statement that he has come "for pleasure of" the clowns strengthens
the implication that he is not there *per accidens* (see note to I. iii. 46), or by his own
will.

36. *Constantinople*] In ch. 22 of *EFB*, Faustus's and Mephastophilis's visit to Rome is fol-
lowed, after intervening stops in other cities of Italy, France, Switzerland, Germany,
Austria, Bohemia and Poland, by a descent on the court of the "Great Turk" in
Constantinople (*EFB* 139-41).

42. *a dog*] Bevington and Rasmussen (170) note that according to Henslowe's *Diary*, the
Admirals' Men possessed "j black dogge" among their props in 1598; this would
probably have been a mask.

ACT IV

Enter Chorus.

When Faustus had with pleasure ta'en the view
Of rarest things and royal courts of kings,
He stay'd his course, and so returned home,
Where such as bare his absence but with grief,
5 I mean his friends and nearest companions,
Did gratulate his safety with kind words,
And in their conference of what befell
Touching his journey through the world and air
They put forth questions of astrology,
10 Which Faustus answer'd with such learned skill
As they admir'd and wonder'd at his wit.
Now is his fame spread forth in every land;
Amongst the rest the Emperor is one,
Carolus the Fifth, at whose palace now

---

11. *as*] that.

14. *Carolus the Fifth*] Charles V (1500-1558), King of Spain and Holy Roman Emperor from 1518 and 1519 respectively until his abdication in 1555.

14-15. *at whose palace now / Faustus is feasted*] The historical Doctor Faustus never made an appearance at the imperial court. Contemporary *magi*, however, had connections with the courts both of the Emperor Maximilian (Charles V's grandfather and immediate predecessor) and of Charles V. The Abbot Johannes Trithemius (1462-1516), author of the first account, written in 1507, of the historical Doctor Faustus, and himself suspected of practising demonic magic, was summoned to the court of Maximilian for extended periods in 1506 and 1507 (Brann 42, 95); his *Liber octo quaestionum* (1508), a work on demonology, is addressed to Maximilian. Several decades later, Martin Luther told of a magician, identified in one report of the conversation as Trithemius, who entertained Maximilian by having demons take on the forms of Alexander the Great and other monarchs (*Tischreden* no. 4450, *WATr* iv. 319). Another humanist *magus*, Henricus Cornelius Agrippa (1486-1535), served Maximilian in diplomatic missions from 1510 or 1511 until at least 1515, and in 1529 was engaged by Margaret of Savoy, regent of the Netherlands, as archivist and historiographer to the Emperor Charles V. The historian André Thevet felt it necessary to refute the opinion that Charles V's military victories had been won by Agrippa's magic (Thevet ii. fol. 542v-543); the same boast, made on behalf of Doctor Faustus, was refuted by Philipp Melanchthon in a lecture given at Wittenberg in the mid-1550s (Palmer and More 103).

Faustus is feasted 'mongst his noblemen.   15
What there he did in trial of his art
I leave untold, your eyes shall see perform'd.

Exit.

— ACT IV SCENE I —

Enter Emperor, Faustus, and a Knight, with attendants.

EMPEROR.

Master Doctor Faustus, I have heard strange report of thy
knowledge in the black art, how that none in my empire, nor
in the whole world, can compare with thee for the rare effects
of magic: they say thou hast a familiar spirit, by whom thou
canst accomplish what thou list. This therefore is my re-   5
quest: that thou let me see some proof of thy skill, that mine
eyes may be witnesses to confirm what mine ears have heard
reported; and here I swear to thee, by the honor of mine imperial crown, that whatever thou doest, thou shalt be no ways
prejudiced or endamaged.   10

KNIGHT. *(aside)*

I'faith, he looks much like a conjurer.

FAUSTUS.

My gracious sovereign, though I must confess myself far inferior to the report men have published, and nothing answerable to the honor of your imperial Majesty, yet for that love
and duty binds me thereunto, I am content to do whatsoever   15
your Majesty shall command me.

EMPEROR.

Then Doctor Faustus, mark what I shall say.
As I was sometime solitary set

---

3. *rare*] remarkable, extraordinary.
5. *what thou list*] whatever you wish.
10. *endamaged*] harmed.
13-14. *nothing answerable*] quite unequal.
14. *for that*] because.

Within my closet, sundry thoughts arose
20 About the honor of mine ancestors:
How they had won by prowess such exploits,
Got such riches, subdu'd so many kingdoms,
As we that do succeed, or they that shall
Hereafter possess our throne shall,
25 I fear me, never attain to that degree
Of high renown and great authority;
Amongst which kings is Alexander the Great,
Chief spectacle of the world's pre-eminence,
The bright shining of whose glorious acts
30 Lightens the world with his reflecting beams,
As when I hear but motion made of him
It grieves my soul I never saw the man.
If therefore thou, by cunning of thine art,
Canst raise this man from hollow vaults below
35 Where lies entomb'd this famous conqueror,
And bring with him his beauteous paramour,
Both in their right shapes, gesture, and attire
They us'd to wear during their time of life,
Thou shalt both satisfy my just desire
40 And give me cause to praise thee whilst I live.

FAUSTUS.

My gracious lord, I am ready to accomplish your request, so
far forth as by art and power of my spirit I am able to perform.

KNIGHT. (*aside*)

I'faith that's just nothing at all.

FAUSTUS.

45 But if it like your Grace, it is not in my ability to present
before your eyes the true substantial bodies of those two
deceased princes, which long since are consumed to dust.

---

19. *closet*] study, inner chamber.

23. *succeed*] follow in dynastic succession.

28. *pre-eminence*] pre-eminent people.

31. *motion*] mention.

36. *paramour*] mistress, consort.

KNIGHT. (aside)

Ay, marry Master Doctor, now there's a sign of grace in you
when you will confess the truth.

FAUSTUS.

But such spirits as can lively resemble Alexander and his   50
paramour shall appear before your Grace, in that manner
that they best lived in, in their most flourishing estate, which
I doubt not shall sufficiently content your imperial Majesty.

EMPEROR.

Go to, Master Doctor, let me see them presently.

KNIGHT.

Do you hear, Master Doctor? You bring Alexander and his   55
paramour before the Emperor?

FAUSTUS.

How then, sir?

KNIGHT.

I'faith, that's as true as Diana turned me to a stag.

FAUSTUS.

No sir, but when Actaeon died, he left the horns for you.
Mephastophilis, be gone.   60

Exit Mephastophilis.

KNIGHT.

Nay, and you go to conjuring, I'll be gone.

50-51. *such spirits as can lively resemble Alexander and his paramour*] A sense of the uncanny
likeness of necromantic magic and theatrical illusion appears in some 16th-century
polemics against magic. For example, Gianfrancesco Pico tells of a magician who
was carried off alive by a devil after having promised to a curious and unwise prince
"that he would present to him the siege of Troy, as on a stage or in a theater, and
that he would show him Achilles and Hector as they were when they fought" (*De
rerum praenotione* [1506-7] IV. 9, retold by Johann Weyer in *De praestigiis daemonum* II.
4 [Weyer 109]).

54. *Go to*] Normally an expression of incredulity, it appears here to express mild demur-
ral, or perhaps encouragement, with the same range of meanings as "Come, come."
presently] at once.

58-59. *Diana, Actaeon*] Actaeon, a hunter, witnessed the goddess Diana and her nymphs
bathing; the goddess transformed him into a stag and he was torn to pieces by his
own dogs. See Ovid, *Metamorphoses* III. 155-252.

61. *and*] if.

Exit Knight.

FAUSTUS.

I'll meet with you anon for interrupting me so. Here they
are, my gracious lord.

Enter Mephastophilis with Alexander and his paramour.

EMPEROR.

65 Master Doctor, I heard this lady while she lived had a wart
or mole in her neck. How shall I know whether it be so or
no?

FAUSTUS.

Your highness may boldly go and see.

[*Emperor does so; then spirits exeunt.*]

EMPEROR.

Sure these are no spirits, but the true substantial bodies of
these two deceased princes.

FAUSTUS.

70 Will't please your highness now to send for the knight
that was so pleasant with me here of late?

EMPEROR.

One of you call him forth.

Enter the Knight with a pair of horns on his head.

How now, sir knight? Why, I had thought thou had'st been
a bachelor, but now I see thou hast a wife, that not only gives
75 thee horns but makes thee wear them. Feel on thy head!

KNIGHT.

Thou damned wretch and execrable dog,
Bred in the concave of some monstrous rock,

---

62. *meet with*] get even with.

77-78. *Bred ... a gentleman?*] These lines are borrowed from *2 Tamburlaine* III. ii. 89:
"Fenc'd with the concave of a monstrous rock," and from *1 Tamburlaine* III. iii. 226:

How dar'st thou thus abuse a gentleman?
Villain, I say, undo what thou hast done!

FAUSTUS.

O not so fast, sir; there's no haste but good. Are you   80
remembered how you crossed me in my conference with the
Emperor? I think I have met with you for it.

EMPEROR.

Good Master Doctor, at my entreaty release him. He hath
done penance sufficient.

FAUSTUS.

My gracious lord, not so much for the injury he offered me   85
here in your presence, as to delight you with some mirth,
hath Faustus worthily requited this injurious knight; which
being all I desire, I am content to release him of his horns.
And sir knight, hereafter speak well of scholars. Mephastophilis, transform him straight. Now, my good lord, having   90
done my duty, I humbly take my leave.

EMPEROR.

Farewell, Master Doctor; yet ere you go, expect from me a
bounteous reward.

Exeunt Emperor, Knight, and attendants;
[manent Faustus and Mephastophilis].

— ACT IV SCENE II —

FAUSTUS.

Now Mephastophilis, the restless course
That time doth run with calm and silent foot,
Shortening my days and thread of vital life,

"How dare you thus abuse my majesty?" Although Marlowe habitually re-worked
images and lines that he had already used in other play-texts, the particularly derivative feel of these lines suggests that this scene was entrusted to a collaborator who
drew upon the *Tamburlaine* plays.
80. *there's ... good*] a common proverb: "No haste but good (speed)." See Tilley H 199.
85. *injury*] insult.
90. *straight*] at once.
93.2.] Faustus and Mephastophilis remain on stage.
3. *vital life*] a tautology, like "final end" in line 34 of this scene.

Calls for the payment of my latest years.

5   Therefore, sweet Mephastophilis,

Let us make haste to Wittenberg.

MEPH.

What, will you go on horseback, or on foot?

FAUSTUS.

Nay, till I am past this fair and pleasant green

I'll walk on foot.

Enter a Horse-courser.

HOR.

10   I have been all this day seeking one Master Fustian; mass,

see where he is. God save you, Master Doctor.

FAUSTUS.

What, horse-courser, you are well met.

HOR.

Do you hear, sir? I have brought you forty dollars for your

horse.

FAUSTUS.

15   I cannot sell him so. If thou lik'st him for fifty, take him.

HOR.

Alas sir, I have no more. I pray you, speak for me.

MEPH.

I pray you, let him have him. He is an honest fellow, and he

has a great charge, neither wife not child.

9.1. Horse-courser] a dealer in horses, the Elizabethan equivalent to a used-car salesman.
In *The Seven Deadly Sins of London* (1606), Dekker singles out "hackneymen and
horse-coursers" as devotees of "politic falsehood and lying" (Dekker 1905: 37), and
in *Lanthorne and Candle-Light* (1608), he adds that "you shall find every Horse-courser
… to be in quality a cozener, by profession a knave.… He will swear anything, but
the faster he swears, the more danger 'tis to believe him" (Dekker 1904: 249).

10. *Fustian*] a clownish deformation of "Faustus." Fustian was a coarse cloth made of
cotton and flax; the word was metaphorically applied to bombastic, inflated, or nonsensical language.

mass] a contraction of "By the Mass."

18. *charge*] burden (of family responsibilities). Mephastophilis promptly contradicts this
claim, thereby mocking transparent falsehoods of the kind used by horse-dealers.

FAUSTUS.

Well, come, give me your money. My boy will deliver him
to you. But I must tell you one thing before you have him: 20
ride him not into the water at any hand.

HOR.

Why sir, will he not drink of all waters?

FAUSTUS.

O yes, he will drink of all waters, but ride him not into the
water. Ride him over hedge or ditch, or where thou wilt, but
not into the water.   25

HOR.

Well, sir, now am I a made man for ever! I'll not leave my
horse for forty. If he had but the quality of hey ding ding,
hey ding ding, I'd make a brave living on him: he has a
buttock so slick as an eel. Well, God-bye sir, your boy will
deliver him me. But hark ye sir, if my horse be sick or ill   30
at ease, if I bring his water to you, you'll tell me what it is?

FAUSTUS.

Away, you villain! What, dost thou think I am a horse-doctor?

Exit Horse-courser.

What art thou, Faustus, but a man condemn'd to die?
Thy fatal time doth draw to final end;
Despair doth drive distrust into my thoughts.   35

---

21. *at any hand*] under any circumstances.
22. *drink of all waters*] go anywhere (Gill). Compare *Twelfth Night* IV. ii. 56: "I am for all
waters."
26. *leave*] sell.
27-28. *hey ding ding*] a common refrain in popular songs; compare *As You Like It* V. iii.
18-19 ("When birds do sing, hey ding-a-ding ding, / Sweet lovers love the spring").
Nashe's use of the phrase in one of his exchanges with Gabriel Harvey—"Yea,
Madame Gabriela, are you such an old jerker? then Hey ding a ding, up with your
petticoat, have at your plum-tree" (Nashe iii. 313)—suggested to Greg that the
phrase has sexual overtones, and that the horse in question is "not a gelding." The
"buttock so slick as an eel" implies sexual potency; the "brave living" the horse-
courser anticipates will presumably come from stud fees.
29. *God-bye*] a contraction of "God be with you."
31. *water*] urine.
34. *fatal time*] time allotted by fate (Ward).

Confound these passions with a quiet sleep:
Tush, Christ did call the thief upon the cross.
Then rest thee, Faustus, quiet in conceit.

Sleeps in his chair.
Enter Horse-courser all wet, crying.

HOR.

Alas, alas, Doctor Fustian, quotha? Mass, Doctor Lopus was
40 never such a doctor: has given me a purgation, has purged me
of forty dollars, I shall never see them more. But yet like an
ass as I was, I would not be ruled my him, for he bade me I
should ride him into no water. Now I, thinking my horse
had had some rare quality that he would not have had me
45 know of, I like a venturous youth rid him into the deep pond
at the town's end. I was no sooner in the middle of the
pond, but my horse vanished away, and I sat upon a bottle of
hay, never so near drowning in my life! But I'll seek out my
doctor, and have my forty dollars again, or I'll make it the

---

37. *the thief upon the cross*] See *Luke* 23: 39-43. Greene in *The Repentance of Robert Greene* quotes what he calls the "golden sentence" of St. Augustine: "There was (saith he) one thief saved and no more, therefore presume not; and there was one saved, and therefore despair not" (Greene 1923: 28). But the gospel texts, taken together, suggest longer odds. In *Mark* 15: 32 and *Matthew* 27: 44, both of the thieves crucified with Jesus taunt him and are presumably damned; in *John* 19: 18, 32, the occupations and eternal destination of the two men crucified with Jesus are not specified. Thus (as one of the two tramps in Samuel Beckett's *Waiting for Godot* notes), in one of the four gospels one of the two thieves was saved.
38. *conceit*] state of mind.
39. *Doctor Lopus*] Doctor Roderigo Lopez, a Portuguese marrano and personal physician to Queen Elizabeth. Lopez incurred the enmity of the Earl of Essex, who in January 1594 accused him of high treason; he was tried (and convicted) on February 28 on charges which included attempting to poison the queen, and was executed on June 7—more than a year after Marlowe's death (see Hotine). The past-tense allusion to him suggests that in its present form this scene must be post-Marlovian. However, the allusion cannot be used to date this passage to the year of Lopez's death: Nashe's two references to Lopez (to his hanging and to his trial) date from 1596 and 1599 respectively (Nashe iii. 18, 216).
40. *a purgation*] an emetic: the horse-dealer has been cleansed "through evacuation of money" (Ormerod and Wortham 122).
47. *bottle*] from the French "botte," meaning bundle.

dearest horse. O, yonder is his snipper-snapper. Do you   50
hear? You, hey-pass, where's your master?

MEPH.

Why sir, what would you? You cannot speak with him.

HOR.

But I will speak with him.

MEPH.

Why, he's fast asleep; come some other time.

HOR.

I'll speak with him now, or I'll break his glass windows   55
about his ears.

MEPH.

I tell thee, he has not slept this eight nights.

HOR.

And he have not slept this eight weeks I'll speak with him.

MEPH.

See where he is, fast asleep.

HOR.

Ay, this is he. God save ye Master Doctor! Master Doctor,   60
Master Doctor Fustian, forty dollars, forty dollars for a
bottle of hay!

MEPH.

Why, thou seest he hears thee not.

HOR.

So ho, ho! So ho, ho! (*Hallow in his ear.*) No, will you not
wake? I'll make you wake ere I go!   65

Pull him by the leg, and pull it away.

Alas, I am undone! What shall I do?

---

50. *dearest*] most expensive. If the horse-courser can't have his money back, he'll take revenge.

50. *snipper-snapper*] conceited young fellow, smart-aleck.

51. *hey-pass*] an expression used by fairground conjurors or jugglers. Nashe uses it in the Induction to *The Unfortunate Traveller*, and in that same fiction describes the deceptive treachery of one character as "heathen heigh-pass and ... intrinsical legerdemain" (Nashe ii. 208, 259)

55. *glass windows*] spectacles.

64. *So ho, ho*] a huntsman's cry to direct hounds to the hare (Gill).

FAUSTUS.

O my leg, my leg! Help, Mephastophilis! Call the officers, my leg, my leg!

MEPH.

Come villain, to the constable.

HOR.

70   O Lord, sir: let me go, and I'll give you forty dollars more.

MEPH.

Where be they?

HOR.

I have none about me; come to my ostry, and I'll give them you.

MEPH.

Be gone, quickly.

Horse-courser runs away.

FAUSTUS.

75   What, is he gone? Farewell he, Faustus has his leg again, and the horse-courser, I take it, a bottle of hay for his labor. Well, this trick shall cost him forty dollars more.

Enter Wagner.

How now, Wagner, what's the news with thee?

WAGNER.

Sir, the Duke of Vanholt doth earnestly entreat your com-
80   pany.

---

72. *ostry*] hostelry, inn.

79. *Duke of Vanholt*] The episode dramatized in the following scene is derived from two chapters in the 1587 *Historia* in which Faustus visits the "Fürst [or Graf] von Anhalt" (Füssel and Kreutzer 89). Given the division of Protestant Germany between states of Lutheran and of Calvinistic orientation, the Lutheran *Historia*'s association of a prince of the Calvinist ruling family of Anhalt with Faustus may well have been intended as a slander. In the *English Faust Book*, the direct source of this episode, Faustus visits "the duke of Anholt" (*EFB* 155-56). The A text's "Vanholt," which is followed by B, suggests that the compositor may have been working aurally, setting type while an assistant read aloud from the manuscript.

FAUSTUS.

The Duke of Vanholt! An honorable gentleman, to whom
I must be no niggard of my cunning. Come Mephastophilis, let's away to him.

Exeunt.

— ACT IV SCENE III —

Enter to them the Duke, and the Duchess; the Duke speaks.

DUKE.

Believe me, Master Doctor, this merriment hath much
pleased me.

FAUSTUS.

My gracious lord, I am glad it contents you so well. But it
may be, madam, you take no delight in this. I have heard
that great-bellied women do long for some dainties or other: 5
what is it, madam? Tell me, and you shall have it.

DUCHESS.

Thanks, good Master Doctor, and for I see your courteous
intent to pleasure me, I will not hide from you the thing my
heart desires; and were it now summer, as it is January, and
the dead time of the winter, I would desire no better meat   10
than a dish of ripe grapes.

---

82. *niggard*] a parsimonious person, one who shares only grudgingly.

0.1. Enter to them] This stage direction appears to contradict the *"Exeunt"* at the end
of IV. ii. That direction suggests that Faustus and Mephastophilis leave the stage
after IV. ii to indicate the passage of time—and then immediately re-enter; this
one suggests that they remain on stage, and that the two scenes are linked by what
has been called dramatic enjambement. Bevington and Rasmussen suggest that an
intervening scene may have been lost.

4. *take no delight in this*] Rasmussen notes that these words and a subsequent phrase from
line 13 of this scene ("Were it a greater thing than this") are echoed in the anonymous *The Taming of a Shrew* (c. 1588-93): "For trust me I take no great delight in it...
/ If that sweet mistress were your harts content, / You should command a greater
thing than that" (vi. 10, 16-17). These verbal echoes suggest that the parallel passage
in B1 is a later revision of A.

10. *meat*] food.

FAUSTUS.

Alas, madam, that's nothing. Mephastophilis, be gone.

Exit Mephastophilis.

Were it a greater thing than this, so it would content you, you should have it.

Enter Mephastophilis with the grapes.

15   Here they be, madam, will't please you taste on them?
DUKE.

Believe me, Master Doctor, this makes me wonder above the rest, that being in the dead time of winter, and in the month of January, how you should come by these grapes.
FAUSTUS.

If it like your Grace, the year is divided into two circles
20   over the whole world, that when it is here winter with us, in the contrary circle it is summer with them, as in India, Saba, and farther countries in the east; and by means of a swift spirit that I have, I had them brought hither, as ye see. How do you like them, madam, be they good?
DUCHESS.

25   Believe me, Master Doctor, they be the best grapes that e'er I tasted in my life before.
FAUSTUS.

I am glad they content you so, madam.

---

12. *Mephastophilis, be gone*] Mephastophilis is presumably invisible to the Duke and Duchess (the explanation Faustus gives in lines 22-24 would otherwise be superfluous).

19-22.] The two "circles" should of course be the northern and southern hemispheres. The writer who adapted this passage for the stage was at least aware that India and Saba lay to the east. Compare *EFB*, ch. 39: "...when with us it is winter, in the contrary circle it is notwithstanding summer, for in India and Saba there falleth or setteth the sun, so that it is so warm that they have twice a year fruit..." (156). To do him justice, the translator responsible for *EFB* managed here to trim down an intractably silly passage in his source, the *Historia von D. Johann Fausten*, ch. 44 (Füssel and Kreutzer 89-90).

21. *Saba*] the land of the Queen of Sheba, now Yemen; see Milton, *Paradise Lost* IV. 161-63.

DUKE.

Come madam, let us in, where you must well reward this
learned man for the kindness he hath showed to you.

DUCHESS.

And so I will, my lord, and whilst I live rest beholding for
this courtesy.

FAUSTUS.

I humbly thank your Grace.

DUKE.

Come Master Doctor, follow us, and receive your reward.

Exeunt.

ACT V

— ACT V SCENE I —

Enter Wagner solus.

WAGNER.
    I think my master means to die shortly,
    For he hath given to me all his goods;
    And yet me thinkes if that death were near
    He would not banquet and carouse and swill
5   Amongst the students, as even now he doth,
    Who are at supper with such belly-cheer
    As Wagner ne'er beheld in all his life.
    See where they come: belike the feast is ended.

Exit.

Enter Faustus with two or three Scholars.

1 SCH.
    Master Doctor Faustus, since our conference about fair
10   ladies, which was the beautiful'st in all the world, we have
    determined with ourselves that Helen of Greece was the
    admirablest lady that ever lived. Therefore, Master Doctor,
    if you will do us that favor as to let us see that peerless
    dame of Greece, whom all the world admires for majesty,
15   we should think ourselves much beholding unto you.
FAUSTUS.
    Gentlemen,
    For that I know your friendship is unfeign'd
    (And Faustus' custom is not to deny
    The just requests of those that wish him well),
20   You shall behold that peerless dame of Greece

---

3. *me thinkes*] Modernized spelling would upset the rhythm of this line.

11. *determined with*] settled among.

17. *for that*] because.

No otherways for pomp and majesty
Than when Sir Paris cross'd the seas with her
And brought the spoils to rich Dardania.
Be silent then, for danger is in words.

Music sounds, and Helen passeth over the stage.

2 SCH.

Too simple is my wit to tell her praise,   25
Whom all the world admires for majesty.

3 SCH.

Not marvel though the angry Greeks pursu'd
With ten years' war the rape of such a queen,
Whose heavenly beauty passeth all compare.

1 SCH.

Since we have seen the pride of nature's works,   30
And only paragon of excellence,

Enter an Old Man.

Let us depart, and for this glorious deed
Happy and blest be Faustus evermore.

FAUSTUS.

Gentlemen, farewell, the same I wish to you.

Exeunt Scholars.

---

22. Sir Paris] Ward identifies "Sir" as "the chivalrous prefix of mediaeval romance," and
notes for comparison Pistol's "Sir Pandarus of Troy" and "Sir Actaeon" in *The Merry
Wives of Windsor* I. iii. 65 and II. i. 105.

23. *spoils*] booty, including Helen, taken from Menelaus, king of Sparta.

Dardania] Troy, referred to here by the name of the founder of the Trojan dynasty,
Dardanus. Compare Shakespeare, *Troilus and Cressida*, Prologue, line 13: "On Dardan
plains".

27. *pursu'd*] sought to punish or avenge (*OED*, v. I. i.b).

28. *rape*] abduction.

29.] This line echoes Spenser, *Faerie Queene* III. i. 26: "Whose sovereign beauty hath no
living peer" (see Cheney 1997: 196).

OLD MAN.

35 Ah Doctor Faustus, that I might prevail
    To guide thy steps unto the way of life,
    By which sweet path thy may'st attain the goal
    That shall conduct thee to celestial rest.
    Break heart, drop blood, and mingle it with tears,
40 Tears falling from repentant heaviness
    Of thy most vile and loathsome filthiness,
    The stench whereof corrupts the inward soul
    With such flagitious crimes of heinous sins
    As no commiseration may expel
45 But mercy, Faustus, of thy Saviour sweet,
    Whose blood alone must wash away thy guilt.

FAUSTUS.

    Where art thou, Faustus? wretch, what hast thou done?

35-46.] This speech, which modulates after line 40 into a harsh denunciation of Faustus's
sinfulness as so disgusting and corrupting that only Christ's mercy and the blood of
his redemptive sacrifice can possibly save him, is replaced in B1 by a longer speech of
a wholly different theological orientation. The Old Man's words in A1 are Calvinist
in their implication that the consequence of sin is "loathsome filthiness," i.e., that
sinful humanity is radically unloveable, and that salvation can come only as a wholly
unmerited consequence of an act of divine mercy. Stachniewski cites many instances
from the period of Calvinist domination of Anglican orthodoxy (from the 1560s
to the mid-seventeenth century) in which Calvinist theology and preaching produced reactions like that of Faustus in line 48 (see Stachniewski 17-54). He notes that
"Many actual suicides resulted from religious despair. Cambridge was notorious for
them in the 1580s and 1590s, the period of its greatest domination by puritan preaching" (49). In B1, in contrast, the Old Man tells Faustus, in Augustinian terms, that
his soul remains loveable unless perverted by the habit or custom of sinfulness, and
he speaks in tones not of "wrath" but of "tender love."

36. *the way of life*] The Old Man's speech, as Ormerod and Wortham note, is laden with
biblical echoes and cadences; these words, for example, resonate with *Psalm* 16: 11,
Proverbs 10: 17, *John* 14: 6, and *Acts* 2: 28.

43. *flagitious*] extremely wicked, infamous.

45-46.] Compare *Revelation* 1: 5: "Jesus Christ ... loved us, and washed us from our sins
in his blood." *The Prayer-Book of Queen Elizabeth* (1559) specifies that if a person in
"extremity of sickness ... do truly repent him of his sins, and steadfastly believe that
Jesus Christ ... shed his blood for his redemption" (135), this is the equivalent of taking communion. Faustus is unable so to believe; one interpretation of the blood-pact
which he made in II. i (and renews in this scene) is that it amounts to a self-exclusion,
through the shedding of his own blood, from the number of those for whom Christ's
redeeming blood was shed. (See the note to II. i. 58.)

47. *Where art thou, Faustus?*] Bevington and Rasmussen (188) suggest a comparison with
Genesis 3: 9: "the Lord God called to the man, and said unto him, Where art thou?"

Damn'd art thou, Faustus, damn'd, despair and die!
Hell calls for right, and with a roaring voice
Says, "Faustus, come, thine hour is come!"   50

Enter Mephastophilis, who gives him a dagger.

And Faustus will come to do thee right.
OLD MAN.
Ah stay, good Faustus, stay thy desperate steps:
I see an angel hovers o'er thy head,
And with a vial full of precious grace
Offers to pour the same into thy soul: 55
Then call for mercy and avoid despair.
FAUSTUS.
Ah my sweet friend, I feel thy words
To comfort my distressed soul.
Leave me awhile to ponder on my sins.

                                                                 60

48.] This line is missing in B1, no doubt deleted as part of the theologically oriented
revision that substituted a mild Augustinian rebuke for the puritanical denunciation
of the Old Man's first speech in A1.

49. *roaring voice*] Bevington and Rasmussen (188) note for comparison *1 Peter* 5: 8: "the
devil as a roaring lion walketh about, seeking whom he may devour...."

50. *thine hour is come*] Cornelius (268) compares *John* 13: 1: "Jesus knew that his hour was
come...."

50.1.] There is a similar demonic temptation to suicide in Spenser, *Faerie Queene* I. ix.
50-51.

54. *a vial full of precious grace*] The Old Man here individualizes an image from *Revelation*
5: 8, in which elders worshipping before the throne of God carry "golden vials full
of odours, which are the prayers of the saints."

55. *Offers to pour*] The gesture which the Old Man purportedly sees would seem to be
conditional in nature. The verb "offer," followed by an infinitive, can mean either
"to propose or express one's readiness (to do something), conditionally on the assent
of the person addressed" (*OED*, "offer," v. 4), or "to make an attempt or show of
intention (to do something)" (v. 5.b). The pouring of grace, if the angel's offering is
more than just a show of intention, appears to be conditional on Faustus calling for
mercy—but Protestant orthodoxy made such a call dependent upon a prior reception
of grace.

57, 60. *sweet friend, sweet Faustus*] The adjective "sweet," which does not appear in the B1
revision of these lines, may to some extent counter the harshness of the Old Man's
first speech: unless debased by overuse, this adjective represents those to whom it is
applied (including "thy Saviour sweet" [line 45]) as objects of delight.

OLD MAN.

60   I go, sweet Faustus, but with heavy cheer,
        Fearing the ruin of thy hopeless soul.

                    Exit.

FAUSTUS.

        Accursed Faustus, where is mercy now?
        I do repent, and yet I do despair:
        Hell strives with grace for conquest in my breast;
65   What shall I do to shun the snares of death?
MEPH.

        Thou traitor, Faustus, I arrest thy soul
        For disobedience to my sovereign lord.
        Revolt, or I'll in piece-meal tear thy flesh!
FAUSTUS.

        Sweet Mephastophilis, entreat thy lord
70   To pardon my unjust presumption,
        And with my blood again I will confirm
        My former vow I made to Lucifer.
MEPH.

        Do it then quickly, with unfeigned heart,

60–62.] These lines are revised in B1 in a way that significantly shifts the meaning of the Old Man's intervention. In line 61 the Old Man fearfully anticipates that Faustus' lack of hope (which in Calvinist terms amounts to the same thing as a lack of the faith necessary for salvation) will lead to his soul's ruin or downfall; B1 has him fear instead "the enemy of thy hapless soul," the demonic agent who he anticipates will victimize this unfortunate man. In line 62 Faustus loses confidence in that mercy which the Old Man's vision of an angel had represented as imminently available; B1 shifts attention from the question of the availability of divine mercy, making Faustus instead blame his own perverse agency by repeating a phrase from line 47: "wretch, what hast thou done?" The focus in A1 is on the divine grace which, if Faustus receives it, will enable him to have faith in his saviour's mercy; B1 deflects our attention instead to the sinful agency of Faustus and of his demonic enemy.

68. *Revolt*] reverse your course of action (*OED*, v. I. 2.b); in religious contexts, the word carries the implication of departing from the truth (*OED*, v. I. 2.a, 2.c). B1 has Faustus say, after this line, "I do repent I e'er offended him"—words which, unlike B1's other deviations from A1 in this scene, alter the meaning only to the extent of making more explicit what is already evident in A1.

73. *unfeigned heart*] Bevington and Rasmussen (189) note an ironic resonance with *1 Timothy* 1: 5: "For the end of the commandment is love out of a pure heart, and of a good conscience, and of faith unfeigned."

Lest greater danger do attend thy drift.

FAUSTUS.

Torment, sweet friend, that base and crooked age   75
That durst dissuade me from thy Lucifer,
With greatest torments that our hell affords.

MEPH.

His faith is great, I cannot touch his soul.
But what I may afflict his body with
I will attempt, which is but little worth.   80

FAUSTUS.

One thing, good servant, let me crave of thee
To glut the longing of my heart's desire:
That I might have unto my paramour
That heavenly Helen which I saw of late,
Whose sweet embracings may extinguish clean   85
These thoughts that do dissuade me from my vow,
And keep mine oath I made to Lucifer.

MEPH.

Faustus, this, or what else thou shalt desire,

---

74. *drift*] conscious or unconscious tendency or aim (*OED*, sb. 3, 4).

77.] This line is paralleled by Thomas Kyd in *The Spanish Tragedy* II. iii. 48: "With greatest pleasure that our court affords."

83. *unto*] as.

84. *heavenly Helen*] The presence of Helen of Troy in the Faustus legend is one sign of that legend's dependence on the patristic legend of Simon Magus, the first-century Gnostic heresiarch and magician. Helen's appearances in *EFB* are heavily moralized. But Marlowe seems to have been aware of Simon Magus's blasphemous identification of his Helen, a redeemed prostitute, with the divine Wisdom, as well as with Helen of Troy. Irenaeus (c. 180 C.E.) states that Simon claimed to be the supreme God, while his companion Helena, whom he had redeemed from prostitution in the city of Tyre, "was the first conception of his mind, the mother of all, by whom, in the beginning, he conceived in his mind [the thought] of forming angels and archangels." These powers, who subsequently created the world, were ignorant of Simon and jealous of his First Thought, whom they imprisoned in human form, so that "for ages [she] passed in succession from one female body to another, as from vessel to vessel. She was, for example, in that Helen on whose account the Trojan war was undertaken..." (Irenaeus 87-88 [I. 23]). According to the pseudo-Clementine *Recognitions*, Simon asserted that his companion was "Wisdom, the mother of all things, for whom, says he, the Greeks and barbarians contending, were able in some measure to see an image of her; but of herself, as she is, the dweller with the first and only God, they were wholly ignorant" (*Recognitions* 199 [II. 12]).

85. *extinguish clean*] Bevington and Rasmussen (189) note that this reading is supported against the B text's "clear" by *2 Tamburlaine* V. iii. 89: "Is almost clean extinguished...."

Shall be performed in twinkling of an eye.

Enter Helen.

FAUSTUS.

90   Was this the face that launch'd a thousand ships
        And burnt the topless towers of Ilium?
        Sweet Helen, make me immortal with a kiss;
        Her lips sucks forth my soul, see where it flies!
        Come Helen, come, give me my soul again;
95   Here will I dwell, for heaven be in these lips,
        And all is dross that is not Helena.

Enter Old Man.

        I will be Paris, and for love of thee
        Instead of Troy shall Wittenberg be sack'd,
        And I will combat with weak Menelaus

---

90. *a thousand ships*] Compare Seneca, *Troades* 26-27: "The plunderer hurries away the
Dardanian spoils, booty which a thousand ships cannot contain." Lucian's *Dialogues
of the Dead* xviii (Loeb edition, v) provides a closer parallel: when Menippus is shown
the skull of Helen, he exclaims, "And for this a thousand ships carried warriors from
every part of Greece...." Marlowe's Tamburlaine compares his Zenocrate to "Helen,
whose beauty summon'd Greece to arms, / And drew a thousand ships to Tenedos"
(*2 Tamburlaine* II. iv. 87-8).

91. *topless*] immensely high. Compare *Edward III* IV. v. 113-15: "a lofty hill / Whose top
seems topless, for the embracing sky / Doth hide his high head in her azure bosom"
(*Shakespeare Apocrypha* 96).

Ilium] Troy.

92. *make ... kiss*] Compare *Dido Queen of Carthage* IV. iv. 122-3: "in his looks I see eternity, / And he'll make me immortal with a kiss."

92-96, 103-04, 109.] Compare the apocryphal *Wisdom of Solomon*, 7: 25-26, 29, 8:2: Wisdom
"is the breath of the power of God, and a pure influence that floweth from the glory of
the Almighty: therefore can no defiled thing come unto her. For she is the brightness of
the everlasting light, the undefiled mirror of the Majesty of God, and the image of his
goodness. [...] For she is more beautiful than the Sun, and is above all the order of the
stars, and the light is not to be compared unto her. [...] I have loved her, and sought her
from my youth: I desired to marry her, such love had I unto her beauty."

96.1.] The Old Man does not re-enter in B1, which cuts the last nine lines of this scene.

99. *weak Menelaus*] Book III of Homer's *Iliad* recounts the duel between Alexandros or
Paris and Menelaus. Paris challenged all the best of the Achaeans to single combat,
but recoiled in fear from Menelaus. Paris was saved from death by Aphrodite, who

And wear thy colours on my plumed crest;   100
Yea, I will wound Achilles in the heel
And then return to Helen for a kiss.
O, thou art fairer than the evening air
Clad in the beauty of a thousand stars;
Brighter art thou than flaming Jupiter   105
When he appear'd to hapless Semele,
More lovely than the monarch of the sky
In wanton Arethusa's azur'd arms,
And none but thou shalt be my paramour.

Exeunt.

OLD MAN.

Accursed Faustus, miserable man,   110
That from thy soul exclud'st the grace of heaven
And fliest the throne of his tribunal seat!

Enter the devils.

Satan begins to sift me with his pride;
As in this furnace God shall try my faith,

---

carried him in a mist into his own bedchamber—where, although shamed in Helen's eyes as in everyone else's, he promptly took Helen to bed.

106. *hapless Semele*] One of Jupiter's human mistresses, she was persuaded by Juno to ask him to come to her in the same form in which he embraced Juno in heaven, and was consumed by fire. See Ovid, *Metamorphoses* III. 259-315.

108. *Arethusa*] a nymph who, bathing in the river Alpheus, aroused the river-god's lust; fleeing from him, she was transformed into a fountain (see Ovid's *Metamorphoses* V. 577-641). No classical myth links her with Jupiter or the sun-god. However, Gill notes that George Sandys in *Ovid's Metamorphoses Englished* (1621) writes in his commentary on this passage that the river-god Alpheus "drew his pedigree from the sun" (Gill 1990: 85).

113. *sift me*] Compare Jesus's words to Peter at the last supper: "Simon, Simon, behold, Satan hath desired to have you, that he may sift you as wheat" (*Luke* 22: 31, *Authorized Version*). Ormerod and Wortham (144), observing that the *Geneva Bible* has "winnow" here, suggest that Marlowe derived "sift" from the *Coverdale Bible* of 1535; "sift" is also used in this verse in William Tyndale's 1526 translation of the New Testament (Tyndale *NT* 184).

114. *furnace*] an allusion, as Bevington and Rasmussen note, to the fiery furnace of *Daniel* 3: 3-28.

115 My faith, vile hell, shall triumph over thee!
     Ambitious fiends, see how the heaven smiles
     At your repulse, and laughs your state to scorn:
     Hence, hell, for hence I fly unto my God.

Exeunt.

— ACT V SCENE II —

Enter Faustus with the Scholars.

FAUSTUS.
   Ah, gentlemen!
I SCH.
   What ails Faustus?
FAUSTUS.
   Ah, my sweet chamber-fellow, had I lived with thee, then had
   I lived still, but now I die eternally. Look, comes he not,
5 comes he not?
2 SCH.
   What means Faustus?
3 SCH.
   Belike he is grown into some sickness, by being over-solitary.
I SCH.
   If it be so, we'll have physicians to cure him. 'Tis but a
   surfeit, never fear, man.
FAUSTUS.
10 A surfeit of deadly sin, that hath damned both body and
    soul.
2 SCH.
   Yet Faustus, look up to heaven; remember, God's mercies
   are infinite.

116-17.] Cornelius (271) notes that the Old Man is echoing *Psalm* 2: 4, in the translation
of the *Bishops' Bible*: "He that dwelleth in heaven will laugh them to scorn...."
10. *surfeit*] an excessive indulgence in food or drink, and the resulting disorder of the
system.

FAUSTUS.

But Faustus' offence can ne'er be pardoned: the serpent
that tempted Eve may be saved, but not Faustus. Ah   15
gentlemen, hear me with patience, and tremble not at my
speeches. Though my heart pants and quivers to remember
that I have been a student here these thirty years, O would
I had never seen Wittenberg, never read book: and what
wonders I have done, all Germany can witness, yea all the   20
world, for which Faustus hath lost both Germany and the
world, yea heaven itself, heaven the seat of God, the throne
of the blessed, the kingdom of joy, and must remain in hell
for ever—hell, ah, hell, for ever! Sweet friends, what shall
become of Faustus, being in hell for ever?   25

3 SCH.

Yet Faustus, call on God.

FAUSTUS.

On God, whom Faustus hath abjured? on God, whom Faustus hath blasphemed? Ah my God, I would weep, but the
devil draws in my tears. Gush forth blood instead of tears,
yea life and soul! Oh, he stays my tongue; I would lift up   30
my hands, but see, they hold them, they hold them!

ALL.

Who, Faustus?

---

14. *Faustus' offence can ne'er be pardoned*] Stachniewski notes that "Despair was the usual
Calvinist interpretation of the unpardonable sin against the Holy Ghost." In relation
to this line he quotes the Anglican (and Calvinist) theologian William Perkins's
opinion that despair "cannot be forgiven … because after a man hath once committed this sin, it is impossible for him to repent" (Stachniewski 317-18, quoting
Perkins, *Works* 118).

20-22.] Cornelius (273) notes a reminiscence here of *Mark* 8: 36: "For what shall it profit
a man, though he should win the whole world, if he lose his soul?"

28-29. *the devil draws in my tears*] An inability to shed penitent tears was interpreted by
Renaissance demonologists as a sign of demonic possession. Heinrich Kramer and
James Sprenger wrote in the *Malleus maleficarum* that "the grace of tears is one of
the chief gifts allowed to the penitent…. Therefore there can be no doubt that they
are displeasing to the devil, and that he uses all his endeavour to restrain them, to
prevent a witch from finally attaining to penitence" (*Malleus* 475 [III. Qn 15]). Jean
Bodin in *De la démonomanie des sorciers* (1580) lists an inability to weep among the
presumptive proofs of a witch's guilt (Bodin 199 [IV. iv]).

FAUSTUS.

Lucifer and Mephastophilis. Ah, gentlemen, I gave them my
soul for my cunning.

ALL.

35   God forbid!

FAUSTUS.

God forbade it indeed, but Faustus hath done it: for the vain
pleasure of four and twenty years hath Faustus lost eternal
joy and felicity. I writ them a bill with mine own blood, the
date is expired, the time will come, and he will fetch me!

1 SCH.

40   Why did not Faustus tell us of this before, that divines
might have prayed for thee?

FAUSTUS.

Oft have I thought to have done so, but the devil threatened
to tear me in pieces if I named God, to fetch both body and
soul if I once gave ear to divinity, and now 'tis too late:
45   gentlemen, away, lest you perish with me.

2 SCH.

O what shall we do to save Faustus?

FAUSTUS.

Talk not of me, but save yourselves, and depart.

3 SCH.

God will strengthen me, I will stay with Faustus.

1 SCH.

Tempt not God, sweet friend, but let us into the next room,
50   and there pray for him.

FAUSTUS.

Ay, pray for me, pray for me; and what noise soever ye hear,
come not unto me, for nothing can rescue me.

2 SCH.

Pray thou, and we will pray that God may have mercy upon
thee.

---

34. *cunning*] knowledge.

38. *bill*] deed.

43. *tear me in pieces*] Compare 1 *Tamburlaine* IV. iv. 38: "legions of devils shall tear thee
in pieces."

46. *save*] This word, missing in A1 but obviously necessary to the sense, is supplied from B1.

FAUSTUS.

Gentlemen, farewell. If I live till morning, I'll visit you; if   55
not, Faustus is gone to hell.

ALL.

Faustus, farewell.

Exeunt Scholars.
The clock strikes eleven.

FAUSTUS.

Ah Faustus,
Now hast thou but one bare hour to live,
And then thou must be damn'd perpetually.   60
Stand still, you ever-moving spheres of heaven,
That time may cease, and midnight never come!
Fair nature's eye, rise, rise again, and make
Perpetual day, or let this hour be but a year,
A month, a week, a natural day,   65
That Faustus may repent, and save his soul.
O lente lente currite noctis equi!
The stars move still, time runs, the clock will strike,
The devil will come, and Faustus must be damn'd.
O, I'll leap up to my God: who pulls me down?   70

61-69.] Compare *Edward II* V. i. 64-70: "Continue ever, thou celestial sun, / Let never silent night possess this clime; / Stand still, you watches of the element, / All times and
seasons rest you at a stay, / That Edward may be still fair England's king. / But day's
bright beams doth vanish fast away, / And needs I must resign my wished crown."

67. O lente ... equi] "O gallop slowly, slowly, you horses of the night!" Faustus is quoting
from Ovid, *Amores* I. xiii. 40. The tone of Ovid's request to Aurora, goddess of the
dawn, to hold back her horses so that he can remain longer in bed with his beloved is
deliberately teasing. In this passage, he tells the goddess that she has left Tithonus' bed
because he is old, but in other circumstances would behave differently: "At si quem
mavis Cephalum complexa teneres, / clamares 'lente currite, noctis equi!'"—lines
which Marlowe translated thus, in *All Ovid's Elegies*: "But heldst thou in thine arms
some Cephalus, / Then wouldst thou cry, stay night and run not thus." The playfully
erotic associations of the line make it especially poignant in this context.

70. O, I'll leap up ... who pulls me down?] As Steane (1964: 282) observed, this line contains another Ovidian resonance, though in this case Faustus echoes a phrase from
Marlowe's translation of *All Ovid's Elegies* rather than Ovid's text. *Amores* I. xv ends
with the boast that, thanks to his poetry, Ovid will outlive his own funeral pyre:
"Ergo etiam cum me supremus adederit ignis, / vivam, parsque mei multa superstes

See, see where Christ's blood streams in the firmament:
One drop would save my soul, half a drop! Ah, my Christ,
Ah rend not my heart for naming of my Christ,
Yet I will call on him, oh spare me Lucifer!
75 Where is it now? 'tis gone,
And see where God stretcheth out his arm
And bends his ireful brows!
Mountains and hills, come, come, and fall on me
And hide me from the heavy wrath of God.
80 No, no?
Then will I headlong run into the earth.
Earth, gape! O no, it will not harbor me.
You stars that reign'd at my nativity,
Whose influence hath allotted death and hell,

---

erit" (I. xv. 41-2: "Then even when the last fire has devoured me, / I shall live on, and my great part will yet survive"—or, in Marlowe's vivid translation, "Then though death rakes my bones in funeral fire, / I'll live, and as he pulls me down mount higher").

71.] Compare *2 Tamburlaine* V. iii. 48-50: "Come let us march against the powers of heaven, / And set black streamers in the firmament / To signify the slaughter of the gods."

73.] This line, addressed to Lucifer, echoes one spoken by Edward II to his lover Gaveston: "Rend not my heart with thy too piercing words" (*Edward II* I. iv. 117). Robert A. H. Smith suggests an allusion in both cases to *Joel* 2: 12-13, where, faced by a terrifying prospect of destruction that makes the earth quake and the heavens tremble, and that darkens the sun, moon and stars, the Israelites are exhorted to repentance: "Turn you unto me with all your heart, and with fasting, and with weeping, and with mourning, And rent ["rend" in the *Authorized Version*] your heart, and not your clothes: and turn unto the Lord your God, for he is gracious, and merciful, slow to anger, and of great kindness, and repenteth him of evil" (see Smith 1997: 483).

78-79.] This is a recurrent motif in apocalyptic writings, e.g. *Luke* 23: 30: "Then shall they begin to say to the mountains, Fall on us; and to the hills, Cover us"; *Revelation* 6: 16: "And said to the mountains and rocks, Fall on us, and hide us from the presence of him that sitteth on the throne, and from the wrath of the Lamb." See also *Hosea* 10: 8.

82. *Earth, gape!*] The imperative has no effect—but Faustus might well recoil from the idea of opening a path between this world and the underworld, which as Bevington and Rasmussen (195) note is what Zabina in her wretchedness hopes for in *1 Tamburlaine* V. i. 241-3: "Gape earth, and let the fiends infernal view / A hell as hopeless and as full of fear / As are the blasted banks of Erebus...."

83.] Bevington and Rasmussen (196) note *1 Tamburlaine* IV. ii. 33: "Smile, stars that reign'd at my nativity...."

83-89.] Having aspired initially to "rend the clouds" (I. i. 60) and to beget himself in divine form (I. i. 63-64), Faustus now begs to undergo a bizarrely literalized reversal

Now draw up Faustus like a foggy mist   85
Into the entrails of yon laboring cloud,
That when you vomit forth into the air
My limbs may issue from your smoky mouths,
So that my soul may but ascend to heaven.

The watch strikes.

Ah, half the hour is past: 'twill all be past anon.   90
Oh God, if thou wilt not have mercy on my soul,
Yet for Christ's sake, whose blood hath ransom'd me,
Impose some end to my incessant pain:
Let Faustus live in hell a thousand years,
A hundred thousand, and at last be sav'd.   95
O, no end is limited to damned souls.
Why wert thou not a creature wanting soul?
Or why is this immortal that thou hast?
Ah, Pythagoras' metempsychosis, were that true
This soul should fly from me, and I be chang'd   100
Unto some brutish beast.
All beasts are happy, for when they die
Their souls are soon dissolv'd in elements,

---

of the process of rebirth that was central to Renaissance Hermetic-Cabalistic magic.
The bargain proposed—of resorption into a dismembering womb and of the regurgitation and dispersal of his body in exchange for the salvation of his soul—is the
most violent expression of despair in the play.

89.1. watch] clock.

96. *no end is limited to damned souls*] i.e., damnation is endless. As Snow remarks, "end"
here suggests purpose and finality as well as temporal conclusiveness. Faustus, who
challenged "the end of every art" (I. i. 4) and set out to transgress the limits fixed
by his human state and his despair, here seems to recognize an absence of limit (and
a corresponding emptying out of purposefulness and temporality) as the defining
conditions of damnation.

99. *metempsychosis*] the doctrine of the transmigration of souls. Feste teases Malvolio with
this doctrine in *Twelfth Night* IV. ii. 50-53: "Thou shalt hold th'opinion of Pythagoras
ere I will allow of thy wits, and fear to kill a woodcock lest thou dispossess the soul
of thy grandam."

102-03.] Nashe restores this thought to an orthodox context in *Christs Teares Over
Jerusalem* (1593): "Let us not glory that we are men, who have put on the shapes of
beasts. Thrice blessed are beasts that die soon, and after this life feel no hell: Woe
unto us, we shall, if we appear to God in the image of beasts..." (Nashe ii. 113).

But mine must live still to be plagu'd in hell.
105 Curst be the parents that engender'd me;
No Faustus, curse thyself, curse Lucifer
That hath depriv'd thee of the joys of heaven!

The clock striketh twelve.

O it strikes, it strikes: now body, turn to air
Or Lucifer will bear thee quick to hell!

Thunder and lightning.

110 O soul, be changed into little water drops
And fall into the ocean, ne'er be found!
My God, my God, look not so fierce on me!

Enter devils.

Adders and serpents, let me breathe awhile!
Ugly hell gape not, come not Lucifer,
115 I'll burn my books, ah Mephastophilis!

Exeunt with him.

---

109. *quick*] alive.

112. *My God, my God*] A. D. Nuttall remarks that after these words, "we can scarcely avoid expecting the rest of the cry of dereliction, 'My God, my God, why hast thou forsaken me?' (*Matthew* 27: 46), but instead we get, 'Look not so fierce on me!' The cry of dereliction is *overtaken* and displaced in the sentence by the face of terror, as the folly of Icarus, in the Prologue, was overtaken by the conspiracy of heaven. It is as if, by a final horror, the feared absence of God proves less dreadful than his presence" (Nuttall 1998: 46).

114.] Snow remarks of II. i. 26-29 and of this line that "The same erotic energy charges both utterances, and the later one is the genuine consummation of the earlier one as well as its ironic inversion" (Snow 72).

EPILOGUE

Enter Chorus.

Cut is the branch that might have grown full straight,
And burned is Apollo's laurel bough
That sometime grew within this learned man:
Faustus is gone, regard his hellish fall,
Whose fiendful fortune may exhort the wise   5
Only to wonder at unlawful things,
Whose deepness doth entice such forward wits
To practice more than heavenly power permits.

Exit.

Terminat hora diem, terminat Author opus.

1.] Troni Grande (170 n. 52) notes that Marlowe here echoes a line from the tale of *Shore's Wife* in *The Mirror for Magistrates*: "And bent the wand that might have grown ful straight" (*Mirror*, line 140). John Stachniewski suggests that this line evokes a Calvinist context: "In the [Epilogue's] opening line the agent has been obscured but the metaphor must prompt the question whether, since the branch is Faustus, or a part of Faustus, he can easily cut it himself. Recollection of biblical parables of pruning and casting unwanted branches into the fire then identifies God as the agent (see *John* 15: 6; *Matt.* 3: 10 and 7: 19). The conclusion invited is that Faustus could have continued to grow ... had not God intervened to destroy him" (Stachniewski 313).

2. *Apollo's laurel bough*] Marlowe makes use of the same image in his Latin dedication of his dead friend Thomas Watson's *Amintae Gaudia* (1592) to Mary, Countess of Pembroke. For the text, see Gill 1987: 218-19; and for commentary, Eriksen 1986 and Cheney 1997: 192-93.

4-8.] Tromly (152) proposes that "These lines place the 'forward wits' of the audience in precisely the situation of Faustus, which is to say that of Tantalus," and leave us "with a vision of enticement and punishment, perhaps enticement as punishment."

6. *Only to wonder*] to be content with wondering.

8.2.] "The hour ends the day; the author ends his work." Bakeless (i. 293) notes that this same sentence occurs in a manuscript in the Archbishop Parker collection at Corpus Christi College, Cambridge, where Marlowe was a student.

Appendix A: Non-parallel Scenes from The Tragical History of the Life and Death of Doctor Faustus *(1616 version) (London: John Wright, 1616)*

[This Appendix is designed to facilitate comparisons between the A and B versions of *Doctor Faustus*. For this purpose it is important to remember that my critical edition of the A version is not a reprint of the 1604 quarto, but incorporates readings from the 1616 quarto at points where there is good reason to believe that it preserves readings that are earlier and more authoritative than those of A. My edition restores displaced comic scenes to their correct places and—where the evidence permits—reverses obvious textual corruptions, with the aim of offering a text close to what London audiences would have seen performed in the early 1590s.

The scenes from the B version offered in this Appendix follow the 1616 quarto closely, the aim in this case being to show how the play was transformed in the early seventeenth century by revision and censorship. Although the 1616 quarto preserves a text close to what would have been performed following the censorship prompted by the Act of Abuses (1606), some of its readings probably stem from editorial work at the time of its printing in 1616.

The B-version scenes offered here differ from the B-version editions of the 1960s and 1970s, most of whose editors restored A-text lines that had been cut or grievously altered in the 1616 quarto as a result of revision or censorship, and thus uncritically conflated the A and B versions of the play. In disguising the extent to which Marlovian scenes were subjected in B to ideologically motivated revisions, these editions give a misleading impression of the B text's orientation.

The comic scene identified here as Act II, scene iv is printed in the recent B-text editions of Bevington and Rasmussen and of Burnett as Act II, scene ii: in those editions it fills the gap in B between the first and second scenes of Act II. Although for purposes of performance this may be an appropriate expedient, the textual evidence suggests that in the B text as written there were originally two comic scenes involving stolen magic books, which followed II. i and II. iii respectively. B's surviving stolen-book scene is linked to the comic stolen-cup scene (III. iii) by the fact that the clowns depart for a tavern at the end of the first of these scenes and emerge from one at the start of the other. It would seem that the scene printed here as II. iv, in the same sequence as in the 1616 quarto, was not displaced in that quarto, and that the B text's II. ii is lost. A relocation of II. iv cannot help but give a misleading impression of the textual integrity of the 1616 quarto.

Spelling and punctuation are modernized in these B version scenes, as in my A-version edition. In my explanatory notes, the spelling in quotations from the early quartos and other Renaissance texts has likewise been modernized.

Readers who wish to compare the complete texts of these two versions of the play should consult my critical edition of the 1604 and 1616 versions, which is being published concurrently with the present edition, with full textual apparatus, by Broadview Press.

Those who want to compare the two substantive quartos of 1604 and 1616 in old spelling can consult the Scolar Press facsimile edition, the electronic facsimiles available from Early English Books Online, or W.W. Greg's parallel-text edition. (Some may hope to discover in those editions a satisfactory reading or performance text: one can only wish them, in the words of Shakespeare's Clown in *Antony and Cleopatra*, "all joy of the worm.")]

1. Act I Scene iv (1616 text)

Enter Wagner and the Clown.

WAGNER.
    Come hither, sirrah boy.
CLOWN.
    Boy? O disgrace to my person! Zounds, boy in your face:

1-4.] Compare the opening exchange with that in scene viii of the anonymous *The Taming of a Shrew* (1594), a play which is derivative from Shakespeare's *The Taming of the Shrew* and which also borrows repeatedly from several Marlovian texts:
Polidor's Boy. Come hither, sirrah boy.
Sander. Boy! O disgrace to my person! Zounds, boy, of your face: you have many boys with such pickedevants, I am sure. Zounds, would you not have a bloody nose for this? (viii. 1-4)
For Greg, the close likeness of these passages indicated that the B-version of *Doctor Faustus* was in existence by 1594 and was plagiarized here by the author or authors of *A Shrew*. However, it seems probable that Samuel Rowley was involved in the writing of *A Shrew* as well as in the 1602 revision of *Doctor Faustus*—and that having in 1594 adapted this exchange from the A-version of *Doctor Faustus* (preserving the unusual word "pickedevant"), he then recycled his own borrowing when in 1602 he was hired to re-work *Doctor Faustus* (see Oliver, and Kuriyama 1975: 175-96).
2. *Zounds*] an abbreviation of the oath "By God's wounds."

you have seen many boys with beards, I am sure.

WAGNER.

Sirrah, hast thou no comings in?

CLOWN.

Yes, and goings out too, you may see, sir.   5

WAGNER.

. Alas, poor slave; see how poverty jests in his nakedness.
I know the villain's out of service, and so hungry that I
know he would give his soul to the devil for a shoulder
of mutton, though it were blood raw.

CLOWN.

Not so neither: I had need to have it well roasted, and   10
good sauce to it, if I pay so dear, I can tell you.

WAGNER.

Sirrah, wilt thou be my man and wait on me? and I will
make thee go like *Qui mihi discipulus.*

CLOWN.

What, in verse?

WAGNER.

No slave, in beaten silk and stavesacre.   15

CLOWN.

Stavesacre? That's good to kill vermin: then belike if I
serve you, I shall be lousy.

WAGNER.

Why, so thou shalt be, whether thou dost it or no. For
sirrah, if thou dost not presently bind thyself to me for
seven years, I'll turn all the lice about thee into familiars   20
and make them tear thee in pieces.

CLOWN.

Nay sir, you may save yourself a labor, for they are as
familiar with me as if they paid for their meat and drink,
I can tell you.

WAGNER.

Well sirrah, leave your jesting, and take these guilders.   25

---

13. Qui mihi discipulus] "You who are my pupil." (See the notes to I. iv. 13-14 and 70-71
in my A-version edition.)

17. *lousy*] infested by lice, filthy, contemptible.

25-30.] This money-exchange jest is loosely paralleled in *A Shrew,* scene viii, where
Polidor's Boy gives Sander two shillings "to pay for the healing of thy left leg which
I mean furiously to invade or to maim at the least." After thanking him for the gift,

CLOWN.

Yes, marry sir, and I thank you too.

WAGNER.

So, now thou art to be at an hour's warning whensoever
and wheresoever the devil shall fetch thee.

CLOWN.

Here, take your guilders: I'll none of 'em!

WAGNER.

30   Not I, thou art pressed. Prepare thyself, for I will presently raise up two devils to carry thee away: Banio, Belcher!

CLOWN.

Belcher? And Belcher come here, I'll belch him; I am
not afraid of a devil.

Enter two devils.

WAGNER.

How now sir, will you serve me now?

CLOWN.

35   Ay, good Wagner, take away the devil then.

WAGNER.

Spirits, away! Now sirrah, follow me.

[*Exeunt devils.*]

CLOWN.

I will, sir. But hark you master, will you teach me this
conjuring occupation?

WAGNER.

Ay sirrah, I'll teach thee to turn thyself to a dog, or a
40   cat, or a mouse, or a rat, or anything.

Sander is alarmed to learn that he won't "bar striking at legs," and returns the money:
"Here, here take your two shillings again. I'll see thee hang'd ere I'll fight with thee"
(viii. 37-43).

30. *pressed*] hired or engaged for service (usually military or naval), having accepted
money in earnest of future wages. Wagner's threat that he will have the Clown
carried off by devils evokes the violence that was commonly involved when lower-
class men were pressed (i.e., seized and abducted) for service in war. Another sense
of "prest" (the spelling in B1) may also be present as an ironic secondary meaning:
"ready for use or action, ready in disposition or will" (see *OED*, "Prest," adj. A).

30-31. *presently*] at once.

CLOWN.

A dog, or a cat, or a mouse, or a rat? O brave Wagner!

WAGNER.

Villain, call me Master Wagner, and see that you walk
attentively, and let your right eye be always diametrally
fixed upon my left heel, that thou maist *quasi vestigiis
nostris insistere.*   45

CLOWN.

Well sir, I warrant you.

Exeunt.

2. Act II Scene iv (1616 text)

Enter the Clown [Robin].

ROBIN.

What, Dick, look to the horses there till I come again. I
have gotten one of Doctor Faustus' conjuring books, and
now we'll have such knavery as't passes.

Enter Dick.

DICK.

What, Robin, you must come away and walk the horses.

ROBIN.

I walk the horses? I scorn't, 'faith, I have other matters   5
in hand; let the horses walk themselves and they will. [*He
attempts to read.*] A, *per se*, a; t, h, e, the; o *per se*, o; deny
orgon, gorgon. Keep further from me, O thou illiterate
and unlearned ostler.

---

43. *diametrally*] See the note to I. iv. 70 in my A-version edition.

44-45. quasi vestigiis nostris insistere] "as if treading in our footsteps (or traces)." (See
the note to I. iv. 70-71 of my A-version edition.)

3. *as't passes*] as beats everything (Boas).

7. *A, per se, a; t,h,e, the; o per se, o*] A by itself spells a; t,h,e, spells the; o by itself spells
o. Robin has spelled out all but the last letter of "atheos" ("atheist"), a word adopted
into Latin from Greek. A dialogue between Euphues and Atheos, an atheist, is among
the epistles and dialogues appended to the narrative of Lyly's *Euphues: The Anatomy
of Wit* (1578) to show the effects of Euphues' studies in Athens. Nashe plays with the
phrase "A per se" in *Have With You to Saffron Walden* (1596); see Nashe iii. 45.

7-8. *deny orgon, gorgon*] a valiant attempt at reading out the name "Demogorgon," which
appeared in Faustus's invocation at I. iii. 18.

DICK.

10   'Snails, what hast thou got there, a book? Why, thou
       can'st not tell ne'er a word on't.

ROBIN.

       That thou shalt see presently. Keep out of the circle, I
       say, lest I send you into the ostry with a vengeance.

DICK.

       That's like, 'faith! You had best leave your foolery, for
15   an my master come he'll conjure you, 'faith.

ROBIN.

       My master conjure me? I'll tell thee what, an my master
       come here, I'll clap as fair a pair of horns on's head as
       e'er thou sawest in thy life.

DICK.

       Thou need'st not do that, for my mistress hath done it.

ROBIN.

20   Ay, there be those of us here that have waded as deep into
       matters as other men, if they were disposed to talk.

DICK.

       A plague take you! I thought you did not sneak up and
       down after her for nothing. But I prithee tell me, in good
       sadness, Robin, is that a conjuring book?

---

10. *'Snails*] a contraction of "by God's nails," and thus an oath which, like "Zounds" or "Swowns," refers to Christ's crucifixion.

11. *tell*] construe, understand.

12. *presently*] at once.

13. *ostry*] hostelry, inn.
with a vengeance] with a curse. The phrase was used as a vehement (and unfriendly) intensifier.

14. *That's like*] an expression of incredulity: "That's likely!" or "Fat chance!"

15. *an*] if.

17. *horns*] cuckold's horns. This would duplicate the trick played by Faustus on the insulting knight in IV. i of the A and B texts.

20-21. *that have waded as deep into matters*] Boas (99) notes for comparison *Julius Caesar* I. i. 21-22: "I meddle with no tradesman's matters, nor women's matters ..." The bawdy *double entendre* in which "matters," referring to general issues and concerns, is made to allude to women's sexuality, rests on a popular awareness of the Aristotelian distinction between "the male and female principles..., the former as containing the efficient cause of generation, the latter the material of it" (*Generation of Animals* I. 2, 716a, Aristotle i. 1112). As Castiglione writes in *The Book of the Courtier* (trans. Thomas Hoby, 1577), it is "the opinion of most wise men" that "man is likened to the Forme, the woman to the Matter..." (Castiglione 467).

23-24. *in good sadness*] seriously speaking.

ROBIN.

> Do but speak what thou't have me do, and I'll do't. If   25
> thou't dance naked, put off thy clothes, and I'll conjure
> thee about presently. Or if thou't go but to the tavern
> with me, I'll give thee white wine, red wine, claret wine,
> sack, muscadine, malmsey and whippincrust, hold-belly-
> hold, and we'll not pay one penny for it.   30

DICK.

> O brave! prithee let's to it presently, for I am as dry as a
> dog.

ROBIN.

> Come then, let's away.

Exeunt.

3. Act III Scene i (1616 text)

[In the opening section of this scene, the 1604 and 1616 texts parallel one another quite closely. However, after line 52 (line 47 in the A version), the two texts diverge: the greater part of the 1616 text beyond this point in the play is evidently constituted by the additions for which Henslowe paid in 1602.]

FAUSTUS.

> Having now, my good Mephostophilis,

---

26. *dance naked*] If Dick were willing to take off his clothes before being conjured, it would not require any very powerful magic to make him dance naked. As Owens notes, Reginald Scot includes "To make one dance naked" as one of a series of "Juggling knacks by confederacy": all one need do is "Make a poor boy confederate with you, so as after charms etc. spoken by you, he unclothe himself..." (Scot 278 [XIII. xxx]; see Owens 89 n.29).

28. *claret*] a light red wine from the Bordeaux region (in the sixteenth century, claret was made in the manner of a modern rosé). The term was also more widely used until the early seventeenth century to distinguish wines of a deep yellow or light reddish colour from red and white wines.

29. *sack*] a class of strong light-coloured wines imported from Spain and the Canary islands.

muscadine] muscatel, a strong sweet wine originally produced in Crete; muscat grapes were subsequently planted in southern France, in Spain, and in Italy.

malmsey] a strong sweet wine; the name is a corruption of Monemvasia or Malvasia, a port in the southern Peloponnese in Greece from which this wine (made on the mainland and on Crete and other islands from a grape variety still known as Malvasia) was shipped.

whippincrust] an ignorant distortion of "hippocras," wine flavored with spices.

29-30. *hold-belly-hold*] a belly-full, or perhaps slightly more.

Pass'd with delight the stately town of Trier,
Environ'd round with airy mountain tops,
With walls of flint, and deep entrenched lakes,
5   Not to be won by any conquering prince;
From Paris next, coasting the realm of France,
We saw the river Main fall into Rhine,
Whose banks are set with groves of fruitful vines.
Then up to Naples, rich Campania,
10   Whose buildings fair and gorgeous to the eye
(The streets straight forth, and pav'd with finest brick)
[Quarters the town in four equivolents.]
There saw we learned Maro's golden tomb,
The way he cut an English mile in length
15   Through a rock of stone in one night's space.
From thence to Venice, Padua and the east,
In one of which a sumptuous temple stands
That threats the stars with her aspiring top,
Whose frame is pav'd with sundry colored stones,
20   And roof'd aloft with curious work in gold.
Thus hitherto hath Faustus spent his time.
But tell me now, what resting place is this?
Hast thou, as erst I did command,
Conducted me within the walls of Rome?

MEPH.

25   I have my Faustus, and for proof thereof,

12.] The versifying of *EFB*'s narrative is at this point very careless. This line, missing in
B1, may have been deleted by Samuel Rowley and William Birde (who in their work
of revision seem to have altered other lines in this speech). They evidently had a copy
of *EFB* at hand, and may have noticed both the syntactical oddity of lines 11-12, and
the fact that line 12 is not based on anything in *EFB*.

16. *the east*] This reading, replacing A1's casual "the rest," is probably a revision.

17. *one*] A1's "midst" makes better sense. Greg characterized the B1 reading as "editorial
tinkering."

19-20.] These lines, which do not appear in A1, are probably an addition by Rowley or
Birde. They echo the wording of *EFB*, ch. 22 ("He wondered not a little at ... the
sumptuous church standing therein called Saint Mark's; how all the pavement was set
with coloured stones and all the roof or loft of the church double gilded over" [*EFB*
129]), but seem comically anticlimactic after the note of quasi-Marlovian rebellion
sounded by line 18, since "Whose frame," though it must logically modify "temple,"
attaches itself clumsily to the nearest antecedent, "top."

25-28.] The corresponding lines in A1 are in prose: "Faustus, I have, and because we will
not be unprovided, I have taken up his Holiness' privy chamber for our use." Here
as elsewhere the B-text revisers were concerned to regularize passages that are not
in decasyllabic verse.

This is the goodly palace of the Pope;
And cause we are no common guests,
I choose his privy chamber for our use.

FAUSTUS.

I hope his Holiness will bid us welcome.

MEPH.

All's one, for we'll be bold with his ven'son.   30
But now my Faustus, that thou may'st perceive
What Rome contains for to delight thine eyes,
Know that this city stands upon seven hills,
That underprop the ground-work of the same;
Just through the midst runs flowing Tiber's stream,   35
With winding banks that cut it in two parts,
Over the which four stately bridges lean
That make safe passage to each part of Rome.
Upon the bridge call'd Ponte Angelo
Erected is a castle passing strong,   40
Where thou shalt see such store of ordinance,
As that the double cannons forg'd of brass
Do match the number of the days contain'd
Within the compass of one complete year—
Beside the gates and high pyramides   45
That Julius Caesar brought from Africa.

FAUSTUS.

Now, by the kingdoms of infernal rule,
Of Styx, of Acheron and the fiery lake
Of ever-burning Phlegethon, I swear
That I do long to see the monuments   50
And situation of bright splendent Rome.
Come therefore, let's away.

MEPH.

Nay stay, my Faustus; I know you'd see the Pope,

30.] This line regularizes the A text's "Tut, 'tis no matter, man, we'll be bold with his
good cheer," while also, as elsewhere, removing the mild expletive "Tut."

37. *four stately bridges*] B1's reading, "two," is probably a compositorial repetition error
conditioned by "two" in the preceding line. In *EFB* (130) and in A1 there are four
bridges.

41-44.] These lines are a somewhat wordy revision of three corresponding lines in A1.

53-56.] These lines echo the last three lines of the Chorus to Act III (which appear both
in A1 and in B1). Bowers suggests that the reviser may have "envisaged the excision
of the Chorus and was awkwardly providing within the scene itself the same infor-
mation" (Bowers, "Additions," 6).

And take some part of holy Peter's feast,
55   The which in state and high solemnity
This day is held through Rome and Italy
In honor of the Pope's triumphant victory.

FAUSTUS.

Sweet Mephostophilis, thou pleasest me;
Whilst I am here on earth, let me be cloy'd
60   With all things that delight the heart of man.
My four and twenty years of liberty
I'll spend in pleasure and in dalliance,
That Faustus' name, whilst this bright frame doth stand,
May be admired through the furthest land.

MEPH.

65   'Tis well said, Faustus. Come then, stand by me,
And thou shalt see them come immediately.

FAUSTUS.

Nay stay, my gentle Mephostophilis,
And grant me my request, and then I go.
Thou know'st within the compass of eight days
70   We view'd the face of heaven, of earth and hell.
So high our dragons soar'd into the air
That looking down the earth appear'd to me
No bigger than my hand in quantity.
There did we view the kingdoms of the world,
75   And what might please mine eye I there beheld.
Then in this show let me an actor be,
That this proud Pope may Faustus' cunning see.

MEPH.

Let it be so, my Faustus, but first stay

---

55. *in state and*] These words are B2's emendation of B1's "this day with." Maguire suggests that B1's repetition of "this day" in this line and the next was probably caused during the printing process "by compositorial eye-skip" (Maguire 170).

57. *triumphant victory*] The Pope has successfully confronted (see line 119) the forces of the Emperor, and has captured the rival pope whom the latter had set up.

63. *this bright frame*] i.e., the earth.

63-64.] Rhyming couplets (which are infrequent in A, occurring for example at II. i. 89-90) are a distinctive feature of the B-text additions.

69-75. *Thou ... beheld*] This passage, while echoing the Chorus to Act III, 1-14, is more distinctly derived from *EFB* ch. xxi. Compare, for example, lines 70-73 with Faustus' statement in *EFB* that "as I came down I looked upon the world and the heavens ... and methought that the whole length of the earth was not a span long..." (*EFB* 126-27).

And view their triumphs as they pass this way,
And then devise what best contents thy mind,   80
By cunning in thine art to cross the Pope
Or dash the pride of this solemnity,
To make his monks and abbots stand like apes
And point like antics at his triple crown,
To beat the beads about the friars' pates   85
Or clap huge horns upon the cardinals' heads,
Or any villainy thou canst devise,
And I'll perform it, Faustus. Hark, they come:
This day shall make thee be admir'd in Rome.

Enter the Cardinals and Bishops, some bearing
crosiers, some the pillars; monks and friars, singing
their procession. Then the Pope, and Raymond, King
of Hungary, with Bruno led in chains.

---

79. *triumphs*] processions celebrating a victory; also public festivities, spectacles or pageants.

84. *antics*] grotesques.

triple crown] the papal tiara, a sign of the pope's sovereign power. In the late 13th century the circlet around its base became a spiked crown; a second circlet or crown was added by pope Boniface VIII (1294-1303), and a third either by his successor Benedict XI or by Clement V (1305-1314). The three crowns were subsequently interpreted as symbolizing authority over the church militant, suffering, and triumphant, or the temporal power of the pope and his power of binding and loosing, or even his authority over earth, heaven and hell.

85. *beads*] prayer beads.

89.2 *crosier*] an episcopal crook.

pillars] devotional emblems commemorating the flagellation of Christ; Cavendish reports that Cardinal Wolsey's many attendants included "two pillar-bearers" (Cavendish 21).

89.3 *procession*] a litany or office sung in a religious procession.

the Pope] Addressed as "Pope Adrian" in line 125 of this scene, he is not named in *EFB* or in the A-text. Adrian VI (1522-23) was a contemporary of the historical Doctor Faustus, but much of the action of this scene is derived from the account in John Foxe's *Acts and Monuments of these Latter Days* (or *Book of Martyrs*) of the conflict between Adrian IV (1154-59) and his successor Alexander III (1159-81) with the Emperor Frederick Barbarossa.

89.3-4. *Raymond, King of Hungary; Bruno*] These are not historical figures, although a "Saxon Bruno" was Pope as Gregory V (996-99). The predicament of the B-text's Bruno may reflect the fact that the Hermetic philosopher Giordano Bruno, who was in England from 1583 to 1585, and who lectured at the University of Wittenberg (in Saxony) from 1586 to 1588, was arrested by the Inquisition in Venice in 1592 and burned at the stake in Rome in 1600. See Eriksen 1985 and Eriksen 1987: 59-89.

POPE.

90   Cast down our footstool.

RAYMOND.

Saxon Bruno, stoop,
Whilst on thy back his Holiness ascends
Saint Peter's chair and state pontifical.

BRUNO.

Proud Lucifer, that state belongs to me;
But thus I fall to Peter, not to thee.

POPE.

95   To me and Peter shalt thou groveling lie,
And crouch before the papal dignity.
Sound trumpets, then, for thus Saint Peter's heir
From Bruno's back ascends Saint Peter's chair.

A flourish while he ascends.

Thus, as the gods creep on with feet of wool
100   Long ere with iron hands they punish men,
So shall our sleeping vengeance now arise
And smite with death thy hated enterprise.
Lord Cardinals of France and Padua,
Go forthwith to our holy consistory,
105   And read amongst the statutes decretal

90-92.] These lines imitate a famous sequence in *1 Tamburlaine*. Having ordered his followers to "Bring out my footstool" (IV. ii. 1), the Scythian tyrant commands Bajazeth, the "Turkish emperor" (III. i. 22), to "Fall prostrate on the low disdainful earth, / And be the footstool of great Tamburlaine, / That I may rise into my royal throne" (IV. ii. 13-15).

92. *state pontifical*] papal throne. Postpositive constructions of this kind, usually placed at the end of a line, are a recurrent feature of Samuel Rowley's play *When You See Me You Know Me* (printed in 1605) and of the B-text additions. See, in this scene, lines 105, 144, 194; and Greg 133-34. One such construction also appears in the A-text: "demonstrations magical" (I. i. 151).

94-98, 136-43.] These passages have no basis in *EFB*, but are derived from Foxe's *Acts and Monuments* (Foxe ii.189, 195-96).

99-100.] a variant form of the proverb: "God comes with leaden (woolen) feet but strikes with iron hands." See Tilley G 182.

104. *consistory*] meeting place of the papal consistory or senate, made up of the Pope and cardinals.

105. *statutes decretal*] that part of canon law which is constituted by the decrees of the popes on matters of doctrine or policy. "Decretal" is evidently understood here as embracing also the decisions of church councils.

What, by the holy council held at Trent,
The sacred synod hath decreed for him
That doth assume the papal government
Without election and a true consent.
Away, and bring us word with speed.   110
I CARD.
    We go, my lord.

                    Exeunt Cardinals.

POPE.
    Lord Raymond—[*They converse together.*]
FAUSTUS.
    Go, haste thee, gentle Mephostophilis:
    Follow the cardinals to the consistory,
    And as they turn their superstitious books   115
    Strike them with sloth and drowsy idleness,
    And make them sleep so sound that in their shapes
    Thy self and I may parley with this Pope,
    This proud confronter of the Emperor,
    And in despite of all his holiness   120
    Restore this Bruno to his liberty
    And bear him to the states of Germany.
MEPH.
    Faustus, I go.
FAUSTUS.
                    Dispatch it soon:
    The Pope shall curse that Faustus came to Rome.

        Exeunt Faustus and Mephostophilis.

BRUNO.
    Pope Adrian, let me have some right of law;   125
    I was elected by the Emperor.
POPE.
    We will depose the Emperor for that deed,

---

106. *council held at Trent*] The Council of Trent sat, with interruptions, from 1545 to
    1563.
107. *synod*] general council of the church.
120. *his holiness*] "(a) his pretensions to saintliness (b) his honorific title of 'his Holiness'"
    (Bevington and Rasmussen).

And curse the people that submit to him.
Both he and thou shalt stand excommunicate
130 And interdict from Church's privilege
And all society of holy men:
He grows too proud in his authority,
Lifting his lofty head above the clouds,
And like a steeple over-peers the Church.
135 But we'll pull down his haughty insolence,
And as Pope Alexander, our progenitor,
Trod on the neck of German Frederick,
Adding this golden sentence to our praise,
"That Peter's heirs should tread on emperors,
140 And walk upon the dreadful adder's back,
Treading the lion and dragon down,
And fearless spurn the killing basilisk";
So we will quell that haughty schismatic,
And by authority apostolical
145 Depose him from his regal government.

BRUNO.

Pope Julius swore to princely Sigismond,
For him and the succeeding popes of Rome,
To hold the emperors their lawful lords.

POPE.

Pope Julius did abuse the Church's rites,
150 And therefore none of his decrees can stand.
Is not all power on earth bestow'd on us?
And therefore, though we would, we cannot err.
Behold this silver belt, whereto is fix'd
Seven golden keys fast seal'd with seven seals,
155 In token of our seven-fold power from heaven
To bind or loose, lock fast, condemn, or judge,

---

130. *interdict*] authoritatively cut off from.

136. *progenitor*] here used in a figurative sense to mean "predecessor." Adrian IV actually
preceded Alexander III, who in 1165 excommunicated the Emperor Frederick.

142. *basilisk*] a mythical reptile whose glance was said to be fatal; it seems appropriate in
this context that the Greek word from which "basilisk" is derived means "kinglet."

146-48.] another instance of the blithe disregard for history that characterizes the B-text
additions. Julius I lived in the fourth century; Julius II and III were popes respectively from 1503 to 1513, and from 1550 to 1555; the German emperor Sigismund lived
from 1368 to 1437.

154. *keys*] of St. Peter.

Resign, or seal, or whatso pleaseth us.
Then he, and thou, and all the world shall stoop,
Or be assured of our dreadful curse
To light as heavy as the pains of hell.   160

Enter Faustus and Mephostophilis,
like the Cardinals.

MEPH.
Now tell me, Faustus, are we not fitted well?
FAUSTUS.
Yes Mephostophilis, and two such cardinals
Ne'er served a holy pope as we shall do.
But whilst they sleep within the consistory
Let us salute his reverend Fatherhood.   165
RAYMOND.
Behold, my lord, the cardinals are return'd.
POPE.
Welcome, grave fathers; answer presently,
What have our holy council there decreed
Concerning Bruno and the Emperor,
In quittance of their late conspiracy   170
Against our state and papal dignity?
FAUSTUS.
Most sacred patron of the Church of Rome,
By full consent of all the synod
Of priests and prelates it is thus decreed:
That Bruno and the German Emperor   175
Be held as lollards and bold schismatics
And proud disturbers of the Church's peace;
And if that Bruno by his own assent,
Without enforcement of the German peers,
Did seek to wear the triple diadem   180

---

157. *resign*] "The word here, in its contrast with 'seal', seems to have almost the meaning
of the Latin 'resignare', unseal" (Boas 110).
160. *light*] alight: to settle on, fall upon (*OED* v. II. 6, 7).
170. *quittance of*] requital for.
176. *lollard*] a name of contempt applied in the fourteenth century to followers of Wyclif;
subsequently synonymous with "heretic."
179. *without enforcement of*] without having been compelled by.

And by your death to climb Saint Peter's chair,
The statutes decretal have thus decreed:
He shall be straight condemn'd of heresy,
And on a pile of faggots burnt to death.

POPE.

185   It is enough. Here, take him to your charge
And bear him straight to Ponte Angelo,
And in the strongest tower enclose him fast.
Tomorrow, sitting in our consistory
With all our college of grave cardinals,
190   We will determine of his life or death.
Here, take his triple crown along with you
And leave it in the Church's treasury.
Make haste again, my good lord Cardinals,
And take our blessing apostolical.

MEPH.

195   So, so: was never devil thus bless'd before.

FAUSTUS.

Away, sweet Mephostophilis, be gone;
The cardinals will be plagu'd for this anon.

Exeunt Faustus and Mephostophilis
[with Bruno].

POPE.

Go presently and bring a banquet forth
That we may solemnize Saint Peter's feast,
200   And with Lord Raymond, King of Hungary,
Drink to our late and happy victory.

Exeunt.

4. Act III Scene ii (1616 text)

A sennet while the banquet is brought in,
and then enter Faustus and Mephostophilis
in their own shapes.

---

186. *Ponte Angelo*] See III. i. 39-40, where the papal castle is said to stand on the bridge; the Castel San Angelo in fact stands at the north end of the bridge.
193. *again*] i.e. to return.
0.1. *sennet*] a flourish on the trumpet to signal a ceremonial entrance.

MEPH.

Now Faustus, come prepare thyself for mirth:
The sleepy cardinals are hard at hand
To censure Bruno, that is posted hence,
And on a proud-pac'd steed as swift as thought
Flies o'er the Alps to fruitful Germany,   5
There to salute the woeful Emperor.

FAUSTUS.

The Pope will curse them for their sloth today,
That slept both Bruno and his crown away!
But now, that Faustus may delight his mind
And by their folly make some merriment,   10
Sweet Mephostophilis, so charm me here
That I may walk invisible to all,
And do whate'er I please, unseen of any.

MEPH.

Faustus, thou shalt; then kneel down presently,
Whilst on thy head I lay my hand   15
And charm thee with this magic wand.
First wear this girdle, then appear
Invisible to all are here:
The planets seven, the gloomy air,
Hell, and the Furies' forked hair,   20
Pluto's blue fire, and Hecate's tree,
With magic spells so compass thee
That no eye may thy body see.
So Faustus, now for all their holiness
Do what thou wilt, thou shalt not be discern'd.   25

FAUSTUS.

Thanks Mephostophilis; now friars, take heed
Lest Faustus make your shaven crowns to bleed.

---

17. girdle] a belt worn around the waist.
20. forked hair] suggested by the forked tongues of the snakes that formed the hair of
    the Furies (Greg).
21. Pluto's blue fire] the sulphurous flames of hell.
Hecate's tree] Possibly the gallows-tree, which was commonly erected at crossroads.
    Hecate was said to appear on moonlit nights at cross-roads (hence her other name
    "Trioditis," or in Latin, "Trivia"), accompanied by the dogs of the Styx and crowds
    of the dead (Greg). Boas suggests emending "tree" to "three," in allusion to Hecate's
    triform deity.
22. compass] encompass.

MEPH.

Faustus, no more: see where the cardinals come.

Enter Pope and all the lords.
Enter the Cardinals with a book.

POPE.

Welcome, lord Cardinals; come, sit down.
30   Lord Raymond, take your seat. Friars, attend,
And see that all things be in readiness
As best beseems this solemn festival.

I CARD.

First may it please your sacred Holiness
To view the sentence of the reverend synod
35   Concerning Bruno and the Emperor?

POPE.

What needs this question? Did I not tell you,
Tomorrow we would sit i'the consistory
And there determine of his punishment?
You brought us word, even now, it was decreed
40   That Bruno and the cursed Emperor
Were by the holy council both condemn'd
For loathed lollards, and base schismatics:
Then wherefore would you have me view that book?

I CARD.

Your Grace mistakes, you gave us no such charge.

RAYMOND.

45   Deny it not: we all are witnesses
That Bruno here was late deliver'd you
With his rich triple crown to be reserv'd
And put into the Church's treasury.

AMBO CARDINALS.

By holy Paul we saw them not!

POPE.

50   By Peter you shall die
Unless you bring them forth immediately!

---

44. *no such charge*] an odd denial: the Pope has made no mention of his instructions to the
Cardinals, or of his having entrusted Bruno to them. Several lines may be missing;
alternatively, this discontinuity may be due to the writer's carelessness.
49. AMBO] both.

Hale them to prison, lade their limbs with gyves.
False prelates, for this hateful treachery
Curs'd be your souls to hellish misery.

[Exeunt attendants with the two Cardinals.]

FAUSTUS.

So, they are safe: now Faustus, to the feast;   55
The Pope had never such a frolic guest.

POPE.

Lord Archbishop of Rheims, sit down with us.

BISH.

I thank your Holiness.

FAUSTUS.

Fall to, the devil choke you an you spare!

POPE.

Who's that spoke? Friars, look about.   60
Lord Raymond, pray fall to; I am beholding
To the Bishop of Milan for this so rare a present.

FAUSTUS.

I thank you, sir.

[Snatch it.]

POPE.

How now? who snatch'd the meat from me?
Villains, why speak you not?   65
My good lord Archbishop, here's a most dainty dish
Was sent me from a cardinal in France.

FAUSTUS.

I'll have that too.

[Snatch it.]

POPE.

What lollards do attend our Holiness
That we receive such great indignity?   70

---

52. *lade*] load.
gyves] fetters.
56. *frolic*] playful, mischievous.

Fetch me some wine.

FAUSTUS.

Ay, pray do, for Faustus is a-dry.

POPE.

Lord Raymond, I drink unto your Grace.

FAUSTUS.

I pledge your Grace.

[*Snatch it.*]

POPE.

75   My wine gone too? Ye lubbers, look about
And find the man that doth this villainy,
Or by our sanctitude you all shall die!
I pray, my lords, have patience at this troublesome banquet.

ARCHBISHOP.

Please it your Holiness, I think it be some ghost crept out
80   of purgatory, and now is come unto your Holiness for his
pardon.

POPE.

It may be so;
Go, then, command our priests to sing a dirge
To lay the fury of this same troublesome ghost.

[*The Pope crosseth himself.*]

FAUSTUS.

85   How now? must every bit be spiced with a cross?
Nay then, take that!

[*Faustus hits him a box of the ear.*]

POPE.

O, I am slain, help me my lords!
O come and help to bear my body hence;
Damn'd be this soul forever for this deed.

Exeunt the Pope and his train.

---

75. *lubbers*] lazy, clumsy louts. The *OED* notes that in medieval usage the word was
commonly applied to monks.

MEPH.

> Now Faustus, what will you do now? for I can tell you,   90
> you'll be cursed with bell, book and candle.

FAUSTUS.

> Bell, book and candle; candle, book and bell,
> Forward and backward, to curse Faustus to hell!

Enter the Friars with bell, book and candle
for the dirge.

I FRIAR.

> Come brethren, let's about our business with good devo-
> tion.   95

[Sing this:]

> *Cursed be he that stole his Holiness' meat from the table.*
> *Maledicat Dominus.*
> *Cursed be he that struck his Holiness a blow on the face.*
> *Maledicat Dominus.*
> *Cursed be he that took Friar Sandelo a blow on the pate.*   100
> *Maledicat Dominus.*
> *Cursed be he that disturbeth our holy dirge.*
> *Maledicat Dominus.*
> *Cursed be he that took away his Holiness' wine.*
> *Maledicat Dominus.*   105

[Faustus and Mephostophilis] beat the Friars,
fling fireworks among them, and Exeunt.

5. Act III Scene iii (1616 text)

Enter Clown [Robin] and Dick, with a cup.

DICK.

> Sirrah Robin, we were best look that your devil can
> answer the stealing of this same cup, for the vintner's boy
> follows us at the hard heels.

---

3. *at the hard heels*] hard at heel, closely.

ROBIN.

    'Tis no matter, let him come: an he follows us, I'll so

5   conjure him as he was never conjured in his life, I warrant
    him. Let me see the cup.

Enter Vintner.

DICK.

    Here 'tis. Yonder he comes; now Robin, now or never
    show thy cunning.

VINTNER.

    O, are you here? I am glad I have found you. You are a

10   couple of fine companions! Pray, where's the cup you
    stole from the tavern?

ROBIN.

    How, how? we steal a cup? Take heed what you say: we
    look not like cup-stealers, I can tell you.

VINTNER.

    Never deny't, for I know you have it, and I'll search you.

ROBIN.

15   Search me? Ay, and spare not—hold the cup, Dick.
    Come, come; search me, search me.

VINTNER.

    [*To Dick*] Come on sirrah; let me search you now.

DICK.

    Ay, ay; do, do—hold the cup, Robin. I fear not your
    searching; we scorn to steal your cups, I can tell you.

VINTNER.

20   Never outface me for the matter, for sure the cup is bet-
    ween you two.

ROBIN.

    Nay, there you lie: 'tis beyond us both.

VINTNER.

    A plague take you! I thought 'twas your knavery to take
    it away. Come, give it me again.

---

4. *an*] if.

20. *Never outface me ... matter*] "don't impudently deny it to me" (Bevington and
    Rasmussen).

22. *beyond us both*] Robin has perhaps thrown it up into the air.

ROBIN.

    Ay, much! when, can you tell? Dick, make me a circle, and   25
    stand close at my back, and stir not for thy life. Vintner,
    you shall have your cup anon—say nothing, Dick! O, per
    se, o; Demogorgon, Belcher and Mephostophilis!

Enter Mephostophilis.

MEPH.

    You princely legions of infernal rule,
    How am I vexed by these villains' charms!   30
    From Constantinople have they brought me now,
    Only for pleasure of these damned slaves.

[Exit Vintner.]

ROBIN.

    By lady sir, you have had a shrewd journey of it: will it
    please you to take a shoulder of mutton to supper, and a
    tester in your purse, and go back again?   35
DICK.

    Ay, I pray you heartily sir, for we called you but in jest,
    I promise you.
MEPH.

    To purge the rashness of this cursed deed,
    First be thou turned to this ugly shape:
    For apish deeds transformed to an ape.   40
ROBIN.

    O brave, an ape! I pray sir, let me have the carrying of
    him about to show some tricks.
MEPH.

    And so thou shalt: be thou transformed to a dog, and
    carry him upon thy back. Away, be gone!
ROBIN.

    A dog? that's excellent: let the maids look well to their   45
    porridge-pots, for I'll into the kitchen presently. Come
    Dick, come.

---

33. *By lady*] By our lady.
shrewd] difficult, irksome.
35. *tester*] a sixpence.

Exeunt the two clowns.

MEPH.

    Now with the flames of ever-burning fire

    I'll wing myself, and forwith fly amain

50   Unto my Faustus, to the Great Turk's court.

Exit.

6. Act IV Scene i (1616 text)

Enter Martino and Frederick at several doors.

MARTINO.

    What ho, officers, gentlemen:

    Hie to the presence to attend the Emperor.

    Good Frederick, see the rooms be voided straight.

    His Majesty is coming to the hall;

5   Go back, and see the state in readiness.

FREDERICK.

    But where is Bruno, our elected Pope,

    That on a fury's back came post from Rome?

    Will not his Grace consort the Emperor?

MARTINO.

    O yes, and with him comes the German conjurer,

10   The learned Faustus, fame of Wittenberg,

    The wonder of the world for magic art;

    And he intends to show great Carolus

    The race of all his stout progenitors,

    And bring in presence of his Majesty

15   The royal shapes and warlike semblances

---

49. *amain*] speedily.

2. *presence*] (a) presence chamber, a place prepared for ceremonial attendance (*OED* 2. c), or (b) the monarch and the space immediately around him (*OED* 2. b). In either case, Martino is instructing other courtiers to attend upon the Emperor offstage.

3. *voided straight*] cleared at once.

5. *state*] throne. It can be assumed that at some point prior to the Emperor's entrance, a throne is to be brought onstage.

8. *consort*] accompany.

12. *Carolus*] the Emperor Charles V.

13. *stout progenitors*] brave ancestors and precursors.

Of Alexander and his beauteous paramour.

FREDERICK.

Where is Benvolio?

MARTINO.

Fast asleep, I warrant you.

He took his rouse with stoups of Rhenish wine

So kindly yesternight to Bruno's health   20

That all this day the sluggard keeps his bed.

FREDERICK.

See, see: his window's ope; we'll call to him.

MARTINO.

What ho, Benvolio!

Enter Benvolio above at a window,
in his nightcap, buttoning.

BENVOLIO.

What a devil ail you two?

MARTINO.

Speak softly sir, lest the devil hear you!   25

For Faustus at the court is late arriv'd,

And at his heels a thousand furies wait

To accomplish whatsoe'er the doctor please.

BENVOLIO.

What of this?

MARTINO.

Come leave thy chamber first, and thou shalt see   30

The conjurer perform such rare exploits

Before the Pope and royal Emperor

As never yet was seen in Germany.

---

19. *took his rouse*] drank heavily, caroused. The line echoes *Hamlet* I. iv. 8-10: "The King
doth wake tonight and takes his rouse, / Keeps wassail, and the swagg'ring upspring
reels, / And as he drains his draughts of Rhenish down...." These lines appear in both
the First and Second Quartos of *Hamlet*; this B-text scene would therefore appear to
have been composed after 1601.

stoups] tankards.

27. *furies*] In classical Greek and Roman cultures, *erinyes* or *furiae* were chthonic god-
desses who avenged crime (cf. Seneca, *Medea* line 13), especially that of murder
within a family. In the late sixteenth century, the word came to refer more generally
to demonic powers, as with Spenser's Ate, who "at first was born of hellish brood, /
And by infernal furies nourished" (*The Faerie Queene* IV. i. 26).

32. *Pope*] i.e. Bruno.

BENVOLIO.

    Has not the Pope enough of conjuring yet?

35   He was on the devil's back late enough,

    And if he be so far in love with him

    I would he would post with him to Rome again.

FREDERICK.

    Speak, wilt thou come and see this sport?

BENVOLIO.

                                      Not I.

MARTINO.

    Wilt thou stand in thy window and see it then?

BENVOLIO.

40   Ay, and I fall not asleep i'the mean time.

MARTINO.

    The Emperor is at hand, who comes to see

    What wonders by black spells may compass'd be.

BENVOLIO.

    Well, go you attend the Emperor.

[Exeunt Frederick and Martino.]

    I am content for this once to thrust my head out at a window,

45   for they say if a man be drunk overnight the devil cannot hurt

    him in the morning. If that be true, I have a charm in my

    head shall control him as well as the conjurer, I warrant you.

A sennet. [Enter] Charles the German Emperor,
Bruno, Saxony, Faustus, Mephostophilis,
Frederick, Martino, and attendants.

EMP.

    Wonder of men, renown'd magician,

    Thrice learned Faustus, welcome to our court.

50   This deed of thine in setting Bruno free

    From his and our professed enemy

    Shall add more excellence unto thine art

    Than if by powerful necromantic spells

    Thou couldst command the world's obedience.

55   Forever be belov'd of Carolus;

---

46. *a charm in my head*] i.e., a hangover.

And if this Bruno thou hast late redeem'd
In peace possess the triple diadem
And sit in Peter's chair, despite of chance,
Thou shalt be famous through all Italy,
And honor'd of the German Emperor.   60

FAUSTUS.

These gracious words, most royal Carolus,
Shall make poor Faustus to his utmost power
Both love and serve the German Emperor
And lay his life at holy Bruno's feet.   65
For proof whereof, if so your Grace be pleas'd,
The doctor stands prepar'd by power of art
To cast his magic charms, that shall pierce through
The ebon gates of ever-burning hell
And hale the stubborn furies from their caves
To compass whatsoe'er your Grace commands.   70

BENVOLIO.

Blood, he speaks terribly! But for all that I do not greatly
believe him: he looks as like a conjurer as the Pope to a
costermonger.

EMP.

Then Faustus, as thou late didst promise us,
We would behold that famous conqueror,   75
Great Alexander, and his paramour,
In their true shapes and state majestical,
That we may wonder at their excellence.

FAUSTUS.

Your Majesty shall see them presently.
Mephostophilis, away,   80
And with a solemn noise of trumpets' sound
Present before this royal Emperor
Great Alexander and his beauteous paramour.

MEPH.

Faustus, I will.

[*Exit.*]

BENVOLIO.

Well, Master Doctor, an your devils come not away quickly, 85

---

68. *ebon*] ebony.
71. *Blood*] a contraction of "By God's blood!"

you shall have me asleep presently; zounds, I could eat my self for anger to think I have been such an ass all this while, to stand gaping after the devil's governor, and can see nothing.

FAUSTUS.

I'll make you feel something anon, if my art fail me not.—

90 My lord, I must forewarn your Majesty
That when my spirits present the royal shapes
Of Alexander and his paramour
Your Grace demand no questions of the King,
But in dumb silence let them come and go.

EMP.

95 Be it as Faustus please, we are content.

BENVOLIO.

Ay, ay, and I am content too: and thou bring Alexander and his paramour before the Emperor, I'll be Actaeon and turn myself to a stag.

FAUSTUS.

And I'll play Diana and send you the horns presently.

Sennet.

Enter at one door the Emperor Alexander, at the other Darius; they meet, Darius is thrown down; Alexander kills him, takes off his crown, and offering to go out, his paramour meets him; he embraceth her and sets Darius' crown upon her head; and coming back, both salute the Emperor, who leaving his state, offers to embrace them, which Faustus seeing suddenly stays him. Then trumpets cease, and music sounds.

FAUSTUS.

100 My gracious Lord, you do forget yourself:
These are but shadows, not substantial.

EMP.

O, pardon me, my thoughts are so ravish'd
With sight of this renowned Emperor
That in mine arms I would have compass'd him.

105 But Faustus, since I may not speak to them
To satisfy my longing thoughts at full,

---

73. *costermonger*] one who sells apples in the open street.

86, 129, 135, 147. *zounds*] a contraction of "By God's wounds!"

99.1–3. Alexander, Darius] Alexander the Great defeated Darius, the emperor of Persia, at the battles of Issus and Arbela (333 and 331 B.C.E.); Darius was killed by his followers in 330 B.C.E. to prevent his capture.

99.3. offering to] as he is about to.

Let me this tell thee: I have heard it said
That this fair lady, whilst she liv'd on earth,
Had on her neck a little wart or mole;
How may I prove that saying to be true?   110
FAUSTUS.

Your Majesty may boldly go and see.
EMP.

Faustus, I see it plain,
And in this sight thou better pleasest me
Than if I gain'd another monarchy.
FAUSTUS.

Away, be gone!   115

Exit show.

See, see, my gracious Lord: what strange beast is yon, that
thrusts his head out at window?
EMP.

O wondrous sight: see, Duke of Saxony,
Two spreading horns most strangely fastened
Upon the head of young Benvolio!   120
SAXONY.

What, is he asleep, or dead?
FAUSTUS.

He sleeps, my Lord, but dreams not of his horns.
EMP.

This sport is excellent: we'll call and wake him.
What ho, Benvolio!
BENVOLIO.

A plague upon you! let me sleep awhile.   125
EMP.

I blame thee not to sleep much, having such a head of
thine own.
SAXONY.

Look up Benvolio, 'tis the Emperor calls.
BENVOLIO.

The Emperor! Where? O zounds, my head!

---

125. *A plague upon you*] He has not recognized the Emperor's voice.
129-31.] Jolted into full awareness by the realization that he has insulted the Emperor,
  Benvolio presumably knocks the back of his head on the window-frame. The

EMP.

130   Nay, and thy horns hold, 'tis no matter for thy head, for
       that's armed sufficiently.

FAUSTUS.

       Why, how now, sir knight; what, hanged by the horns?
       This is most horrible; fie, fie, pull in your head for shame,
       let not all the world wonder at you.

BENVOLIO.

135   Zounds Doctor, is this your villainy?

FAUSTUS.

       O say not so, sir: the doctor has no skill,
       No art, no cunning to present these lords
       Or bring before this royal Emperor
       The mighty monarch, warlike Alexander.

140   If Faustus do it, you are straight resolv'd
       In bold Actaeon's shape to turn a stag.
       And therefore my Lord, so please your Majesty,
       I'll raise a kennel of hounds shall hunt him so
       As all his footmanship shall scarce prevail

145   To keep his carcase from their bloody fangs.
       Ho, Belimote, Argiron, Asterote!

BENVOLIO.

       Hold, hold! Zounds, he'll raise up a kennel of devils, I
       think, anon. Good my Lord, entreat for me: 'sblood, I am
       never able to endure these torments.

EMP.

150   Then, good Master Doctor,
       Let me entreat you to remove his horns;
       He has done penance now sufficiently.

    Emperor mockingly tells him not to be concerned, for his head is well protected so
    long as his horns remain in place.

144. *footmanship*] speed in running.

146. *Belimote, Argiron, Asterote*] Astoreth or Astarte, the Phoenician goddess of fertility,
    is mentioned by Johann Weyer in *De praestigiis daemonum* (I. v, I. vi, I. xi, V. xvi),
    and by Milton in *Paradise Lost* I. 437-46. However, the author of this scene appears
    to have derived these names, not from the learned sources upon which Milton drew,
    but rather from one or another of the grimoires from which Reginald Scot mock-
    ingly quotes in *The Discoverie of Witchcraft* (1584). Greg suggests that Argiron may be
    a corruption of Acheron (Greg 366).

148, 158. *'Sblood*] a contraction of "By God's blood!"

FAUSTUS.

My gracious Lord, not so much for injury done to me as to
delight your Majesty with some mirth hath Faustus justly re-
quited this injurious knight, which being all I desire, I am   155
content to remove his horns. Mephostophilis, transform him;

[*Mephostophilis removes the horns.*]

and hereafter, sir, look well you speak well of scholars.

BENVOLIO.

Speak well of ye? 'Sblood, and scholars be such cuckold-
makers to clap horns of honest men's heads o'this order,
I'll ne'er trust smooth faces and small ruffs more. But an   160
I be not revenged for this, would I might be turned to a
gaping oyster, and drink nothing but salt water.

EMP.

Come Faustus, while the Emperor lives,
In recompense of this thy high desert
Thou shalt command the state of Germany   165
And live belov'd of mighty Carolus.

Exeunt omnes.

---

153. *injury*] insult.

155. *injurious*] insulting, offensive.

159. *of*] on.

o *'this order*] in this manner.

160. *smooth faces and small ruffs*] "beardless scholars in academical garb" (Boas). In the
following B-text scene, Faustus is evidently bearded (see B: IV. ii. 59-61); Bevington
and Rasmussen (256) suggest that this line reflects "the conventional pejorative use
of 'smooth-faced'," and cite *King John* II. i. 574: "That smooth-faced gentleman,
tickling commodity...." (The image is pejorative only when the face in question is
imagined as masculine: compare *Richard III* V. viii. 33: "Enrich the time to come
with smooth-faced peace....")

160-62. *an I be not revenged ... salt water*] These words appear to imitate a form of jest
that is characteristic of Falstaff in *1 Henry IV* (first printed in 1598). Compare, for
example, "An I have not ballads made on you all and sung to filthy tunes, let a cup of
sack be my poison"; "An I have not forgotten what the inside of a church is made of,
I am a peppercorn, a brewer's horse" (*1 Henry IV* II. ii. 40-41, III. iii. 6-8). Benvolio's
Falstaffian self-mockery in this speech contrasts strongly with the sensitivity to public mockery expressed in his first speech in B: IV. ii, and in the concluding lines of
B: IV. iii.

165. *Thou shalt command the state of Germany*] Leah Marcus understands this to mean
that "At the end of the scene, Charles invests Faustus with command over all of

7. Act IV Scene ii (1616 text)

Enter Benvolio, Martino, Frederick, with soldiers.

MARTINO.

    Nay sweet Benvolio, let us sway thy thoughts

    From this attempt against the conjurer.

BENVOLIO.

    Away, you love me not to urge me thus.

    Shall I let slip so great an injury,

5   When every servile groom jests at my wrongs,

    And in their rustic gambols proudly say,

    "Benvolio's head was grac'd with horns today"?

    O, may these eyelids never close again

    Till with my sword I have that conjurer slain!

10   If you will aid me in this enterprise

    Then draw your weapons and be resolute;

    If not, depart: here will Benvolio die,

    But Faustus' death shall quit my infamy.

FREDERICK.

    Nay, we will stay with thee, betide what may,

15   And kill that doctor if he come this way.

BENVOLIO.

    Then gentle Frederick, hie thee to the grove

    And place our servants and our followers

    Close in an ambush there behind the trees.

    By this, I know, the conjurer is near;

20   I saw him kneel and kiss the Emperor's hand

    And take his leave, laden with rich rewards.

Germany" (Marcus 1996: 59). But since there is no subsequent indication that Faustus bears authority over any state in this political sense (*OED*, "state," 29), and since he is at this point about to depart from the Emperor's German court, or state (*OED*, 26), the Emperor is more probably using "state" in the sense of "throne" (*OED*, 20; see line 5 of this scene), and is therefore telling Faustus that any request he makes of his regal power will be acceded to as instantly as if it were a command. Compare the Duke's use of "command" in this sense (*OED*, 12) in *Two Gentlemen of Verona* III. i. 22-23: "Proteus, I thank thee for thine honest care, / Which to requite command me while I live."

4. *let slip*] overlook.

13. *quit*] requite, pay for.

18. *close*] hidden.

19. *by this*] by this time, by now.

Then soldiers, boldly fight: if Faustus die,
Take you the wealth, leave us the victory.

FREDERICK.

Come soldiers, follow me unto the grove;
Who kills him shall have gold and endless love.   25

Exit Frederick with the soldiers.

BENVOLIO.

My head is lighter than it was by th'horns,
But yet my heart's more ponderous than my head
And pants until I see that conjurer dead.

MARTINO.

Where shall we place ourselves, Benvolio?

BENVOLIO.

Here will we stay to bide the first assault.   30
O, were that damned hell-hound but in place,
Thou soon shouldst see me quit my foul disgrace.

Enter Frederick.

FREDERICK.

Close, close: the conjurer is at hand,
And all alone comes walking in his gown;
Be ready then and strike the peasant down.   35

BENVOLIO.

Mine be that honor, then. Now sword, strike home:
For horns he gave, I'll have his head anon.

Enter Faustus with the false head.

MARTINO.

See, see: he comes.

BENVOLIO.

                    No words: this blow ends all;
Hell take his soul, his body thus must fall!

---

27. *But ... head*] Bevington and Rasmussen (73-74) note the similarity of this line to the
First Folio text of *King Lear* I. i. 75-6: "my love's / More ponderous [Q1: richer] than
my tongue." *King Lear* was first performed in 1606, and Q1 of *King Lear* was printed
in 1607-8; this line, if it is indebted to the revised text of *Lear* that was printed in the
First Folio, would indicate that some features of the B text date from 1609 or later.

[*Strikes.*]

FAUSTUS.

40   Oh!

FREDERICK.

Groan you, Master Doctor?

BENVOLIO.

Break may his heart with groans! Dear Frederick, see;
Thus will I end his griefs immediately.

MARTINO.

Strike with a willing hand: his head is off.

BENVOLIO.

45   The devil's dead: the furies now may laugh.

FREDERICK.

Was this that stern aspect, that awful frown,
Made the grim monarch of infernal spirits
Tremble and quake at his commanding charms?

MARTINO.

Was this that damned head whose heart conspir'd
50   Benvolio's shame before the Emperor?

BENVOLIO.

Ay, that's the head; and here the body lies,
Justly rewarded for his villainies.

FREDERICK.

Come, let's devise how we may add more shame
To the black scandal of his hated name.

BENVOLIO.

55   First on his head, in quittance of my wrongs,
I'll nail huge forked horns, and let them hang
Within the window where he yok'd me first,
That all the world may see my just revenge.

MARTINO.

What use shall we put his beard to?

---

43. *griefs*] sufferings.

46-50. *Was this ... Emperor?*] This double echo of the most famous line in the play ("Was
this the face that launch'd a thousand ships...?" [V. i. 90, B: V. i. 93]) provides one
indication of the derivative and secondary nature of these B-version passages.

46. *awful*] awe-inspiring.

57. *yok'd me*] held me fast, as though in a yoke.

BENVOLIO.

    We'll sell it to a chimney-sweeper: it will wear out ten   60
    birchen brooms, I warrant you.

FREDERICK.

    What shall his eyes do?

BENVOLIO.

    We'll put out his eyes, and they shall serve for buttons
    to his lips, to keep his tongue from catching cold.

MARTINO.

    An excellent policy! And now sirs, having divided him,   65
    what shall the body do?

[Faustus gets up.]

BENVOLIO.

    Zounds, the devil's alive again!

FREDERICK.

    Give him his head, for God's sake!

FAUSTUS.

    Nay, keep it: Faustus will have heads and hands,
    Ay, all your hearts, to recompense this deed.   70
    Knew you not, traitors, I was limited
    For four and twenty years to breathe on earth?
    And had you cut my body with your swords,
    Or hew'd this flesh and bones as small as sand,
    Yet in a minute had my spirit return'd   75
    And I had breath'd a man made free from harm.
    But wherefore do I dally my revenge?
    Asteroth, Belimoth, Mephostophilis!

---

60. *wear out*] outlast.

61. *birchen*] made of birch twigs.

71-72.] Bevington and Rasmussen note that although Faustus here speaks as though his
    twenty-four year contract were generally known, at V. ii. 33-39 (B: V. ii. 59-65) the
    scholars learn of it for the first time.

73-74.] Compare *The Taming of a Shrew* (1594) xvi. 60-61: "This angry sword should
    rip thy hateful chest, / And hew'd thee smaller than the Libyan sands." Gill argues
    that the Libyan sands detail, which can be traced back to Catullus ("quam magnus
    numerus Libyssae harena": "as great as is the number of the Libyan sand" [poem 7, l.
    3]), shows the B-text lines to be derivative: she finds it "most unlikely" that a writer
    borrowing from the B text "would add this magic ingredient of his own accord; it is
    more probable that the borrowing is in the other direction" (Gill 1990: 141-42).

Enter Mephostophilis and other devils.

Go horse these traitors on your fiery backs
80   And mount aloft with them as high as heaven;
Thence pitch them headlong to the lowest hell!
Yet stay: the world shall see their misery,
And hell shall after plague their treachery.
Go Belimoth, and take this caitiff hence
85   And hurl him in some lake of mud and dirt;
Take thou this other, drag him through the woods
Amongst the pricking thorns and sharpest briars,
Whilst with my gentle Mephostophilis
This traitor flies unto some steepy rock,
90   That rolling down may break the villain's bones
As he intended to dismember me.
Fly hence, dispatch my charge immediately.

FREDERICK.

Pity us, gentle Faustus, save our lives!

FAUSTUS.

Away!

FREDERICK.

He must needs go that the devil drives.

Exeunt spirits with the knights.
Enter the ambushed soldiers.

1 SOLD.

95   Come sirs, prepare yourselves in readiness,
Make haste to help these noble gentlemen;
I heard them parley with the conjurer.

2 SOLD.

See where he comes: dispatch, and kill the slave.

FAUSTUS.

What's here? an ambush to betray my life!

79.] The motif of devils carrying their victims off on their backs was popular in morality plays, and remained current in the late 1580s and early 1590s; cf. *Friar Bacon and Friar Bungay*, vi. 170, ix. 161, and xv. 1-64; *A Looking-Glass*, scene xiv. 1716-17.

84. *this caitiff*] Martino (cf. B: IV. iii. 3-5).

86, 89. *this other … This traitor*] Frederick and Benvolio respectively, since it was the latter who sought to dismember Faustus.

94. *He … drives*] a common proverb. See Tilley D278.

Then Faustus, try thy skill. Base peasants, stand!   100
For lo, these trees remove at my command
And stand as bulwarks 'twixt yourselves and me
To shield me from your hated treachery.
Yet to encounter this your weak attempt,
Behold, an army comes incontinent.   105

> *Faustus strikes the door, and enter a devil playing on*
> *a drum; after him another bearing an ensign, and*
> *divers with weapons; Mephostophilis with fireworks;*
> *they set upon the soldiers and drive them out.*

> [*Exit Faustus.*]

8. Act IV Scene iii (1616 text)

> *Enter at several doors Benvolio, Frederick, and*
> *Martino, their heads and faces bloody and besmeared*
> *with mud and dirt, all having horns on their heads.*

MARTINO.
    What ho, Benvolio!
BENVOLIO.
                Here! What, Frederick, ho!
FREDERICK.
    O help me, gentle friend; where is Martino?
MARTINO.
    Dear Frederick, here,
    Half-smothered in a lake of mud and dirt
    Through which the furies dragg'd me by the heels.   5
FREDERICK.
    Martino, see: Benvolio's horns again!
MARTINO.
    O misery! How now, Benvolio?

101-03.] Bevington and Rasmussen (260) remark that "some spectacular stage device" is
    implied by these words: presumably the stage properties used to indicate the grove
    of trees within which the soldiers were placed in ambush are suddenly animated by
    extras concealed within them.
101. *remove*] shift their position.
105. *incontinent*] at once.
105.1. *door*] i.e., of the stage.

BENVOLIO.

Defend me, heaven; shall I be haunted still?

MARTINO.

Nay, fear not, man: we have no power to kill.

BENVOLIO.

10   My friends transformed thus: O hellish spite,
Your heads are all set with horns.

FREDERICK.

You hit it right, it is your own you mean:
Fell on your head.

BENVOLIO.

                    Zounds, horns again!

MARTINO.

Nay, chafe not, man, we all are sped.

BENVOLIO.

15   What devil attends this damn'd magician,
That, spite of spite, our wrongs are doubled?

FREDERICK.

What may we do that we may hide our shames?

BENVOLIO.

If we should follow him to work revenge,
He'd join long asses' ears to these huge horns

20   And make us laughing stocks to all the world.

MARTINO.

What shall we then do, dear Benvolio?

BENVOLIO.

I have a castle joining near these woods,
And thither we'll repair and live obscure
Till time shall alter this our brutish shapes.

25   Sith black disgrace hath thus eclips'd our fame,
We'll rather die with grief than live with shame.

Exeunt omnes.

8.] Benvolio, on first seeing his friends, mistakes them for demonic apparitions.

14. *sped*] done for.

16. *spite of spite*] despite everything.

doubled] a trisyllable.

24. *this*] these.

25. *Sith*] since.

9. Act IV Scene iv (1616 text)

Enter Faustus, and the Horse-courser,
and Mephostophilis.

HOR.

I beseech your worship accept of these forty dollars.

FAUSTUS.

Friend, thou canst not buy so good a horse for so small
a price. I have no great need to sell him, but if thou likest
him for ten dollars more, take him, because I see thou
hast a good mind to him.   5

HOR.

I beseech you sir, accept of this. I am a very poor man,
and have lost very much of late by horseflesh, and this
bargain will set me up again.

FAUSTUS.

Well, I will not stand with thee; give me the money. Now
sirrah, I must tell you that you may ride him o'er hedge   10
and ditch, and spare him not, but do you hear? in any
case, ride him not into the water.

HOR.

How sir, not into the water? Why, will he not drink of
all waters?

FAUSTUS.

Yes, he will drink of all waters, but ride him not into the   15
water: o'er hedge and ditch, or where thou wilt, but not
into the water. Go, bid the ostler deliver him unto you,
and remember what I say.

HOR.

I warrant you, sir. O joyful day, now am I a made man
for ever!   20

Exit.

FAUSTUS.

What art thou, Faustus, but a man condemn'd to die?
Thy fatal time draws to a final end;

0.2] Mephostophilis does not speak in this scene. Boas, Greg, Kirschbaum, Jump and
  Bowers drop him from the stage direction.
9. *stand*] haggle.

Despair doth drive distrust into my thoughts.
Confound these passions with a quiet sleep:
25 Tush, Christ did call the thief upon the cross.
Then rest thee, Faustus, quiet in conceit.

He sits to sleep.
Enter the Horse-courser, wet.

HOR.

O what a cozening doctor was this! I riding my horse into
the water, thinking some hidden mystery had been in the
horse, I had nothing under me but a little straw, and had
30 much ado to escape drowning. Well, I'll go rouse him, and
make him give me my forty dollars again. Ho, sirrah Doctor,
you cozening scab! Master Doctor, awake, and rise, and give
me my money again, for your horse is turned to a bottle of
hay. Master Doctor!

He pulls off his leg.

35 Alas, I am undone, what shall I do? I have pulled off his leg!

FAUSTUS.

O help, help, the villain hath murdered me!

HOR.

Murder or not murder, now he has but one leg I'll outrun
him, and cast this leg into some ditch or other.

[*Exit.*]

FAUSTUS.

Stop him, stop him, stop him!—Ha, ha, ha: Faustus hath
40 his leg again, and the horse-courser a bundle of hay for
his forty dollars!

Enter Wagner.

27. *cozening*] cheating.
32. *scab*] rascal, scoundrel. "Scab" referred primarily to diseases affecting the skin
    (among them scabies, syphilis, and eczema) and to the pustules and crusts associated
    with them.
33. *bottle*] bundle.

How now, Wagner, what news with thee?

WAGNER.

If it please you, the Duke of Vanholt doth earnestly
entreat your company, and hath sent some of his men to
attend you with provision fit for your journey.   45

FAUSTUS.

The Duke of Vanholt's an honorable gentleman, and one
to whom I must be no niggard of my cunning. Come
away!

Exeunt.

10. Act IV Scene v (1616 text)

*Enter Clown [Robin], Dick, Horse-courser,
and a carter.*

CARTER.

Come my masters, I'll bring you to the best beer in
Europe. What ho, hostess! Where be these whores?

Enter Hostess.

HOSTESS.

How now, what lack you? What, my old guests, welcome!

CLOWN.

Sirrah Dick, dost thou know why I stand so mute?

DICK.

No Robin, why is't?   5

CLOWN.

I am eighteen pence on the score. But say nothing; see if
she have forgotten me.

HOSTESS.

Who's this, that stands so solemnly by himself? What,
my old guest!

CLOWN.

O hostess, how do you? I hope my score stands still.   10

6. *on the score*] in debt for unpaid drinks.
10.] When the Hostess promptly recognizes him, the Clown seeks to ingratiate himself
   by being the first to mention his debt.

HOSTESS.

Ay, there's no doubt of that, for methinks you make no
haste to wipe it out.

DICK.

Why Hostess, I say, fetch us some beer.

HOSTESS.

You shall presently: look up into th'hall there, ho!

Exit.

DICK.

15   Come sirs, what shall we do now till mine hostess comes?

CARTER.

Marry sir, I'll tell you the bravest tale how a conjurer
served me. You know Doctor Fauster?

HOR.

Ay, a plague take him! Here's some on's have cause to
know him. Did he conjure thee too?

CARTER.

20   I'll tell you how he served me. As I was going to Wittenberg t'other day with a load of hay, he met me and asked
me what he should give me for as much hay as he could
eat. Now sir, I thinking that a little would serve his turn,
bade him take as much as he would for three farthings.

25   So he presently gave me my money and fell to eating, and
as I am a cursen man, he never left eating till he had eat up
all my load of hay.

ALL.

O monstrous: eat a whole load of hay!

CLOWN.

Yes, yes, that may be, for I have heard of one that has eat
30   a load of logs.

---

14. *look ... ho!*] The hostess is summoning her staff. Jump (80) notes a parallel construction in *1 Henry IV* II. v. 33-34: "Look down into the Pomegranate, Ralph!" (At some
point during the following exchanges, beer is served, since at line 52 the Carter calls
for another round.)

17, 36. *Fauster*] a clownish corruption of "Faustus"; it reappears in a familiar nursery
rhyme: "Doctor Foster went to Gloucester / In a shower of rain; / He stepped in a
puddle right up to his middle, / And never went back again."

24. *farthing*] a small copper coin, worth one-quarter of a penny.

26. *cursen*] a deformation of "Christian" into something like its opposite: an irregular
form of the past participle "cursed."

eat] eaten.

HOR.

> Now sirs, you shall hear how villainously he served me. I
> went to him yesterday to buy a horse of him, and he would
> by no means sell him under forty dollars; so sir, because I
> knew him to be such a horse as would run over hedge and
> ditch and never tire, I gave him his money. So when I had   35
> my horse, Doctor Fauster bade me ride him night and day
> and spare him no time. "But," quoth he, "in any case ride
> him not into the water." Now sir, I, thinking the horse had
> had some quality that he would not have me know of, what
> did I but rid him into a great river, and when I came just in   40
> the midst my horse vanished away, and I sat straddling
> upon a bottle of hay.

ALL.

> O brave doctor!

HOR.

> But you shall hear how bravely I served him for it. I went
> me home to his house, and there I found him asleep; I kept   45
> a hallowing and whooping in his ears, but all could not
> wake him. I, seeing that, took him by the leg and never
> rested pulling till I had pulled me his leg quite off, and
> now 'tis at home in mine hostry!

CLOWN.

> And has the doctor but one leg, then? That's excellent, for   50
> one of his devils turned me into the likeness of an ape's face.

CARTER.

> Some more drink, Hostess.

CLOWN.

> Hark you, we'll into another room and drink awhile, and
> then we'll go seek out the doctor.

Exeunt omnes.

43, 44. *brave, bravely*] worthy, worthily.
51. *ape's face*] Bevington and Rasmussen note that Robin seems here to be recalling the
   A-version of the play, in which at III. ii. 41-46 he is transformed into an ape, and his
   companion Rafe into a dog. In the corresponding B-version scene (B: III. iii. 38-47),
   Mephostophilis transforms Dick into an ape and Robin into a dog. Here, as also at
   B: IV. vi. 104 and 108-09 below, it is apparent that the transformations involved the
   wearing of masks or headpieces.

II. Act IV Scene vi (1616 text)

Enter the Duke of Vanholt, his Duchess,
Faustus, and Mephostophilis; [also a servant].

DUKE.

    Thanks, Master Doctor, for these pleasant sights.
    Nor know I how sufficiently to recompense your great
    deserts in erecting that enchanted castle in the air,
    The sight whereof so delighted me
5   As nothing in the world could please me more.

FAUSTUS.

    I do think myself, my good lord, highly recompensed in
    that it pleaseth your Grace to think but well of that which
    Faustus hath performed. But gracious Lady, it may be that
    you have taken no pleasure in those sights; therefore I pray
10   you tell me, what is the thing you most desire to have? Be
    it in the world, it shall be yours. I have heard that great-
    bellied women do long for things are rare and dainty.

LADY.

    True, Master Doctor, and since I find you so kind, I will
    make known unto you what my heart desires to have; and
15   were it now summer, as it is January, a dead time of the
    winter, I would request no better meat than a dish of ripe
    grapes.

FAUSTUS.

    This is but a small matter. Go Mephostophilis, away!

Exit Mephostophilis.

    Madam, I will do more than this for your content.

Enter Mephostophilis again with the grapes.

20   Here: now taste ye these. They should be good,
    For they come from a far country, I can tell you.

1-5.] Lines 1, 4 and 5 (here lineated as in B2) are blank verse. (Noting that the emendation of line 4 to "hath so delighted me" would make it metrically regular, Bevington
and Rasmussen speculate that parts of this scene may once have been in verse.)
12. *are*] that are.

DUKE.

    This makes me wonder more than all the rest, that at this
    time of the year, when every tree is barren of his fruit, from
    whence you had these ripe grapes.

FAUSTUS.

    Please it your Grace, the year is divided into two circles   25
    over the whole world, so that when it is winter with us, in
    the contrary circle it is likewise summer with them, as in
    India, Saba, and such countries that lie far east, where they
    have fruit twice a year. From whence, by means of a swift
    spirit that I have, I had these grapes brought, as you see.   30

LADY.

    And trust me, they are the sweetest grapes that e'er I tasted.

The Clowns bounce at the gate within.

DUKE.

    What rude disturbers have we at the gate?
    Go, pacify their fury, set it ope,
    And then demand of them what they would have.

They knock again, and call out to talk with Faustus.

SERVANT.

    Why, how now masters, what a coil is there!   35
    What is the reason you disturb the Duke?

DICK.

    We have no reason for it, therefore a fig for him!

SERVANT.

    Wht, saucy varlets, dare you be so bold?

HOR.

    I hope, sir, we have wit enough to be more bold than wel-
    come.   40

31.1. bounce] to knock, or thump.

35. *masters*] an ironic or derisive inversion of what was normally a term of respect (*OED*
    sb. 20), a plural equivalent to the vocative singular "sirrah."

coil] tumult, noisy disturbance.

37. *a fig*] an expression of contempt, commonly accompanied by an obscene gesture (of
    closing the hand with the thumb thrust between the first and second fingers, or of
    thrusting the thumb into the mouth).

SERVANT.

    It appears so: pray be bold elsewhere,

    And trouble not the Duke.

DUKE.

                    What would they have?

SERVANT.

    They all cry out to speak with Doctor Faustus.

CARTER.

    Ay, and we will speak with him.

DUKE.

45   Will you, sir? Commit the rascals.

DICK.

    Commit with us? he were as good commit with his father

    as commit with us.

FAUSTUS.

    I do beseech your Grace, let them come in;

    They are good subject for a merriment.

DUKE.

50   Do as thou wilt, Faustus, I give thee leave.

FAUSTUS.

    I thank your Grace.

Enter the Clown, Dick, Carter, and Horse-courser.

              Why, how now, my good friends?

    'Faith, you are too outrageous. But come near,

    I have procur'd your pardons; welcome all!

CLOWN.

    Nay sir, we will be welcome for our money, and we will

55   pay for what we take. What ho, give's half a dozen of beer

    here, and be hanged!

FAUSTUS.

    Nay, hark you, can you tell me where you are?

---

45. *Commit the rascals*] Take them to prison.

46. *Commit with*] engage in sexual intercourse with.

54–62.] The clowns believe that they have found Faustus in a tavern like the one where
they were drinking in B: IV. v. Although there is no early indication as to whether
their confusion of a ducal residence with a public house stems from drunkenness or
from Faustus's magic, the entrance of the Hostess at line 92.1 suggests that it must be
the latter (she evidently thinks she is still in her own tavern).

CARTER.

Ay marry, can I: we are under heaven.

SERVANT.

Ay, but sir sauce-box, know you in what place?

HOR.

Ay, ay, the house is good enough to drink in. Zounds, fill   60
us some beer, or we'll break all the barrels in the house
and dash out all your brains with your bottles.

FAUSTUS.

Be not so furious; come, you shall have beer.
My Lord, beseech you give me leave a while;
I'll gage my credit 'twill content your Grace.   65

DUKE.

With all my heart, kind Doctor. Please thyself:
Our servants and our court's at thy command.

FAUSTUS.

I humbly thank your Grace. Then fetch some beer.

[*Exit Mephostophilis.*]

HOR.

Ay marry, there spake a doctor indeed, and 'faith I'll drink
a health to thy wooden leg for that word.   70

FAUSTUS.

My wooden leg? What dost thou mean by that?

CARTER.

Ha, ha, ha! Dost hear him, Dick? He has forgot his leg.

HOR.

Ay, ay, he does not stand much upon that.

FAUSTUS.

No, faith, not much upon a wooden leg.

CARTER.

Good lord, that flesh and blood should be so frail with your   75
worship! Do you not remember a horse-courser you sold
a horse to?

---

68. *Then fetch some beer*] This command must be addressed to Mephostophilis rather than
to one of the Duke's servants, since it is fulfilled by the appearance of the Hostess.
(She presumably enters, for comic effect, in a manner that makes clear she has been
magically transported.)

73. *stand much upon*] with a quibble on the figurative sense of "attach much importance
to."

FAUSTUS.

Yes, I remember I sold one a horse.

CARTER.

80   And do you remember you bid he should not ride into the
water?

FAUSTUS.

Yes, I do very well remember that.

CARTER.

And do you remember nothing of your leg?

FAUSTUS.

No, in good sooth.

CARTER.

Then I pray, remember your curtsy.

FAUSTUS.

85   I thank you, sir.

[*Bows.*]

CARTER.

'Tis not so much worth. I pray you tell me one thing.

FAUSTUS.

What's that?

CARTER.

Be both your legs bedfellows every night together?

FAUSTUS.

Wouldst thou make a Colossus of me, that thou askest me
90   such questions?

CARTER.

No truly, sir, I would make nothing of you; but I would fain
know that.

Enter Hostess with drink.

FAUSTUS.

Then I assure thee certainly they are.

82, 84. *leg, curtsy*] The Carter is playing on the metaphorical sense of "leg" (i.e. "to make
a leg") as "bow."

86. *'Tis ... worth*] Faustus's bow hasn't helped the Carter tell whether or not he has a
wooden leg.

89. *Colossus*] The legs of the Colossus at Rhodes were said to have straddled the entrance
to the harbor.

CARTER.

I thank you, I am fully satisfied.

FAUSTUS.

But wherefore dost thou ask?   95

CARTER.

For nothing, sir; but methinks you should have a wooden
bedfellow of one of 'em.

HOR.

Why, do you hear, sir, did not I pull off one of your legs
when you were asleep?

FAUSTUS.

But I have it again now I am awake: look you here, sir.   100

ALL.

O horrible! Had the doctor three legs?

CARTER.

Do you remember, sir, how you cozened me and eat up my
load of—

Faustus charms him dumb.

DICK.

Do you remember how you made me wear an ape's—

[*Faustus charms him dumb.*]

HOR.

You whoreson conjuring scab, do you remember how you   105
cozened me with a ho—

[*Faustus charms him dumb.*]

CLOWN.

Ha' you forgotten me? You think to carry it away with your
"hey-pass" and "Re-pass". Do you remember the dog's
fa—

---

100. *look you here, sir*] Bevington and Rasmussen propose that Faustus is wearing an
   academic gown, which at this point he opens to display his legs; he may, alternatively, make some display of agility to demonstrate that neither of his legs is artificial.
   (An actor could choose to combine the two: no effect that might enliven this scene
   should be disdained.)

102. *eat*] ate.

[Faustus charms him dumb.]
Exeunt Clowns.

HOSTESS.

110   Who pays for the ale? Hear you, Master Doctor, now you
have sent away my guests, I pray you who shall pay me for
my a—

[Faustus charms her dumb.]
Exit Hostess.

LADY.

My Lord, we are much beholding to this learned man.

DUKE.

So are we, Madam, which we will recompense
115   With all the love and kindness that we may.
His artful sport drives all sad thoughts away.

Exeunt.

12. Act V Scene i (1616 text)

Thunder and lightning. Enter devils with convered dishes;
Mephostophilis leads them into Faustus' study.
Then enter Wagner.

WAGNER.

I think my master means to die shortly:
He hath made his will, and given me his wealth,
His house, his goods, and store of golden plate,
Besides two thousand ducats ready coin'd.
5   I wonder what he means; if death were nigh
He would not frolic thus. He's now at supper
With the scholars, where there's such belly-cheer
As Wagner in his life ne'er saw the like;
And see where they come, belike the feast is done.

Exit.

1-9.] printed as prose in B1; verse here as in Boas.

Enter Faustus, Mephostophilis,
and two or three Scholars.

1 SCH.

    Master Doctor Faustus, since our conference about fair   10
ladies, which was the beautifullest in all the world, we have
determined with ourselves that Helen of Greece was the
admirablest lady that ever lived. Therefore, Master Doctor,
if you will do us so much favor as to let us see that peerless dame of Greece, whom all the world admires for ma-   15
jesty, we should think ourselves much beholding unto you.

FAUSTUS.

    Gentlemen,
For that I know your friendship is unfeign'd,
It is not Faustus' custom to deny
The just request of those that wish him well,   20
You shall behold that peerless dame of Greece
No otherwise for pomp or majesty
Than when sir Paris cross'd the seas with her
And brought the spoils to rich Dardania.
Be silent then, for danger is in words.   25

Music sound; Mephosto brings in Helen;
she passeth over the stage.

2 SCH.

    Was this fair Helen, whose admired worth
Made Greece with ten years' war afflict poor Troy?

3 SCH.

    Too simple is my wit too tell her worth,
Whom all the world admires for majesty.

1 SCH.

    Now we have seen the pride of nature's work,   30
We'll take our leaves, and for this blessed sight
Happy and blest be Faustus evermore.

Exeunt Scholars.

26-27. Was … Troy?] Another anticipation (as in B: IV. ii. 46-50) of the first two lines
of Faustus's speech to Helen. Greg (383) remarks that "poor Troy" has "a feebly
sentimental effect that, to us at least, is almost comic." Compare "poor Faustus" (B:
IV. i. 62).

FAUSTUS.

Gentlemen, farewell, the same wish I to you.

Enter an Old Man.

OLD MAN.

O gentle Faustus, leave this damned art,
35   This magic, that will charm thy soul to hell
And quite bereave thee of salvation.
Though thou hast now offended like a man,
Do not persever in it like a devil:
Yet, yet, thou hast an amiable soul,
40   If sin by custom grow not into nature:
Then, Faustus, will repentance come too late,
Then thou art banish'd from the sight of heaven;
No mortal can express the pains of hell.
It may be this my exhortation
45   Seems harsh and all unpleasant; let it not,
For, gentle son, I speak it not in wrath
Or envy of thee, but in tender love
And pity of thy future misery,
And so have hope that this my kind rebuke,
50   Checking thy body, may amend thy soul.

FAUSTUS.

Where art thou, Faustus? wretch, what hast thou done!

---

38. *persever*] accented on the second syllable.

39-40. *Yet ... nature*] i.e., Your soul is still worthy of love so long as sin does not through
force of habit become second nature. These lines are strongly Augustinian in tone.
In his *Confessions*, St. Augustine explained the soul's vacillation between opposing
wills, the mind's monstrous inability to command itself to will one thing, in terms
of the contrary pulls of truth and of custom (*Confessions* VIII. ix. 21), and told how
he had himself been bound by the chains of custom or habit: "The enemy had a
grip on my will and so made a chain for me to hold me a prisoner. The consequence
of a distorted will is passion. By servitude to passion, habit is formed, and habit to
which there is no resistance becomes necessity" (*Confessions* VIII. v. 10). This sort of
custom, "created for the soul by its own act of sin" (Augustine, *Acta contra Fortunatum
Manichaeum* 22; see Brown 150), also becomes part of our nature, as a matter both
of the pleasure derived from the memory of past sins and also of the increasing ease
with which they are repeated.

44. *exhortation*] pronounced as a word of five syllables.

50. *Checking*] reproving.

51.] B1 omits the line which follows this line in A1: "Damn'd art thou, Faustus, damn'd,
despair and die!"

Hell claims his right, and with a roaring voice
Says, "Faustus, come, thine hour is almost come!"

Mephostophilis gives him a dagger.

And Faustus now will come to do thee right.
OLD MAN.
    O stay, good Faustus, stay thy desperate steps!   55
    I see an angel hover o'er thy head,
    And with a vial full of precious grace
    Offers to pour the same into thy soul:
    Then call for mercy and avoid despair.
FAUSTUS.
    O friend, I feel thy words to comfort my distressed soul;   60
    Leave me awhile to ponder on my sins.
OLD MAN.
    Faustus, I leave thee, but with grief of heart,
    Fearing the enemy of thy hapless soul.

Exit.

FAUSTUS.
    Accursed Faustus: wretch, what hast thou done?
    I do repent, and yet I do despair;   65
    Hell strives with grace for conquest in my breast:
    What shall I do to shun the snares of death?
MEPH.
    Thou traitor, Faustus, I arrest thy soul
    For disobedience to my sovereign Lord.
    Revolt, or I'll in piece-meal tear thy flesh.   70

---

63. *the enemy of thy hapless soul*] The Old Man in A1 fears "the ruin of thy hopeless soul."
The B1 revisers have shifted the emphasis from Faustus's hopelessness (i.e., his lack
of the faith necessary for salvation) to the agency of the demonic enemy who will
victimize this unfortunate man.

64. *wretch, what hast thou done?*] This question, recycled from line 51 above, replaces
A1's "where is mercy now?" In A1 the Old Man told Faustus that only his Savior's
mercy and redeeming blood could cleanse him of his sins, and then diverted him
from suicidal despair by his account of an angelic vision suggesting that he could
receive mercy; after the Old Man's departure, Faustus wonders whether this mercy is
indeed accessible to him. The B1 revision shifts attention from this question to that
of Faustus's perverse agency.

FAUSTUS.

    I do repent I ere offended him.

    Sweet Mephostophilis, entreat thy lord

    To pardon my unjust presumption,

    And with my blood again I will confirm

75   The former vow I made to Lucifer.

MEPH.

    Do it then, Faustus, with unfeigned heart,

    Lest greater dangers do attend thy drift.

FAUSTUS.

    Torment, sweet friend, that base and aged man

    That durst dissuade me from thy Lucifer,

80   With greatest torment that our hell affords.

MEPH.

    His faith is great, I cannot touch his soul.

    But what I may afflict his body with

    I will attempt, which is but little worth.

FAUSTUS.

    One thing, good servant, let me crave of thee,

85   To glut the longing of my heart's desire:

    That I may have unto my paramour

    That heavenly Helen which I saw of late,

    Whose sweet embraces may extinguish cleare

    Those thoughts that do dissuade me from my vow,

90   And keep my vow I made to Lucifer.

MEPH.

    This, or what else my Faustus shall desire,

    Shall be performed in twinkling of an eye.

        Enter Helen again, passing over between two cupids.

FAUSTUS.

    Was this the face that launch'd a thousand ships

    And burnt the topless towers of Ilium?

95   Sweet Helen, make me immortal with a kiss;

    Her lips suck forth my soul, see where it flies!

71.] This line does not appear in A1.

78. *aged man*] This is arguably a normalizing revision of A1's "crooked age."

90. *my vow*] This reading is probably a compositorial repetition error, conditioned by "my vow" in the preceding line. A1 has "mine oath."

Come Helen, come, give me my soul again;
Here will I dwell, for heaven is in these lips,
And all is dross that is not Helena.
I will be Paris, and for love of thee   100
Instead of Troy shall Wittenberg be sack'd,
And I will combat with weak Menelaus
And wear thy colours on my plumed crest;
Yea, I will wound Achilles in the heel
And then return to Helen for a kiss.   105
O, thou art fairer than the evening's air
Clad in the beauty of a thousand stars;
Brighter art thou than flaming Jupiter
When he appear'd to hapless Semele,
More lovely than the monarch of the sky   110
In wanton Arethusa's azure arms,
And none but thou shalt be my paramour.

Exeunt.

13. Act V Scene ii (1616 text)

Thunder.
Enter Lucifer, Belzebub, and Mephostophilis.

LUCIFER.

Thus from infernal Dis do we ascend
To view the subjects of our monarchy,
Those souls which sin seals the black sons of hell,
'Mong which as chief, Faustus, we come to thee,
Bringing with us lasting damnation   5

---

98. *heaven is in these lips*] This appears to be a normalizing revision of A1's subjunctive
    construction: "heaven be in these lips...."
99.] In A1 the Old Man re-enters after this line, and concludes the scene after the departure
    of Faustus and Helen with a nine-line speech that both judges Faustus as "accursed"
    and offers a strong contrast to the last four lines of Faustus's final speech in V. ii.
0.1.] As in I.iii (where A's stage direction "Enter Faustus to conjure" is replaced in B by
    "Thunder. Enter Lucifer and four devils, Faustus to them with this speech"), the
    B-text introduces a second, demonic audience, which one must presume remains
    invisible to Faustus.
1. *Dis*] a name given to Pluto and, by transference, to the underworld over which he rules.

To wait upon thy soul; the time is come
Which makes it forfeit.

MEPH.
                                        And this gloomy night
Here in this room will wretched Faustus be.

BEL.
                    And here we'll stay
10   To mark him how he doth demean himself.

MEPH.
        How should he but in desperate lunacy?
Fond worldling, now his heart-blood dries with grief;
His conscience kills it, and his laboring brain
Begets a world of idle fantasies
15   To overreach the devil: but all in vain,
His store of pleasures must be sauc'd with pain.
He and his servant Wagner are at hand;
Both come from drawing Faustus' latest will.
See where they come.

Enter Faustus and Wagner.

FAUSTUS.
20   Say Wagner, thou hast perus'd my will;
How dost thou like it?

WAGNER.
                        Sir, so wondrous well
As in all humble duty I do yield
My life and lasting service for your love.

Enter the Scholars.

---

6. *wait upon*] lie in wait for (*OED* 14.b). Compare, from *The Lamentable Tragedie of Locrine* (1595), "Millions of devils wait upon thy soul! / Legions of spirits vex thy impious ghost!" (IV. i. 183-84; *Shakespeare Apocrypha* 57).

10. *demean himself*] conduct or govern himself. (The modern meaning of debasing or humbling oneself seems also to be present, though this sense, first cited by *OED* from a text of 1601, apparently remained rare until the eighteenth century.)

12. *Fond*] foolish.

18. *latest*] most recent, or final.

18-24.] This discussion of Faustus's will is both redundant (Wagner has already said all that need be said at the outset of V. i), and also dramatically clumsy, since it obliges Faustus to move from calmness to a state of panic within two lines.

FAUSTUS.

Gramercies, Wagner. Welcome, gentlemen.

[*Exit Wagner.*]

1 SCH.

Now, worthy Faustus, methinks your looks are chang'd.   25

FAUSTUS.

Oh gentlemen!

2 SCH.

What ails Faustus?

FAUSTUS.

Ah my sweet chamber-fellow, had I liv'd with thee,
Then had I liv'd still, but now must die eternally.
Look sirs, comes he not, comes he not?   30

1 SCH.

O my dear Faustus, what imports this fear?

2 SCH.

Is all our pleasure turn'd to melancholy?

3 SCH.

He is not well with being over solitary.

2 SCH.

If it be so, we'll have physicians, and Faustus shall be
cured.   35

3 SCH.

'Tis but a surfeit, sir, fear nothing.

FAUSTUS.

A surfeit of deadly sin, that hath damned both body and
soul.

2 SCH.

Yet Faustus, look up to heaven, and remember mercy is infinite.   40

---

24. *Gramercies*] thank you.

24.1.] B1 does not indicate an exit for Wagner; this is the obvious place for it.

24-26. *Welcome ... Oh gentlemen!*] This abrupt shift in Faustus's mood would make dramatic sense if one could assume that the B1 revisers intended him at this point to become aware of the devils. Faustus's questions in line 30 (which are carried over from
A1) indicate that the revisers did not think of the demonic audience as being visible
to him. One can imagine stage effects of a poltergeist kind that could go unremarked
by the Scholars as they enter, while striking terror into Faustus.

39. *mercy*] The A text has "God's mercy"; B1's deletion of "God's" is an instance of the

FAUSTUS.

But Faustus' offense can ne'er be pardoned: the serpent
that tempted Eve may be saved, but not Faustus. O
gentlemen, hear with patience, and tremble not at my
speeches. Though my heart pant and quiver to remember
45   that I have been a student here these thirty years, O would
I had never seen Wittenberg, never read book: and what
wonders I have done, all Germany can witness: yea, all
the world, for which Faustus hath lost both Germany and
the world, yea heaven itself, heaven the seat of God, the
50   throne of the blessed, the kingdom of joy, and must remain
in hell for ever—hell, O hell for ever. Sweet friends, what
shall become of Faustus, being in hell for ever?

2 SCH.

Yet Faustus, call on God.

FAUSTUS.

On God, whom Faustus hath abjured? on God, whom Faus-
55   tus hath blasphemed? O my God, I would weep, but the
devil draws in my tears. Gush forth blood instead of tears,
yea life and soul! Oh, he stays my tongue; I would lift up
my hands, but see, they hold 'em, they hold 'em.

ALL.

Who, Faustus?

FAUSTUS.

60   Why, Lucifer and Mephostophilis. O gentlemen, I gave
them my soul for my cunning.

ALL.

O God forbid!

FAUSTUS.

God forbade it indeed, but Faustus hath done it: for the vain
pleasure of four and twenty years hath Faustus lost eternal
65   joy and felicity. I writ them a bill with mine own blood, the
date is expired: this is the time, and he will fetch me!

1 SCH.

Why did not Faustus tell us of this before, that divines
might have prayed for thee?

---

expunging of words that might have been thought offensive under the 1606 Act of
Abuses.

55-58.] The presence of the devils (whether on stage or on an upper gallery or balcony)
raises the question of how their participation in or response to these lines should be
staged. This is one sign of B1's literalizing of the horror of Faustus's predicament.

FAUSTUS.

Oft have I thought to have done so, but the devil
threatened to tear me in pieces if I named God, to fetch 70
me body and soul if I once gave ear to divinity, and now
'tis too late: gentlemen, away, lest you perish with me.

2 SCH.

O what may we do to save Faustus?

FAUSTUS.

Talk not of me, but save yourselves, and depart.

3 SCH.

God will strengthen me, I will stay with Faustus. 75

1 SCH.

Tempt not God, sweet friend, but let us into the next
room, and pray for him.

FAUSTUS.

Ay, pray for me, pray for me; and what noise soever you
hear, come not unto me, for nothing can rescue me.

2 SCH.

Pray thou, and we will pray that God may have mercy 80
upon thee.

FAUSTUS.

Gentlemen, farewell. If I live till morning, I'll visit you;
if not, Faustus is gone to hell.

ALL.

Faustus, farewell.

Exeunt Scholars.

MEPH.

Ay Faustus, now thou hast no hope of heaven, 85
Therefore despair, think only upon hell,
For that must be thy mansion, there to dwell.

FAUSTUS.

O thou bewitching fiend, 'twas thy temptation
Hath robb'd me of eternal happiness.

MEPH.

I do confess it Faustus, and rejoice; 90

85.] Mephostophilis has presumably descended from the gallery to the stage before
speaking.

90-94. *I do confess it ... And led thine eye*] This passage flatly contradicts Mephostophilis's
statement in the B-text variant at II. iii. 4, where in response to Faustus's declaration,

'Twas I, that when thou wert i'the way to heaven
Damm'd up thy passage: when thou took'st the book
To view the scriptures, then I turn'd the leaves
And led thine eye.

95   What, weep'st thou? 'tis too late, despair, farewell;
Fools that will laugh on earth must weep in hell!

Exit.

*Enter the Good Angel and the Bad Angel
at several doors.*

GOOD.

Oh Faustus, if thou hadst given ear to me,
Innumerable joys had follow'd thee,
But thou didst love the world.

BAD.

Gave ear to me,

100   And now must taste hell's pains perpetually.

GOOD.

O what will all thy riches, pleasures, pomps,
Avail thee now?

BAD.

Nothing but vex thee more,
To want in hell, that had on earth such store.

Music while the throne descends.

"When I behold the heavens then I repent / And curse thee wicked Mephostophilis, / Because thou hast depriv'd me of those joys," he says: "'Twas thine own seeking Faustus, thank thy self." Eric Rasmussen notes that with the addition of these contradictory statements ("'Twas thine own seeking," "'Twas I"), Mephostophilis in the B-text "lies to Faustus—something that he never does in the A-text" (Rasmussen 80).

96. *must weep*] B1's "most weep" produces an acceptable sense, but the B2 emendation followed here gives a contrast between "will laugh" and "must weep" that was probably the original reading.

96.2. *several*] different. Although their entrance appears to indicate a continuing adversarial relationship, the angels promptly show themselves to be "so frankly in cahoots that they finish one another's sentences" (Empson 172; see also Tromly 148-49).

103.1] The throne would have been let down from the theater's canopy or "heavens" by means of a winch (see Astington). Tromly proposes that the spectacle of its descent might suggest for Faustus, if only momentarily, a hope of escape: "Since the play has been almost totally devoid of unproblematic signs of saving grace, the allurement

GOOD.

> O, thou hast lost celestial happiness,
> Pleasures unspeakable, bliss without end.   105
> Hadst thou affected sweet divinity,
> Hell or the devil had had no power on thee.
> Hadst thou kept on that way, Faustus, behold
> In what resplendent glory thou hadst sat
> In yonder throne, like those bright shining saints,   110
> And triumph'd over hell; that hast thou lost,
> And now, poor soul, must thy good angel leave thee:
> The jaws of hell are open to receive thee.

Exit.

[*The throne ascends.*] *Hell is discovered.*

BAD.

> Now Faustus, let thine eyes with horror stare
> Into that vast perpetual torture-house: 115
> There are the furies, tossing damned souls
> On burning forks; their bodies broil in lead.
> There are live quarters broiling on the coals,
> That ne'er can die; this ever-burning chair

---

of this glittering throne which descends to the harmonies of ravishing music would be difficult to exaggerate" (149). This throne, the only physical sign of heaven to appear in either version of the play, can also be seen as "an emblem of state control" (Shepherd 96). A throne appears to be indicated as a stage property for the scene in the imperial court (see note to B: IV. i. 5); it seems unlikely that the company would have provided itself with separate thrones for that scene and this.

106. *affected*] been drawn to, preferred, loved.

110. *bright shining saints*] Bevington and Rasmussen suggest that the throne would have been accompanied by "some pictorial representation of the saints, or possibly representation by mute actors."

113.1.] The re-ascent of the throne is not marked in B1. Tromly suggests that it may be drawn up "with the Good Angel sitting smugly in it" (149), and notes for comparison a stage direction in the epilogue of Greene's *Alphonsus, King of Arragon* (c. 1587): "*Exit, Venus. Or, if you can conveniently, let a chair come down from the top of the stage, and draw her up.*"

Hell is discovered] A curtain may have been drawn to reveal a painted backcloth (presumably the "Hell mouth" listed by Henslowe's *Diary* among the Admiral's Men's props), or perhaps a trap door was uncovered with smoke rising from it.

118. *live quarters*] Executions for high treason could involve the victim being hanged, and then being taken down while still alive, partially eviscerated, and chopped into quarters, which were then publicly displayed.

120 Is for o'er tortur'd souls to rest them in.
These that are fed with sops of flaming fire
Were gluttons and lov'd only delicates,
And laugh'd to see the poor starve at their gates.
But yet all these are nothing: thou shalt see
125 Ten thousand tortures that more horrid be.
FAUSTUS.
O, I have seen enough to torture me!
BAD.
Nay, thou must feel them, taste the smart of all;
He that loves pleasure must for pleasure fall.
And so I leave thee, Faustus, till anon,
130 Then wilt thou tumble in confusion.

Exit.

The clock strikes eleven.

FAUSTUS.
O Faustus,
Now hast thou but one bare hour to live,
And then thou must be damn'd perpetually.
Stand still, you ever-moving spheres of heaven,
135 That time may cease, and midnight never come!
Fair nature's eye, rise, rise again, and make
Perpetual day, or let this hour be but a year,
A month, a week, a natural day,
That Faustus may repent, and save his soul.
140 *O lente lente currite noctis equi!*
The stars move still, time runs, the clock will strike,
The devil will come, and Faustus must be damn'd.
O I'll leap up to heaven: who pulls me down?

121-23.] These lines sadistically revise the parable of the rich man and Lazarus the beggar (*Luke* 16: 19-26). Tromly (149-50) notes that according to the gloss in the *Geneva Bible*, Jesus's parable concerns "those who live deliciously and neglect the poor," while here, in contrast, gluttons have taken delight "in actually *watching* the poor people starve at their gates." The punishment, Tromly observes, is likewise more cruel: the biblical rich man, tormented after his death in the flames of hell, cannot be given the cooling drops of water for which he begs, but he is told so by Abraham in a manner far removed from the sadism of these lines.

122. *delicates*] delicacies.

143. *heaven*] an instance of censorship in B1: this word replaces A1's "my God."

One drop of blood will save me; oh my Christ,
Rend not my heart for naming of my Christ.   145
Yet will I call on him: O spare me Lucifer!
Where is it now? 'tis gone,
And see, a threatening arm, an angry brow!
Mountains and hills, come, come, and fall on me,
And hide me from the heavy wrath of heaven.   150
No? Then will I headlong run into the earth.
Gape earth! O no, it will not harbor me.
You stars that reign'd at my nativity,
Whose influence hath allotted death and hell,
Now draw up Faustus like a foggy mist   155
Into the entrails of yon laboring cloud,
That when you vomit forth into the air
My limbs may issue from your smoky mouths,
But let my soul mount, and ascend to heaven.

The watch strikes.

O, half the hour is past: 'twill all be past anon.   160
O, if my soul must suffer for my sin,
Impose some end to my incessant pain:
Let Faustus live in hell a thousand years,

144.] In the most flagrant instance of a revisionary censorship in B1, this line replaces
two lines in the A text: "See, see where Christ's blood streams in the firmament, /
One drop would save my soul, half a drop, ah my Christ...." While the change may
have been made out of anxiety that the lines might cause offense under the provisions
of the 1606 Act of Abuses, it can be noted that the B1 revisers removed the strong
reference to Christ's blood in the Old Man's first speech (see V. i. 46 in my A-version
edition).

148.] This line, the product once again of censorship, replaces two lines in the A text:
"And see where God stretcheth out his arm / And bends his ireful brows...."

150. *heaven*] The B1 censor has substituted this word for A1's "God."

161.] This line replaces two lines in the A text: "O God, if thou wilt not have mercy on
my soul, / Yet for Christ's sake, whose blood hath ransom'd me...." The motives of
the B1 revisers and of the hypothetical censor overlap here in a way that may cast
doubt on attempts to distinguish between the two. A1's references to God and Christ
are removed, arguably in response to the 1606 Act of Abuses. At the same time, the
B1 revision erases (as in the Old Man's speech and in line 144 above) a reference to
Christ's blood, expunges from the text the question of whether divine mercy is being
refused to Faustus by an act of divine will, and has Faustus seem to acknowledge that
the horrible suffering his soul will shortly experience in the "vast perpetual torture-
house" (line 115) the Bad Angel has shown him follows appropriately from his sin.

A hundred thousand, and at last be sav'd.
165   No end is limited to damned souls.
Why wert thou not a creature wanting soul?
Or why is this immortal that thou hast?
Oh, Pythagoras' metempsychosis, were that true
This soul should fly from me, and I be chang'd
170   Into some brutish beast.
All beasts are happy, for when they die
Their souls are soon dissolv'd in elements,
But mine must live still to be plagu'd in hell.
Curst be the parents that engender'd me;
175   No Faustus, curse thyself, curse Lucifer
That hath depriv'd thee of the joys of heaven!

The clock strikes twelve.

It strikes, it strikes: now body, turn to air,
Or Lucifer will bear thee quick to hell!
O soul, be chang'd into small water drops,
180   And fall into the ocean, ne'er be found!

Thunder, and enter the devils.

O mercy, heaven: look not so fierce on me!
Adders and serpents, let me breathe awhile!
Ugly hell gape not, come not Lucifer,
I'll burn my books, oh Mephostophilis!

Exeunt.

14. Act V Scene iii (1616 text)

Enter the Scholars.

1 SCH.

Come gentlemen, let us go visit Faustus,
For such a dreadful night was never seen
Since first the world's creation did begin;

---

179. *small*] B1 substitutes this word for A1's "little."
181. *O mercy heaven*] B1's replacement, in a last small act of censorship, for A1's "My God, my God."

Such fearful shrieks and cries were never heard.
Pray heaven the doctor have escap'd the danger. 5

2 SCH.

O help us heaven! See, here are Faustus' limbs
All torn asunder by the hand of death!

3 SCH.

The devils whom Faustus serv'd have torn him thus,
For 'twixt the hours of twelve and one me thought
I heard him shriek and call aloud for help, 10
At which self time the house seem'd all on fire
With dreadful horror of these damned fiends.

2 SCH.

Well gentlemen, though Faustus' end be such
As every Christian heart laments to think on,
Yet for he was a scholar once admir'd 15
For wondrous knowledge in our German schools,
We'll give his mangl'd limbs due burial,
And all the students, cloth'd in mourning black,
Shall wait upon his heavy funeral.

Exeunt.

---

11. *self*] same.

15. *for*] since, because.

19. *wait upon*] to observe, behold attentively (*OED*, "wait" 14. a); also to escort, to accompany on its way (*OED*, 14. k).

heavy] sad, sorrowful.

19.1.] This stage direction is followed by the final Chorus.

Appendix B: Excerpts from The Historie of the damnable life, and deserved death of Doctor John Faustus *(London, 1592)*

[The standard edition of this text is *The English Faust Book*, ed. John Henry Jones (1994), cited in my notes as *EFB*. For critical commentary, see Jones's excellent introduction, and also Butler 1952: 31-41.

The principal passages of this source text drawn upon in the A-version of Marlowe's play and in the B-text revisions are reproduced here, in modernized form, and with obvious misprints silently corrected. In these excerpts from the 1592 *Historie of the damnable life*, I have been rather more conservative in modernizing punctuation than has Jones in his edition. To facilitate comparisons, I have indicated the passages in Marlowe's *Doctor Faustus* which correspond to these excerpts.]

1. *Doctor Faustus*, **Prologue, 11-27; I. i; I. iii**

EFB, Chap. 1.
John Faustus, born in the town of Rhode, lying in the province of Weimar in Germ[any], his father a poor husbandman and not [able] well to bring him up: but having an uncle at Wittenberg, a rich man and without issue, took this J. Faustus from his father and made him his heir, in so much that his father was no more troubled with him, for he remained with his uncle at Wittenberg, where he was kept at the university in the same city to study divinity. But Faustus, being of a naughty mind and otherwise addicted, applied not his studies, but took himself to other exercises: the which his uncle oftentimes hearing, rebuked him for it, as Eli oft times rebuked his children for sinning against the Lord: even so this good man labored to have Faustus apply his study of divinity, that he might come to the knowledge of God and his laws. But it is manifest that many virtuous parents have wicked children, as Cain, Reuben, Absolom and such like have been to their parents: so this Faustus having godly parents, and seeing him to be of a toward wit, were very desirous to bring him up in those virtuous studies, namely, of divinity: but he gave himself secretly to study necromancy and conjuration, in so much that few or none could perceive his profession.

But to the purpose: Faustus continued at study in the university, and was by the Rectors and sixteen Masters afterwards examined how he had profited in his studies; and being found by them that none for his time were able to argue with him in divinity, or for the excellency of his wisdom to compare with him, with one consent they made him Doctor of Divinity. But Doctor Faustus, within short time after he had obtained his degree, fell into such fantasies and deep cogitations that he was marked of many, and of the most part of the students was called the Speculator; and sometime he would throw the scriptures from him as though he had no care of his former profession: so that he began a very ungodly life, as hereafter more at large may appear; for the old proverb saith, Who can hold that will away? So who can hold Faustus from the devil, that seeks after him with all his endeavor? For he accompanied himself with divers that were seen in those devilish arts, and that had the Chaldean, Persian, Hebrew, Arabian, and Greek tongues, using figures, characters, conjurations, incantations, with many other ceremonies belonging to those infernal arts, as necromancy, charms, soothsaying, witchcraft, enchantment, being delighted with their books, words, and names so well that he studied day and night therein: in so much that he could not abide to be called doctor of divinity, but waxed a worldly man, and named himself an astrologian, and a mathematician: and for a shadow sometimes a physician, and did great cures, namely with herbs, roots, waters, drinks, receipts, and clisters. And without doubt he was passing wise, and excellent perfect in the holy scriptures: but he that knoweth his master's will and doth it not, is worthy to be beaten with many stripes. It is written, No man can serve two masters, and Thou shalt not tempt the Lord thy God: but Faustus threw all this in the wind, and made his soul of no estimation, regarding more his worldly pleasure than the joys to come: therefore at the day of judgment there is no hope of his redemption.

EFB, Chap. 2.

You have heard before, that all Faustus' mind was set to study the arts of necromancy and conjuration, the which exercise he followed day and night: and taking to him the wings of an eagle, thought to fly over the whole world, and to know the secrets of heaven and earth; for his speculation was so wonderful, being expert in using his *vocabula*, figures, characters, conjurations, and other ceremonial actions, that in all the haste he put in practice to bring the devil before him. And taking his way to a thick wood near to Wittenberg, called in the German tongue *Spisser Waldt* [...], he came into the same wood towards evening to a cross way, where he made with a wand a circle in the dust, and within that many more circles and characters: and thus he passed away the time, until it was nine or ten of the clock in the night, then began Doctor Faustus to call for Mephostophiles the spirit, and to charge him in the name of Beelzebub to appear there personally without any long stay: then presently the devil began so great a rumor in the wood, as if heaven and earth would have come together with wind, the trees bowing their tops to the ground; then fell the devil to bleat as if the whole wood had been full of lions, and suddenly about the circle ran the devil as if a thousand wagons had been running together on paved stones. After this at the four corners of the wood it thundered horribly, with such lightnings as if the whole world, to his seeming, had been on fire. Faustus all this while half amazed at the devil's so long tarrying, and doubting whether he were best to abide any more such horrible conjurings, thought to leave his circle and depart; whereupon the devil made him music of all sorts, as if the nymphs themselves had been in place: whereat Faustus was revived and stood stoutly in his circle aspecting his purpose, and began again to conjure the spirit Mephostophiles in the name of the prince of devils to appear in his likeness: whereat suddenly over his head hanged hovering in the air a mighty dragon: then calls Faustus again after his devilish manner, at which there was a monstrous cry in the wood, as if hell had been open, and all the tormented souls crying to God for mercy; presently not three fathom above his head fell a flame in manner of a lightning, and changed itself into a globe: yet Faustus feared it not, but did persuade himself that the devil should give him his request before he would leave [...]. Faustus, vexed at the spirit's so long tarrying, used his charms with full purpose not to depart before he had his intent, and crying on Mephostophiles the spirit, suddenly the globe opened and sprang up in height of a man: so burning a time, in the end it converted to the shape of a fiery man. This pleasant beast ran about the circle a great while, and appeared in manner of a grey friar, asking Faustus what was his request. Faustus commanded that the next morning at twelve of the clock he should appear to him at his house, but the devil would in no wise grant. Faustus began again to conjure him in the name of Beelzebub, that he should fulfil his request: whereupon the spirit agreed, and so they departed each one his way.

EFB, Chap. 3.

Doctor Faustus having commanded the spirit to be with him, at his hour appointed he came and appeared in his chamber, demanding of Faustus what his desire was: then began Doctor Faustus anew with him to conjure him that he should be obedient unto him, and to answer him certain articles, and to fulfil them in all points.

1   That the spirit should serve him and be obedient unto him in all things that he asked of him from that hour until the hour of

his death.

2 Farther, any thing that he desired of him he should bring it to him.

3 Also, that in all Faustus his demands or interrogations the spirit should tell him nothing but that which is true.

Hereupon the spirit answered and laid his case forth, that he had no power of himself, until he had first given his prince (that was ruler over him) to understand thereof, and to know if he could obtain so much of his lord: Therefore speak farther that I may do thy whole desire to my prince: for it is not in my power to fulfil without his leave....

Doctor Faustus upon this arose where he sat, and said, I will have my request, and yet I will not be damned. The spirit answered, Then shalt thou want thy desire, and yet art thou mine notwithstanding: if any man would detain thee it is in vain, for thine infidelity hath confounded thee.

Hereupon spake Faustus: Get thee hence from me, and take Saint Valentine's farewell and Crisam with thee, yet I conjure thee that thou be here at evening, and bethink thyself on that I have asked thee, and ask thy prince's counsel therein. Mephostophiles the spirit, thus answered, vanished away, leaving Faustus in his study, where he sat pondering with himself how he might obtain his request of the devil without loss of his soul: yet fully he was resolved in himself rather than to want his pleasure, to do whatsoever the spirit and his lord should condition upon.

EFB, Chap. 10.
[...] Here Faustus said: But how came thy lord and master Lucifer to have so great a fall from heaven? Mephostophiles answered: My lord Lucifer was a fair angel, created of God as immortal, and being placed in the seraphins, which are above the cherubins, he would have presumed unto the throne of God, with intent to have thrust God out of his seat. Upon this presumption the Lord cast him down headlong, and where before he was an angel of light, now dwells he in darkness....

EFB, Chap. 13.
[...] Faustus, my lord Lucifer (so called now, for that he was banished out of the clear light of heaven) was at the first an angel of God; he sat on the cherubins, and saw all the wonderful works of God, yea he was so of God ordained for shape, pomp, authority, worthiness, and dwelling, that he far exceeded all the other creatures of God, yea our gold and precious stones: and so illuminated, that he far surpassed the brightness

of the sun and all other stars: wherefore God placed him on the cherubins, where he had a kingly office, and was always before God's seat, to the end he might be the more perfect in all his beings: but when he began to be high-minded, proud, and so presumptuous that he would usurp the seat of his Majesty, then was he banished out from amongst the heavenly powers....

2. *Doctor Faustus*, II. i. 30-157

EFB, Chap. 4.

Faustus continuing in his devilish cogitations, never moving out of the place where the spirit left him (such was his fervent love to the devil), the night approaching, this swift flying spirit appeared to Faustus, offering himself with all submission to his service, with full authority from his prince to do whatsoever he would request, if so be Faustus would promise to be his: This answer I bring thee, and an answer must thou make by me again, yet will I hear what is thy desire, because thou hast sworn me to be here at this time. Doctor Faustus gave him this answer, though faintly (for his soul's sake): That his request was none other but to become a devil, or at least a limb of him, and that the spirit should agree unto these articles as followeth.

1   That he might be a spirit in shape and quality.
2   That Mephostophiles should be his servant, and at his commandment.
3   That Mephostophiles should bring him any thing, and do for him whatsoever.
4   That at all times he should be in his house, invisible to all men, except only to himself, and at his commandment to show himself.
5   Lastly, that Mephostophiles should at all times appear at his command, in what form or shape soever he would.

Upon these points the spirit answered Doctor Faustus, that all this should be granted him and fulfilled, and more if he would agree unto him upon certain articles as followeth.

First, that Doctor Faustus should give himself to his lord Lucifer, body and soul.
Secondly, for confirmation of the same, he should make him a writing, written with his own blood.

Thirdly, that he would be an enemy to all Christian people.

Fourthly, that he would deny his Christian belief.

Fifthly, that he let not any man change his opinion, if so be any man should go about to dissuade or withdraw him from it.

Further, the spirit promised Faustus to give him certain years to live in health and pleasure, and when such years were expired, that then Faustus should be fetched away, and if he should hold these articles and conditions, then he should have all whatsoever his heart would wish or desire; and that Faustus should quickly perceive himself to be a spirit in all manner of actions whatsoever. Hereupon Doctor Faustus his mind was so inflamed that he forgot his soul, and promised Mephostophiles to hold all things as he had mentioned them: he thought the devil was not so black as they use to paint him, nor hell so hot as the people say, etc.

EFB, Chap. 5.

[...] After a while, Faustus promised Mephostophiles to write and make his obligation, with full assurance of the articles in the chapter before rehearsed. A pitiful case (Christian reader), for certainly this letter or obligation was found in his house after his most lamentable end, with all the rest of his damnable practices used in his whole life. Therefore I wish all Christians to take an example by this wicked Faustus, and to be comforted in Christ, contenting themselves with that vocation whereunto it hath pleased God to call them, and not to esteem the vain delights of this life, as did this unhappy Faustus, in giving his soul to the devil: and to confirm it the more assuredly, he took a small penknife, and pricked a vein in his left hand, and for certainty thereupon were seen on his hand these words written, as if they had been written with blood, *O homo fuge:* whereat the spirit vanished, but Faustus continued in his damnable mind, and made his writing as followeth.

EFB, Chap. 6.

How Doctor Faustus set his blood in a saucer on warm ashes, and writ as followeth.

I Johannes Faustus, Doctor, do openly acknowledge with mine own hand, to the greater force and strengthening of this letter, that sithence I began to study and speculate the course and order of the elements, I have not found through the gift that is given me from above any such learning and wisdom that can bring me to my desires: and for that I find that men are unable to instruct me any farther in the matter, now have I, Doctor John Faustus, unto the hellish prince of Orient and his messenger Mephostophiles, given both body and soul, upon such condition that they shall learn me, and fulfil my desire in all things, as they have promised and vowed unto me, with due obedience unto me, according to the articles mentioned between us.

Further, I covenant and grant them by these presents, that at the end of 24 years next ensuing the date of this present letter […] I give them full power to do with me at their pleasure, to rule, to send, fetch, or carry me or mine, be it either body, soul, flesh, blood, or goods, into their habitation, be it wheresoever: and hereupon, I defy God and his Christ, all the host of heaven, and all living creatures that bear the shape of God, yea all that lives; and again I say it, and it shall be so. And to the more strengthening of this writing, I have written it with mine own hand and blood […].

EFB, Chap. 7.
[Faustus is treated to a series of magical spectacles in which spirits assume the forms of animals, and is given a sack of gold and another of silver.] Lastly, was heard by Faustus all manner instruments of music[…], the which so ravished his mind, that he thought he had been in another world, forgot both body and soul, in so much that he was minded never to change his opinion concerning that which he had done. Hereat came Mephostophiles into the hall to Faustus, in apparel like unto a friar, to whom Faustus spake: Thou hast done me a wonderful pleasure in showing me this pastime; if thou continue as thou hast begun, thou shalt win my heart and soul, yea and have it. Mephostophiles answered, This is nothing, I will please thee better: yet that thou maist know my power and all, ask what thou wilt request of me, that shalt thou have, conditionally hold thy promise, and give me thy hand-writing: at which words, the wretch thrust forth his hand, saying, Hold thee, there hast thou my promise: Mephostophiles took the writing […].

EFB, Chap 11.
The night following, after Faustus his communication had with Mephostophiles as concerning the fall of Lucifer, Doctor Faustus dreamed that he had seen a part of hell: but in what manner it was, or in what place he knew not: whereupon he was greatly troubled in mind, and called unto him Mephostophiles his spirit, saying to him, My Mephostophiles, I pray thee resolve me in this doubt: what is hell, what substance is it of, in what place stands it, and when was it made? Mephostophiles answered: My Faustus, thou shalt know that before the fall of my lord Lucifer there was no hell, but even then was hell or-

dained: it is of no substance, but a confused thing [...]: in this confused hell is nought to find but a filthy, sulphurish, firie, stinking mist or fog [...]. Further, we devils know not how God hath laid the foundation of our hell, nor whereof it is: but to be short with thee, Faustus, we know that hell hath neither bottom nor end.

EFB, Chap. 9.

Doctor Faustus continued thus in his epicurish life day and night, and believed not that there was a God, hell, or devil: he thought that body and soul died together, and had quite forgotten divinity or the immortality of his soul, but stood in his damnable heresy day and night. And bethinking himself of a wife, called Mephostophiles to counsel; which would in no wise agree, demanding of him if he would break the covenant made with him, or if he had forgot it. Hast not thou (quoth Mephostophiles) sworn thyself an enemy to God and all creatures? To this I answer thee, thou canst not marry; thou canst not serve two masters, God, and my prince: for wedlock is a chief institution ordained of God, and that hast thou promised to defy, as we do all, and that hast thou also done: and moreover thou hast confirmed it with thy blood: persuade thyself that what thou dost in contempt of wedlock, it is all to thine own delight. Therefore, Faustus, look well about thee, and bethink thyself better, and I wish thee to change thy mind: for if thou keep not what thou hast promised in thy writing, we will tear thee in pieces like the dust under thy feet [...]. But shortly, and that within two hours after, Faustus called his spirit, which came in his old manner like a friar. Then Faustus said unto him, I am not able to resist nor bridle my fantasy, I must and will have a wife, and I pray thee give thy consent to it. Suddenly upon these words came such a whirlwind about the place, that Faustus thought the whole house would come down; all the doors in the house flew off the hooks: after all this, his house was full of smoke, and the floor covered over with ashes: which when Doctor Faustus perceived, he would have gone up the stairs: and flying up, he was taken and thrown into the hall, that he was not able to stir hand nor foot: then round about him ran a monstrous circle of fire, never standing still, that Faustus fried as he lay, and thought there to have been burned. Then cried he out to his spirit Mephostophiles for help, promising him he would live in all things as he had vowed in his handwriting. Hereupon appeared unto him an ugly devil, so fearful and monstrous to behold, that Faustus durst not look on him. The devil said, What wouldst thou have, Faustus? how likest thou thy wedding? what mind art thou in now? Faustus answered, he had forgot his promise, desiring him of pardon, and he would talk no more of such things. The devil answered, Thou wert best so to do, and so vanished.

After appeared unto him his friar Mephostophiles with a bell in his hand, and spake to Faustus: It is no jesting with us; hold thou that which thou hast vowed, and we will perform as we have promised: and more than that, thou shalt have thy heart's desire of what woman soever thou wilt, be she alive or dead, and so long as thou wilt, thou shalt keep her by thee.

These words pleased Faustus wonderful well, and repented himself that he was so foolish to wish himself married, that might have any woman in the whole city brought to him at his command; the which he practised and persevered in a long time.

EFB, Chap. 10.
Doctor Faustus living in all manner of pleasure that his heart could desire, continuing in his amorous drifts, his delicate fare, and costly apparel, called on a time his Mephostophiles to him: which being come, brought with him a book in his hand of all manner of devilish and enchanted arts, the which he gave Faustus, saying: Hold, my Faustus, work now thy heart's desire [...].

3. *Doctor Faustus*, II. iii

EFB, Chap. 18.
Doctor Faustus [...] called unto him Mephostophiles his spirit, saying: [...] when I confer *Astronomia* and *Astrologia*, as the mathematicians and ancient writers have left in memory, I find them to vary and very much to disagree: wherefore I pray thee to teach me the truth in this matter.

EFB, Chap. 19.

Doctor Faustus revolving with himself the speeches of his spirit, he became so woeful and sorrowful in his cogitations that he thought himself already frying in the hottest flames of hell; and lying in his muse, suddenly there appeared unto him his spirit, demanding what things so grieved and troubled his conscience [...]. To whom Faustus answered, I have taken thee unto me as a servant to do me service, and thy service will be very dear unto me; yet I cannot have any diligence of thee farther than thou list thyself, neither dost thou in any thing as it becometh thee. The spirit replied, My Faustus, thou knowest that I was never against thy commandments as yet, but ready to serve and resolve thy questions; although I am not bound unto thee in such respects as concern the hurt of our kingdom, yet was I always willing to answer thee, and so I am still: therefore, my Faustus, say on boldly, what is thy will and pleasure? At which words, the spirit stole away the heart of Faustus, who spake in this sort: Mephostophiles, tell me how and after what sort God made the world, and all the creatures in them, and why man was made after the image of God? The spirit, hearing this, answered: Faustus, thou knowest that all this is in vain for thee to ask. I know that thou art sorry for that thou hast done, but it availeth thee not, for I will tear thee in thousands of pieces if thou change not thine opinions, and hereat he vanished away. Whereat Faustus, all sorrowful for that he had put forth such a question, fell to weeping and to howling bitterly, not for his sins towards God, but for that the devil was departed from him so suddenly, and in such a rage. And being in this perplexity, he was suddenly taken in such an extreme cold, as if he should have frozen in the place where he sat, in which the greatest devil in hell appeared unto him, with certain of his hideous and infernal company in the most ugliest shapes that it was possible to think upon, and traversing the chamber round about where Faustus sat, Faustus thought to himself, Now are they come for me though my time be not come, and that because I have asked such questions of my servant Mephostophiles: at whose cogitations, the chiefest devil, which was his lord unto whom he gave his soul, that was Lucifer, spake in this sort: Faustus, I have seen thy thoughts, which are not as thou hast vowed unto me, by virtue of this letter, and showed him the obligation that he had written with his own blood; wherefore I am come to visit thee and to show thee some of our hellish pastimes, in hope that will draw and confirm thy mind a little more steadfast unto us. Content, quoth Faustus, go to, let me see what pastime you can make.

[There follows a pageant, not of the Seven Deadly Sins, but of grotesquely shaped devils, the last of whom, Mephostophiles, appears first as a dragon, and then transforms himself into the shape of a friar, saying, "Faustus, what wilt thou?"] Saith Faustus, I will that thou teach me to transform myself in like sort as thou and the rest have done: then Lucifer put forth his paw, and gave Faustus a book, saying, Hold, do what thou wilt, which he looking upon, straightways changed himself into a hog, then into a worm, then into a dragon, and finding this for his purpose, it liked him well. Quoth he to Lucifer, And how cometh it that all these filthy forms are in the world? Lucifer answered, They are ordained of God as plagues unto men, and so shalt thou be plagued (quoth he), whereupon came scorpions, wasps, emmets, bees, and gnats, which fell to stinging and biting him [...]; wherefore he cried for help, saying, Mephostophiles my faithful servant, where art thou, help, help I pray thee! Hereat his spirit answered nothing, but Lucifer himself said, Ho ho ho, Faustus, how likest thou the creation of the world? And incontinent it was clear again, and the devils and all the filthy cattle were vanished; only Faustus was left alone, seeing nothing, but hearing the sweetest music that ever he heard before, at which he was so ravished with delight that he forgot the fears he was in before: and it repented him that he had seen no more of their pastime.

EFB, Chap. 20.
[...] on a time he called his spirit Mephostophiles, and said unto him, Bring thou hither unto me thy lord Lucifer, or Belial. He brought him (notwithstanding) one that was called Beelzebub, the which asked Faustus his pleasure. Quoth Faustus, I would know of thee if I may see hell and take a view thereof. That thou shalt (said the devil), and at midnight I will fetch thee.

Doctor Faustus, **Act III, Chorus**

EFB, Chap. 21.
[This chapter takes the form of a letter written by Faustus to a friend.] I being once laid on my bed, and could not sleep for thinking on my calendar and practice, I marveled with myself how it were possible that the firmament should be known and so largely written of men, or whether they write true or false, by their own opinions or supposition, or by due observations and true course of the heavens. Behold, being in these my muses, suddenly I heard [...] a groaning voice which said, Get up, the desire of thy heart, mind, and thought shalt thou see [...] and behold, there stood a wagon, with two dragons before it to draw the same, and all the wagon was of a light burning fire [...]. Hereupon I got me into the wagon, so that the dragons carried me upright into the air [....] on the Tuesday went I out, and on Tuesday seven-nights following I came home again, that is, eight days, in which time I slept not [...]. And farther, my good schoolfellow, I was thus nigh the heavens, where me thought every planet was but as half the earth [...], and as I came down I looked upon the world and the heavens, and me thought that the earth was enclosed in comparison with the firmament, as the yolk of an egg within the white, and me thought that the whole length of the earth was not a span long [...].

Doctor Faustus, III. i

EFB, Chap. 22.

[...] All these kingdoms, provinces, and countries he passed in 25 days, in which time he saw very little that delighted his mind: wherefore he took a little rest at home, and burning in desire to see more at large, and to behold the secrets of each kingdom, he set forward again on his journey upon his swift horse Mephostophiles, and came to Trier, for that he chiefly desired to see this town, and the monuments thereof; but there he saw not many wonders, except one fair palace that belonged unto the bishop, and also a mighty large castle that was built of brick, with three walls and three great trenches, so strong that it was impossible for any prince's power to win it [...]: from whence he departed to Paris, where he liked well the academy; and what place or kingdom soever fell in his mind, the same he visited. He came from Paris to Mentz, where the river of Maine falls into the Rhine; notwithstanding he tarried not long there, but went to Campania in the kingdom of Neapolis, in which he saw an innumerable sort of cloisters, nunneries, and churches, great and high houses of stone, the streets fair and large, and straight forth from one end of the town to the other as a line, and all the pavement of the city was of brick, and the more it rained in the town, the fairer the streets were; there saw he the tomb of Virgil, and the high way that he cut through that mighty hill of stone in one night, the whole length of an English mile [...]. From thence he came to Venice [...]. He wondered not a little at the fairness of Saint Mark's place, and the sumptuous church standing therein called Saint Mark's; how all the pavement was set with coloured stones, and all the rood or loft of the church double gilded over. Leaving this, he came to Padoa, beholding the manner of their academy, which is called the mother or nurse of Christendom; there he heard the doctors, and saw the most monuments in the town, entered his name into the university of the German nation, and wrote himself Doctor Faustus, the insatiable Speculator [...]. Well, forward he went to Rome, which lay, and doth yet lie, on the river Tybris, the which divideth the city in two parts: over the river are four great stone bridges, and upon the one bridge called Ponte S. Angelo is the castle of S. Angelo, wherein are so many great cast pieces as there are days in a year, and such pieces that will shoot seven bullets off with one fire [...]. Hard by this he visited the churchyard of S. Peter's, where he saw the pyramid that Julius Caesar brought out of Africa; it stood in Faustus his time leaning against the church wall of Saint Peter's, but now Papa Sixtus hath erected it in the middle of S. Peter's churchyard

[…]. Other monuments he saw, too many to recite, but amongst the rest he was desirous to see the Pope's palace, and his manner of service at his table, wherefore he and his spirit made themselves invisible, and came into the Pope's court and privy chamber where he was; there saw he many servants attendant on his Holiness, with many a flattering sycophant carrying of his meat […]. Faustus saw notwithstanding in that place those that were like to himself, proud, stout, wilful, gluttons, drunkards, whoremongers, breakers of wedlock, and followers of all manner of ungodly exercises: wherefore he said to his spirit, I thought I had been alone a hog, or pork of the devil's, but he must bear with me a little longer, for these hogs of Rome are already fattened, and fitted to make his roast-meat […]. On a time the Pope would have a feast prepared for the Cardinal of Pavia, and for his first welcome the Cardinal was bidden to dinner: and as he sat at meat, the Pope would ever be blessing and crossing over his mouth. Faustus could suffer it no longer, but up with his fist and smote the Pope on the face, and withal he laughed that the whole house might hear him, yet none of them saw him nor knew where he was. The Pope persuaded his company that it was a damned soul, commanding a mass presently to be said for his delivery out of purgatory, which was done; the Pope sat still at meat, but when the latter mess came in to the Pope's board, Doctor Faustus laid hands thereon, saying: This is mine; and so he took both dish and meat and fled unto the Capitol or Campidoglio, calling his spirit unto him and said: Come, let us be merry, for thou must fetch me some wine, and the cup that the Pope drinks of […]. His spirit, hearing this, departed towards the Pope's chamber, where he found them yet sitting and quaffing: wherefore he took from before the Pope the fairest piece of plate or drinking goblet, and a flagon of wine, and brought it to Faustus; but when the Pope and the rest of his crew perceived they were robbed, and knew not after what sort, they persuaded themselves that it was the damned soul that before had vexed the Pope so, and that smote him on the face, wherefore he sent commandment through all the whole city of Rome, that they should say mass in every church, and ring all the bells for to lay the walking spirit, and to curse him with bell, book, and candle, that so invisibly had misused the Pope's Holiness, with the Cardinal of Pavia, and the rest of their company.

Doctor Faustus, **IV. i**

EFB, Chap. 29.
The Emperor Carolus the fifth of that name was personally with the rest

of his nobles and gentlemen at the town of Inszbruck where he kept his court, unto the which also Doctor Faustus resorted, and being there well known of divers nobles and gentlemen, he was invited into the court to meat, even in the presence of the Emperor: whom when the Emperor saw, he looked earnestly on him, thinking him by his looks to be some wonderful fellow, wherefore he asked one of his nobles whom he should be: who answered that he was called Doctor Faustus. Whereupon the Emperor held his peace until he had taken his repast, after which he called unto him Faustus, into the privy chamber, whither being come, he said unto him: Faustus, I have heard much of thee, that thou art excellent in the black art, and none like thee in mine empire, for men say that thou hast a familiar spirit with thee and that thou canst do what thou list: it is therefore (saith the Emperor) my request of thee that thou let me see a proof of thine experience, and I vow unto thee by the honor of mine imperial crown, none evil shall happen unto thee for so doing. Hereupon Doctor Faustus answered his Majesty, that upon those conditions he was ready in any thing that he could, to do his highness' commandment in what service he would appoint him. Well, then hear what I say (quoth the Emperor). Being once solitary in my house, I called to mind mine elders and ancestors, how it was possible for them to attain unto so great a degree of authority, yea so high, that we the successors of that line are never able to come near. As for example, the great and mighty monarch of the world Alexander magnus was such a lantern and spectacle to all his successors, as the chronicles makes mention of so great riches, conquering and subduing so many kingdoms, the which I and those that follow me (I fear) shall never be able to attain unto: wherefore, Faustus, my hearty desire is that thou wouldst vouchsafe to let me see that Alexander, and his paramour, the which was praised to be so fair; and I pray thee show me them in such sort that I may see their personages, shape, gesture and apparel, as they used in their life time, and that here before my face, to the end that I may say I have my long desire fulfilled, and to praise thee to be a famous man in thine art and experience. Doctor Faustus answered: My most excellent lord, I am ready to accomplish your request in all things, so far forth as I and my spirit are able to perform: yet your Majesty shall know that their dead bodies are not able substantially to be brought before you, but such spirits as have seen Alexander and his paramour alive shall appear unto you in manner and form as they both lived in their most flourishing time: and herewith I hope to please your imperial Majesty. Then Faustus went a little aside to speak to his spirit, but he returned again presently, saying: Now if it please your Majesty you shall see them, yet upon this condition that you demand no question of them, nor speak unto them, which the Emperor agreed unto. Wherewith Doctor Faustus opened the privy chamber door, where presently entered the great and mighty Emperor Alexander magnus, in all things to look upon as if he had been alive, in proportion a strong thick-set man, of a middle stature, black hair, and that both thick and curled head and beard, red cheeks, and a broad face, with eyes like a basilisk; he had on a complete harness burnished and graven, exceeding rich to look upon; and so passing towards the Emperor Carolus, he made low and reverent curtesie: whereat the Emperor Carolus would have stood up to receive and greet him with the like reverence, but Faustus took hold of him and would not permit him to do it. Shortly after Alexander made humble reverence and went out again, and coming to the door his paramour met him; she coming in, she made the Emperor likewise reverence; she was clothed in blue velvet, wrought and embroidered with pearl and gold; she was also excellent fair like milk and blood mixed, tall and slender, with a face round as an apple, and thus she passed certain times up and down the house, which the Emperor marking, said to himself: Now have I seen two persons which my heart hath long wished for to behold, and sure it cannot otherwise be, said he to himself, but that the spirits have changed themselves into these forms, and have not deceived me, calling to his mind the woman that raised the prophet Samuel: and for that the Emperor would be the more satisfied in the matter, he thought, I have heard say that behind her neck she had a great wart or wen, wherefore he took Faustus by the hand without any words, and went to see if it were also to be seen on her or not; but she perceiving that he came to her, bowed down her neck, where he saw a great wart, and hereupon she vanished, leaving the Emperor and the rest well contented.

EFB, Chap. 30.

When Doctor Faustus had accomplished the Emperor's desire in all things as he was requested, he went forth into a gallery, and leaning over a rail to look into the privy garden, he saw many of the Emperor's courtiers walking and talking together, and casting his eyes now this way, now that way, he espied a knight leaning out at a window of the great hall, who was fast asleep (for in those days it was hot); but the person shall be nameless that slept, for he was a knight, although it was done to a little disgrace of the gentleman. It pleased Doctor Faustus, through the help of his spirit Mephostophiles, to firm upon his head as he slept an huge pair of hart's horns, and as the knight awaked thinking to pull in his head, he hit his horns against the glass, that the panes thereof flew about his ears. Think here how this good gentleman was vexed, for he could neither get backward nor forward: which when the Emperor heard all the courtiers laugh, and came forth to see what was happened, the Emperor also when he beheld the knight with so fair a head laughed heartily thereat, and was therewithal well pleased. At last Faustus made him quit of his horns again, but the knight perceived how they came, etc.

1616 text, IV.ii

EFB, Chap. 31.

Doctor Faustus took his leave of the emperor and the rest of the courtiers, at whose departure they were sorry, giving him many rewards and gifts: but being a league and a half from the city he came into a wood, where he beheld the knight that he had jested with at the court with other in harness, mounted on fair palfreys, and running with full charge towards Faustus, but he seeing their intent, ran towards the bushes, and before he came amongst the bushes he returned again, running as it were to meet them that chased him, whereupon suddenly all the bushes were turned into horsemen, which also ran to encounter with the knight and his company, and coming to them, they closed the knight and the rest, and told them that they must pay their ransom before they departed. Whereupon the knight, seeing himself in such distress, besought Faustus to be good to them, which he denied not, but let them loose, yet he so charmed them that everyone, knight and other, for the space of a whole month did wear a pair of goat's horns on their brows, and every palfrey a pair of ox horns on their head: and this was their penance appointed by Faustus, etc.

EFB, Chap. 52.

Doctor Faustus travelled towards Eyszleben, and when he was nigh half the way, he espied seven horsemen, and the chief of them he knew to be the knight to whom he had played a jest in the Emperor's court […]: and when the knight now saw that he had fit opportunity to be revenged of Faustus he ran upon him himself […]: which when Doctor Faustus espied, he vanished away into the wood which was hard by them. But when the knight perceived that he was vanished away, he caused his men to stand still, where as they remained they heard all manner of warlike instruments of music, as drums, flutes, trumpets, and such like, and a certain troop of horsemen running towards them. Then they turned another way, and there also were assaulted on the same side: then another way, and yet they were freshly assaulted, so that which way soever they turned themselves, he was encountered […].

The knight, that knew no other but that he was environed with an host of men (where indeed they were none other than devils), yielded: then Faustus took away his sword, his piece, and horse, with all the rest of his companions. And further he said unto him: Sir, the chief general of our army hath commanded to deal with you according to the law of arms; you shall depart in peace whither you please; and then he gave the knight an horse after the manner, and set him thereon. So he rode, the rest went on foot, until they came to their inn, where being alighted, his page rode on his horse to the water, and presently the horse vanished away, the page being almost sunk and drowned, but he escaped: and coming home, the knight perceived his page so bemired and on foot, asked where his horse was become. Who answered that he was vanished away: which when the knight heard, he said, Of a truth this is Faustus his doing, for he serveth me now as he did before at the court, only to make me a scorn and a laughing-stock.

Doctor Faustus, **IV. ii**

EFB, Chap. 34.
[In the previous chapter Faustus tricks a Jewish money-lender by offering him one of his legs as a surety for a loan. The usurer having thrown the leg away as useless, Faustus announces that he is ready to repay the money. Demanding either his own leg back or one of the usurer's in its place, he finally accepts a sum equal to the loan in return for his illusory dismemberment.] In like manner he served an horse-courser at a fair called Pheiffring, for Doctor Faustus through his cunning had gotten an excellent fair horse, whereupon he rid to the fair, where he had many chap-men that offered him money: lastly, he sold him for 40 dollars, willing him that bought him that in any wise he should not ride him over any water, but the horse-courser marvelled with himself that Faustus bade him ride him over no water. But (quoth he), I will prove, and forthwith he rid him into the river; presently the horse vanished from under him, and he sat on a bundle of straw, in so much that the man was almost drowned. The horse-courser knew well where he lay that had sold him his horse, wherefore he went angrily to his inn, where he found Doctor Faustus fast asleep, and snorting on a bed, but the horse-courser could no longer forbear him, took him by the leg and began to pull him off the bed; but he pulled him so, that he pulled his leg from his body, in so much that the horse-courser fell down backwards in the place, then began Doctor Faustus to cry with an open throat, He hath murdered me. Hereat the horsecourser was afraid, and gave the flight,

thinking none other with himself, but that he had pulled his leg from his body; by this means Doctor Faustus kept his money.

1616 text, IV. v. 20-27

EFB, Chap. 35.

Doctor Faustus being in a town of Germany called Zwickaw, where he was accompanied with many Doctors and Masters, and going forth to walk after supper, they met with a clown that drove a load of hay. Good-even, good fellow, said Faustus to the clown, What shall I give thee to let me eat my belly full of hay? The clown thought with himself, What a mad man is this to eat hay, thought he with himself, thou wilt not eat much. They agreed for three farthings he should eat as much as he could: wherefore Doctor Faustus began to eat, and that so ravenously that all the rest of the company fell a-laughing, blinding so the poor clown, that he was sorry at his heart, for he seemed to have eaten more than the half of his hay, wherefore the clown began to speak him fair, for fear he should have eaten the other half also. Faustus made as though he had pity on the clown, and went his way. When the clown came in place where he would be, he had his hay again as he had before, a full load.

1616 text, IV. vi. 2-5

EFB, Chap. 40.

Doctor Faustus desired the Duke of Anholt to walk a little forth of the court with him, wherefore they went both together into the field, where Doctor Faustus through his skill had placed a mighty castle: which when the Duke saw, he wondered thereat, so did the Duchess, and all the beholders [...]. But as they were in their palace they looked towards the castle, and behold it was all in a flame of fire [....] and thus the castle burned and consumed away clean.

Doctor Faustus, IV. iii

EFB, Chap. 39.

Doctor Faustus on a time came to the Duke of Anholt, the which wel-comed him very courteously; this was in the month of January, where sit-ting at the table, he perceived the Duchess to be with child, and forbearing himself until the meat was taken from the table, and that they brought in the banqueting dishes, said Doctor Faustus to the Duchess, Gracious lady, I have always heard that the great-bellied women do always long for some dainties; I beseech therefore your Grace hide not your mind from me, but tell me what you desire to eat. She answered him: Doctor Faustus, now truly I will not hide from you what my heart doth most desire, namely, that if it were now harvest, I would eat my belly full of ripe grapes and other dainty fruit. Doctor Faustus answered hereupon, Gracious lady, this is a small thing for me to do, for I can do more than this; wherefore he took a plate, and made open one of the casements of the window, holding it forth, where incontinent he had his dish full of all manner of fruits, as red and white grapes, pears, and apples, the which came from out of strange countries; all these he presented the Duchess, saying: Madam, I pray you vouchsafe to taste of this dainty fruit, the which came from a far country, for there the summer is not yet ended. The Duchess thanked Faustus highly, and she fell to her fruit with full appetite. The Duke of Anholt notwithstanding could not withhold to ask Faustus with what reason there were such young fruit to be had at that time of the year. Doctor Faustus told him, May it please your Grace to understand that the year is divided into two circles over the whole world, that when with us it is winter, in the contrary circle it is notwithstanding summer, for in India and Saba there falleth or setteth the sun, so that it is so warm, that they have twice a year fruit: and, gracious lord, I have a swift spirit, the which can in the twinkling of an eye fulfil my desire in any thing, wherefore I sent him into those countries, who hath brought this fruit as you see: whereat the Duke was in great admiration.

1616 text, IV. vi. 102-111

EFB, Chap. 37.
Doctor Faustus went into an inn, wherein were many tables full of clowns, the which were tippling can after can of excellent wine, and to be short, they were all drunken; and as they sat, they so sung and hallowed that one could not hear a man speak for them. This angered Doctor Faustus, wherefore he said to those that had called him in, Mark, my masters, I will show you a merry jest. The clowns continuing still hallowing and singing, he so conjured them that their mouths stood as wide open as it was possible for them to hold them, and never a one of them was able to close his mouth again. By and by the noise was gone, the clowns notwithstanding looked earnestly one upon another, and wist not what was happened; wherefore one by one they went out, and so soon as they came without they were as well as ever they were: but none of them desired to go in any more.

Doctor Faustus, Act V. i. 1-8

EFB, Chap. 56.
Doctor Faustus was now in his 24 and last year, and he had a pretty
stripling to his servant, the which had studied also at the University
of Wittenberg: this youth was very well acquainted with his knaveries
and sorceries, so that he was hated as well for his own knaveries, as
also for his master's, for no man would give him entertainment into
his service, because of his unhappiness, but Faustus. This Wagner was
so well beloved with Faustus, that he used him as his son: for do what
he would his master was always therewith well content. And when the
time drew nigh that Faustus should end, he called unto him a notary
and certain masters the which were his friends and often conversant
with him, in whose presence he gave this Wagner his house and garden.
Item, he gave him in ready money 1600 guilders. Item, a farm. Item,
a gold chain, much plate, and other household stuff. This gave he all
to his servant, and the rest of his time he meant to spend in inns and
students' company, drinking and eating, with other jollity: and thus he
finished his will for that time.

Doctor Faustus, V. i. 9-118

EFB, Chap. 45.
The Sunday following came these students home to Doctor Faustus
his own house, and brought their meat and drink with them: these
men were right welcome guests unto Faustus, wherefore they all fell to
drinking of wine smoothly: and being merry, they began some of them
to talk of the beauty of women, and everyone gave forth his verdict
what he had seen and what he had heard. So one among the rest said, I
never was so desirous of any thing in this world, as to have a sight (if it
were possible) of fair Helena of Greece, for whom the worthy town of
Troie was destroyed [...].

Doctor Faustus answered: For that you are all my friends and are
so desirous to see that famous pearl of Greece, fair Helena [...], I will
therefore bring her into your presence personally, and in the same form
of attire as she used to go when she was in her chiefest flowers and
pleasantest prime of youth [...]. But (said Doctor Faustus) I charge you
all that upon your perils you speak not a word, nor rise up from the
table so long as she is in your presence. And so he went out of the hall,
returning presently again, after whom immediately followed the fair
and beautiful Helena, whose beauty was such that the students were all

amazed to see her, esteeming her rather to be a heavenly than an earthly creature. This lady appeared before them in a most sumptuous gown of purple velvet, richly embroidered; her hair hanged down loose as fair as the beaten gold, and of such length that it reached down to her hams, with amorous coal-black eyes, a sweet and pleasant round face, her lips red as a cherry, her cheeks of rose all colour, her mouth small, her neck as white as the swan, tall and slender of personage; and in sum, there was not one imperfect part in her: she looked round about her with a rolling hawk's eye, a smiling and wanton countenance, which near hand inflamed the hearts of the students, but that they persuaded themselves she was a spirit, wherefore such fantasies passed away lightly with them: and thus fair Helena and Doctor Faustus went out again [...]. The students departed from Faustus' home everyone to his house, but they were not able to sleep the whole night for thinking on the beauty of fair Helena. Wherefore a man may see that the devil blindeth and inflameth the heart with lust oftentimes, that men fall in love with harlots, nay even with furies, which afterward cannot lightly be removed.

EFB, Chap. 48.

A good Christian, an honest and virtuous old man, a lover of the holy scriptures, who was neighbor unto Doctor Faustus, when he perceived that many students had their recourse in and out unto Doctor Faustus, he suspected his evil life, wherefore like a friend he invited Doctor Faustus to supper unto his house, unto the which he agreed; and having ended their banquet, the old man began with these words. My loving friend and neighbour Doctor Faustus, I have to desire of you a friendly and Christian request, beseeching you that you will vouchsafe not to be angry with me, but friendly resolve me in my doubt, and take my poor inviting in good part. To whom Doctor Faustus answered: My loving neighbour, I pray you say your mind. Then began the old patron to say: My good neighbour, you know in the beginning how that you have defied God, and all the host [of] heaven, and given your soul to the devil, wherewith you have incurred God's high displeasure, and are become from a Christian far worse than a heathen person: Oh consider what you have done, it is not only the pleasure of the body, but the safety of the soul that you must have respect unto: of which if you be careless, then are you cast away, and shall remain in the anger of almighty God. But yet is it time enough, Doctor Faustus, if you repent and call unto the Lord for mercy, as we have example in the Acts of the Apostles, the eight Chap. of Simon in Samaria, who was led out of the way, affirming that he was *Simon homo sanctus*. This man was notwithstanding in the end converted, after that he had heard the sermon of Philip, for he was baptized, and saw his sins, and repented. Likewise I beseech you, good brother Doctor Faustus, let my rude sermon be unto you a conversion; and forget the filthy life that you have led; repent, ask mercy, and live. For Christ saith, Come unto me all ye that are weary and heavy laden, and I will refresh you. And in Ezechiel: I desire not the death of a sinner, but rather that he convert and live. Let my words, good brother Faustus, pierce into your adamant heart, and desire God for his son Christ his sake to forgive you. Wherefore have you so long lived in your devilish practices, knowing that in the Old and New Testament you are forbidden, and that men should not suffer any such to live, neither have any conversation with them, for it is an abomination unto the Lord; and that such persons have no part in the Kingdom of God? All this while Doctor Faustus heard him very attentively, and replied: Father, your persuasions like me wondrous well, and I thank you with all my heart for your good will and counsel, promising you so far as I may to follow your discipline: whereupon he took his leave. And being come home, he laid him very pensive on his bed, bethinking himself of the words of the good old man, and in a manner began to repent that he had given his soul to the devil, intending to deny all that he had promised unto Lucifer. Continuing in these cogitations, suddenly his spirit appeared unto him, clapping him upon the head, and wrung it as though he would have pulled the head from the shoulders, saying unto him: Thou knowest, Faustus, that thou hast given thyself body and soul unto my lord Lucifer, and hast vowed thyself an enemy unto God and unto all men; and now thou beginnest to harken to an old doting fool which persuadeth thee as it were unto God, when indeed it is too late, for that thou art the devil's, and he hath good power presently to fetch thee: wherefore he hath sent me unto thee, to tell thee that seeing thou hast sorrowed for what thou hast done, begin again and write another writing with thine own blood; if not, then will I tear thee all to pieces. Hereat Doctor Faustus was sore afraid, and said: My Mephostophiles, I will write again what thou wilt [...].

EFB, Chap. 49.
[...] And presently upon the making of this letter, he became so great an enemy unto the poor old man that he sought his life by all means possible; but this godly man was strong in the holy Ghost, that he could not be vanquished by any means [...]. Thus doth God defend the hearts of all honest Christians that betake themselves under his tuition.

EFB, Chap. 55.

To the end that this miserable Faustus might fill the lust of his flesh, and live in all manner of voluptuous pleasures, it came in his mind [...] in the 23 year past of his time, that he had a great desire to lie with fair Helena of Greece, especially her whom he had seen and showed unto the students of Wittenberg, wherefore he called unto him his spirit Mephostophiles, commanding him to bring him the fair Helena, which he did. Whereupon he fell in love with her, and made her his common concubine and bedfellow, for she was so beautiful and delightful a piece that he could not be one hour from her, if he should therefore have suffered death, she had so stolen away his heart [...].

Doctor Faustus, V. ii

EFB, Chap. 63.
An Oration of Faustus to the students.
My trusty and well-beloved friends, the cause why I have invited you into this place is this: forasmuch as you have known me this many years, in what manner of life I have lived, practising all manner of conjurations and wicked exercises, the which I have obtained through the help of the devil, into whose devilish fellowship they have brought me, the which use the like art and practice, urged by the detestable provocation of my flesh, my stiff-necked and rebellious will, with my filthy infernal thoughts, the which were ever before me, pricking me forward so earnestly, that I must perforce have the consent of the devil to aid me in my devices. And to the end I might the better bring my purpose to pass, to have the devil's aid and furtherance, which I never have wanted in mine actions, I have promised unto him at the end and accomplishing of 24 years, both body and soul, to do therewith at his pleasure: and this day, this dismal day, those 24 years are fully expired, for night beginning, my hour-glass is at an end, the direful finishing whereof I carefully expect: for out of all doubt this night he will fetch me, to whom I have given myself in recompense of his service, both body and soul, and twice confirmed writings with my proper blood. Now have I called you, my well-beloved lords, friends, brethren, and fellows, before that fatal hour to take my friendly farewell, to the end that my departing may not hereafter be hidden from you, beseeching you herewith, courteous and loving lords and brethren, not to take in evil part any thing done by me, but with friendly commendations to salute all my friends and companions wheresoever, desiring both you and them, if ever I have trespassed against your minds in any thing, that you would all heartily forgive me: and as for those lewd practices the

which this full 24 years I have followed, you shall hereafter find them in writing: and I beseech you, let this my lamentable end to the residue of your lives be a sufficient warning, that you have God always before your eyes, praying unto him that he would ever defend you from the temptation of the devil and all his false deceits, not falling altogether from God, as I wretched and ungodly damned creature have done, having denied and defied baptism, the sacraments of Christ's body, God himself, all heavenly powers, and earthly men; yea, I have denied such a God, that desireth not to have one lost. Neither let the evil fellowship of wicked companions mislead you as it hath done me: visit earnestly and oft the church, war and strive continually against the devil with a good and steadfast belief on God and Jesus Christ, and use your vocation in holiness. Lastly, to knit up my troubled oration, this is my friendly request, that you would to rest, and let nothing trouble you; also if you chance to hear any noise, or rumbling about the house, be not therewith afraid, for there shall no evil happen unto you; also I pray you arise not out of your beds. But above all things I entreat you, if you hereafter find my dead carcase, convey it unto the earth, for I die both a good and bad Christian: a good Christian, for that I am heartily sorry, and in my heart always pray for mercy, that my soul may be delivered; a bad Christian, for that I know the devil will have my body, and that would I willingly give him so he would leave my soul in quiet: wherefore I pray you that you would depart to bed, and so I wish you a quiet night, which unto me notwithstanding will be horrible and fearful.

This oration or declaration was made by Doctor Faustus, and that with a hearty and resolute mind, to the end he might not discomfort them: but the students wondered greatly thereat, that he was so blinded for knavery, conjuration, and such like foolish things to give his body and soul unto the devil: for they loved him entirely, and never suspected any such thing before he had opened his mind to them: wherefore one of them said unto him: Ah, friend Faustus, what have you done to conceal this matter so long from us? We would by the help of good divines, and the grace of God, have brought you out of this net, and have torn you out of the bondage and chains of Satan, whereas now we fear it is too late, to the utter ruin of your body and soul. Doctor Faustus answered, I durst never do it, although I often minded to settle myself unto godly people, to desire counsel and help, as once mine old neighbour counselled me, that I should follow his learning and leave all my conjurations, yet when I was minded to amend, and to follow that good man's counsel, then came the devil and would have had me away, as this night he is like to do, and said so soon as I turned again to God he would despatch me altogether. Thus, even thus (good gentlemen, and my dear friends), was I enthralled in that satanical band, all good desires drowned, all piety banished, all purpose of amendment utterly exiled, by the tyrannous threatenings of my deadly enemy. But when the students heard his words, they gave him counsel to do naught else but call upon God, desiring him for the love of his sweet son Jesus Christ's sake to have mercy upon him, teaching him this form of prayer: O God be merciful unto me, poor and miserable sinner, and enter not into judgment with me, for no flesh is able to stand before thee. Although, O Lord, I must leave my sinful body unto the devil, being by him deluded, yet thou in mercy mayest preserve my soul.

This they repeated unto him, yet it could take no hold, but even as Cain he also said his sins were greater than God was able to forgive; for all his thought was on his writing, he meant he had made it too filthy in writing it with his own blood. The students and the other that were there, when they had prayed for him, they wept, and so went forth, but Faustus tarried in the hall [...].

EFB, Chap. 59.
This sorrowful time drawing near so troubled Doctor Faustus, that he began to write his mind [...] in manner as followeth. Ah Faustus, thou sorrowful and woeful man, now must thou go to the damned company in unquenchable fire, whereas thou mightest have had the joyful immortality of the soul, the which thou now hast lost. Ah gross understanding and wilful will, what seizeth on my limbs other than a robbing of my life? Bewail with me my sound and healthful body, wit and soul, bewail with me my senses, for you have had your part and pleasure as well as I. Oh envy and disdain, how have you crept both at once into me, and now for your sakes I must suffer all these torments? Ah, whither is pity and mercy fled? Upon what occasion hath heaven repaid me with this reward by sufferance to suffer me to perish? Wherefore was I created a man? The punishment that I see prepared for me of my self now must I suffer. Ah miserable wretch, there is nothing in this world to show me comfort: then woe is me, what helpeth my wailing?

EFB, Chap. 60.
Another complaint of Doctor Faustus.
Oh poor, woeful, and weary wretch: oh sorrowful soul of Faustus, now art thou in the number of the damned, for now must I wait for unmeasurable pains of death, yea far more lamentable than ever yet any creature hath suffered. Ah senseless, wilful and desperate forgetfulness!

O cursed and unstable life! O blind and careless wretch, that so hast abused thy body, sense and soul! O foolish pleasure, into what a weary labyrinth hast thou brought me, blinding mine eyes in the clearest day? Ah weak heart! O troubled soul, where is become thy knowledge to comfort thee? O pitiful weariness! O desperate hope, now shall I never more be thought upon! Oh, care upon carelessness, and sorrows on heaps: Ah grievous pains that pierce my panting heart, whom is there now that can deliver me? Would God that I knew where to hide me, or into what place to creep or fly. Ah, woe, woe is me, be where I will, yet am I taken. Herewith poor Faustus was so sorrowfully troubled, that he could not speak or utter his mind any further.

EFB, Chap. 61.

How Doctor Faustus bewailed to think on hell [...]
Now thou Faustus, damned wretch, how happy wert thou if as an un-reasonable beast thou mightest die without soul? So shouldest thou not feel any more doubts. But now the devil will take thee away both body and soul, and set thee in an unspeakable place of darkness [...]. Ah thou perpetual damned wretch, now art thou thrown into the everlasting fiery lake that never shall be quenched, there must I dwell in all manner of wailing, sorrow, misery, pain, torment, grief, howling, sighing, sobbing, blubbering, running of eyes, stinking at nose, gnashing of teeth, fear to the ears, horror to the conscience, and shaking both of hand and foot. Ah, that I could carry the heavens on my shoulders, so that there were time at last to quit me of this everlasting damnation! [....] Where is my hold? knowledge dare I not trust: and for a soul to God-wards that have I not, for I shame to speak unto him: if I do, no answer shall be made me, but he will hide his face from me, to the end that I should not behold the joys of the chosen. What mean I then to complain where no help is? No, I know no hope resteth in my groanings. I have desired that it should be so, and God hath said Amen to my misdoings: for now I must have shame to comfort me in my calamities.

1616 text, V. iii

EFB, Chap. 63.
It happened between twelve and one o'clock at midnight, there blew a mighty storm of wind against the house, as though it would have blown the foundation thereof out of his place. Hereupon the students began to fear, and got out of their beds, comforting one another, but they would

not stir out of the chamber: and the host of the house ran out of doors, thinking the house would fall. The students lay near unto that hall wherein Doctor Faustus lay, and they heard a mighty noise and hissing, as if the hall had been full of snakes and adders: with that the door flew open wherein Doctor Faustus was, then he began to cry for help, saying: Murther, murther, but it came forth with half a voice hollowly; shortly after they heard him no more. But when it was day, the students, that had taken no rest that night, arose and went into the hall in the which they left Doctor Faustus, where notwithstanding they found no Faustus, but all the hall lay besprinkled with blood, his brains cleaving to the wall: for the devil had beaten him from one wall against another; in one corner lay his eyes, in another his teeth, a pitiful and fearful sight to behold. Then began the students to bewail and weep for him, and sought for his body in many places: lastly they came into the yard, where they found his body lying on the horse dung, most monstrously torn, and fearful to behold, for his head and all his joints were dashed in pieces.

The forenamed students and masters that were at his death, have obtained so much, that they buried him in the village where he was so grievously tormented. After the which, they returned to Wittenberg […].

Doctor Faustus, Epilogue

EFB, Chap. 63.
And thus ended the whole history of Doctor Faustus his conjuration, and other acts that he did in his life; out of the which example every Christian may learn, but chiefly the stiff-necked and high-minded may thereby learn to fear God, and to be careful of their vocation, and to be at defiance with all devilish works, as God hath most precisely forbidden, to the end we should not invite the devil as a guest, nor give him place as that wicked Faustus hath done: for here we have a fearful example of his writing, promise, and end, that we may remember him: that we go not astray, but take God always before our eyes, to call alone upon him, and to honour him all the days of our life, with heart and hearty prayer, and with all our strength and soul to glorify his holy name, defying the devil and all his works, to the end we may remain with Christ in all endless joy: Amen, Amen, that wish I unto every Christian heart, and God's name to be glorified. Amen.

Appendix C: Excerpts from Henricus Cornelius Agrippa, De incertitudine et vanitate scientiarum et artium atque excellentia verbi dei declamatio *(1530), and* De occulta philosophia libri tres *(1533)*

[Henricus Cornelius Agrippa (1486-1535), whom Marlowe's *Doctor Faustus* aspires to emulate (I. i. 118-19), was a contemporary of the historical Doctor Faustus—with whose name his was frequently paired after the mid-sixteenth century by demonologists and polemicists against magic. Agrippa's *De occulta philosophia* is an encyclopaedic survey of magical beliefs and practices which also expounds a syncretic, magical form of Christianity: he finds in the emphasis of Hermetic, Cabalistic and Neoplatonic writings upon rebirth and deification a key to the saving message of the canonical scriptures. This book, which by implicitly challenging the uniqueness of the Judaeo-Christian tradition effectively decenters it, earned Agrippa the reputation of having been (as Jean Bodin wrote in 1581), "le plus grand Sorcier qui fut oncques de son aage" (fol. 219v).

Agrippa's other major work, *De vanitate*, is a high-spirited attack upon all human arts and sciences, from logic to courtly place-seeking, and from whore-mongering to scholastic theology. Despite the evangelical posture which gives shape to its satire, and its rejection of the more obviously demonic magical practices, this book was suspected of having been intended as a kind of ground-clearing operation for the magical doctrines espoused in *De occulta philosophia*. Such suspicions could find support in the fact that Agrippa praises natural and celestial magic; moreover, the same conflation of Christian and Hermetic notions of rebirth and deification that animates Book III of *De occulta philosophia* is also evident in *De vanitate* (Keefer 1988: 614-53).

Jean Calvin in his *De scandalis* (1550) denounced Agrippa as an atheist and a Lucianic mocker of religious truths; and in 1584 André Thevet lamented that there was "no corner or secret of any discipline where he had not nosed about and there vomited some overflow of his mortal poison" (ii. fol. 544). While Agrippa claimed to be "professing divinity," he was thus believed to have done so only "in show" (*Doctor Faustus*, I. i. 3). The relationship between Agrippa's two major works seen by some sixteenth-century readers is arguably parodied by the pattern of Faustus's first soliloquy, in which a sophistical demolition of the orthodox academic disciplines, including theology, is succeeded by a rhapsodic praise of magic. The connection between these works is complicated by the fact that Agrippa wrote an early version of *De occulta philosophia* in 1510, published *De vanitate* in 1530, and then in 1533 had printed a much expanded version of *De occulta philosophia*.

The standard edition of *De occulta philosophia* is that of Vittoria Perrone Compagni (1992). Several of Agrippa's works are available in English translations: *Three Books of Occult Philosophy*, ed. Donald Tyson (1993, based on James Freake's 1651 translation); Catherine Dunne's edition (1974) of the 1569 Sanford translation of *De vanitate*; and Albert Rabil's translation of Agrippa's *Declamation on the Nobility and Preeminence of the Female Sex* (1996). Important critical studies include Charles Nauert's biography, Paola Zambelli's many articles on Agrippa, and Gary Tomlinson's *Music in Renaissance Magic* (1993), ch. 2.

The excerpts from *De occulta philosophia* given here appear in what after many years I have come to think of as my own translation (though its clumsier features are certainly mine, any more elegant turns of phrase are in fact A. D. Nuttall's); the others are taken (with spelling and punctuation modernized, and with certain translator's errors amended) from James Sanford's translation, *Of the Vanitie and Uncertaintie of Artes and Sciences* (1569).]

Of the Vanity

Of the Vanity, *Translator's Preface*
[...] The author hereof walked in darkness, and together with his excellency of wit, he declareth in some places his blindness of understanding [...]. Some peradventure will object that it is impossible for so excellent a man to err and be deceived, who in all learnings (as appeareth) was conversant and well-exercised: unto whom may be said that which Tully writeth in the first of his *Offices*, where he saith: To be deceived, to slide, to err, and to be beguiled is man's property [...]. Socrates, who by the oracle of Apollo was judged the wisest of his age, confessed that he knew nothing at all, beside a certain slender discipline of love. If Socrates knew so few things, then cannot this author know all things, whose knowledge, though it were great, yet greatly he erred, and no marvel, for he gave his mind to unlawful arts, contrary to the laws of God and man. For it is said, and his works testify the same, that he exercised the art magic, and therein far excelled all other of his time. But in the end, his wicked knowledge was the cause of his miserable death: for as John Manlius, a German writer, doth record, when he was at the point of death he called to him a dog which went about with him,

and spake to him with these words: *Abi a me perdita bestia, quae me per-didisti*: that is, Depart from me, thou wicked beast which hast destroyed me. So forthwith the dog, departing from him, cast himself headlong into a river; this dog was without doubt a devil of hell [...].

Of the Vanity, *Author's Preface*
Will not this my enterprise (studious reader) seem unto thee valiant and adventurous, and almost comparable to the attempts of Hercules, to take up weapons against all that giant force of sciences and arts, and to challenge into the field all these most hardy hunters of arts and sciences? [....] to draw Cerberus bound in chains, to take away the golden apples of Hesperides, and many other noble adventures of this sort which were done by Hercules with great labors, and with no less danger, being of no less travail than peril to overcome these monsters of studies and schools. And I well perceive what a bloody battle I have to fight with them hand to hand, and how dangerous this fight will be, seeing that I am beset on every side with an army of so mighty enemies. O with how many engines will they assail me, and with how many shames and villainies will they load me? [....] The obstinate Logicians will cast against me infinite darts of syllogisms; the long-tongued Sophisters, which wrest to every part their talk, with intricate snares of words, like a bridle, will stop my mouth [...]. The Musicians with their many tunes will [make] me a laughing-stock through the streets, and with jarring sounds and unpleasant ringing of pans, basins and dishes will trouble me more than they are wont at their weddings which be twice married [...]; the dancing player will make a tragedy of me upon his bawdy stage [...]. The vain worker in the art Perspective will engrave and depaint me more brutish and deformed than an ape, or Thersites; the wandering Cosmographers will banish me beyond Moscovie and the frozen sea; the Daedalean builder, with his most mighty engines, will privily undermine me, and compel me to wander in confused labyrinths [...]. The fatal Astrologers will threaten me to be hanged, and with the unstable turning of the heavens will forbid me paradise; the threatening Diviners will wish me all evil; the unreasonable Physiognomer will defame me for a cold man, and of small force in the act of venery [...]. The monstrous Gunner will cast against me the reveng-ing flames of Jupiter, and the fire of lightning. The Interpreter of dark dreams will fear me with his horrible night sprites; the furious Prophet will deceive me with his doubtful oracle; the monstrous Magicians will transform me, as it were another Apuleius or Lucian, into an ass, yet not of gold, but perchance of dirt. The black Necromancer will persecute me with spirits and devils; the church-robbing Theurgist will offer my head

to the crows, or perhaps to the jakes; the circumcised Cabalists will wish me their foreskin; the vain and foolish Juggler will make me appear either headless or without stones. The contentious Philosophers will tear me in pieces with most repugnant opinions; the juggling Pythagoreans will make me go into a dog, and a crocodile [...]. The politic Lawmaker will forbid me to bear office in the public weal; the voluptuous Prince will banish me the court; the ambitious Nobleman will put me out of the senate; the brainless people will exclaim on me in the streets [...]. The covetous Priests will excommunicate me; the Hooded Masquers and spiteful Hypocrites will rail against me out of the pulpit; the almighty Bishops will reserve my sins for everlasting fire [...]. The perbrake [i.e., spewing] Physicians will embrue me with urine and ordure, of the which the babbling Logicianer, disputing of sickness, will take from me a remedy in season; the rash Practicer, with a doubtful experiment, will put me in danger of death; the subtle old-beaten Physician, deferring the remedies, will prolong the sickness for his own avail [...]. The lofty Lawyers will accuse me of treason; the arrogant Canonists will excommunicate me with cruel cursings; the brawling Advocates will bring against me five hundred accusations [...]. The obstinate Divine Sophistical Doctors will call me heretic, or compel me to worship their idols; our grim Masters will enforce me to recant [...].

Now, reader, thou perceivest through how many dangers I shall pass. Yet I hope easily to escape these assaults if thou, supporting the truth, and setting envy apart, shalt come with a gentle mind to the reading of these things. Beside this, I have the Word of God wherewith to defend myself, which boldly I will hold against these for a buckler and shield [...]. And I would have thee understand that I wrote not these things for hatred, for ambition, for deceit, or for error: neither a wicked desire, nor the arrogancy of a lewd mind hath moved me to write this, but the cause of all men, most just and righteous, because I see many [wax] proud in human learning and knowledge, that therefore they do despise and loathe the sacred and canonical scriptures of the holy Ghost as rude and rustical, because they have no ornaments of words, force of syllogisms, and affectate persuasions, nor the strange doctrine of the philosophers: but are simply grounded upon the operation of virtue, and upon bare faith [...]. We see other also, the which although they seem to themselves very godly, notwithstanding will prove and confirm the Laws with the decrees of philosophers, attributing more to them than to the holy prophets of God, or to the evangelists and apostles, they being as contrary to them as white is to black. Furthermore, in many, and almost in all places of study, a perverse custom and damnable use is grown, in that they bind with an oath the scholars which they receive to teach, never to speak against Aristotle, Boethius, Thomas, Albert, or against any other of their scholars, being accounted as a god, from whom if a man differ a finger's breadth in thought immediately they will call him heretic, a sinful person, an offender of godly ears, and worthy to be burned. These then so unadvised giants and enemies of the holy scriptures are to be assaulted, and their fortresses and castles ransacked; and to declare how great the blindness of men is, with so many sciences and arts, and with so many masters and authors, always to err from the knowledge of the truth: and how great a rashness and presumptuous arrogancy it is to prefer the schools of philosophers before the Church of Christ, and to set before, and make equivalent, the opinions of men with the Word of God. Finally, what a wicked tyranny it is, to bind the wits of students to certain appointed authors, and to take from scholars the liberty to search and trace out truth. All which things, sith they are so apparent that they cannot be denied, I must have pardon if to any I shall seem to have declaimed somewhat largely, and peradventure sharply, against any kind of learning, or against their professors.

Cap. 1 (Of Sciences in General)
It is an ancient, and almost an agreeable and common opinion of all the philosophers, by the which they think that every science doth bring unto man some divinity, according to the capacity and value of them both, so that oftentimes, beyond the limits of humanity, they may be reckoned among the fellowship of the gods. From thence arose the divers and infinite commendations of sciences [...]. Notwithstanding I, being persuaded with other kind of reasons, am of opinion that there can chance to the life and salvation of our souls nothing more hurtful and pestilent than these arts and sciences [...], pardon me if herein I disagree from others, until I shall begin this mine opinion at every science by the order of the letters, not only with common arguments, and taken from the outward show of things, but with very strong reasons, and such as are sifted out of the inward bowels of things: not with any subtle eloquence of Demosthenes or Chrysippus (the which should be a shameful thing for me, professing divinity) [...]: for that a professor of the holy scripture ought to speak properly, and not eloquently, and to search out the verity of the matter, and not the garnishing of speech [...].

And that I may not suffer you to give ear in vain, I will now set before your eyes with what footing and tracing (as though with hounds) I have found out this my said opinion. If first I shall admonish you that all sciences be as well naught as good, and that they bring to us, above the limit of humanity, none other blessing of the deity but that perchance which that ancient serpent promised to our first parents, saying, Ye shall be as gods, and shall know good and ill. He shall then vaunt himself in this serpent which boasteth himself to have knowledge, as we read indeed that the heretics Ophiti did, which worshipped the serpent in their sacrifices, saying, That he hath brought the knowledge of virtue into paradise. With these agreeth the history of Plato that a certain spirit called Theutus, enemy to mankind, was the first deviser of sciences no less hurtful than profitable: as very wisely said Thamus, king of Egypt, reasoning of the inventors of sciences and letters.

[...] And so large is the liberty of the truth, and the largeness thereof so free, that it cannot be perceived with the speculations of any science, nor with any strait judgment of the senses, nor with any arguments of the art of logic, nor with any evident proof, with no syllogisms of demonstration, nor with any discourse of man's reason, but with faith only [...]. For every science hath in it some certain principles, which must be believed, and cannot by any means be declared: which if any will obstinately deny, the philosophers have not wherewith to dispute against him, and immediately they will say that there is no disputation against him which denieth the principles: or else will constrain him to flee unto some other things, without the limits of learning: As if any (say they) shall deny the fire is hot, let him be cast into the fire, and let him be demanded what he feeleth: so finally of philosophers they are made tormenters and hangmen, for they will by force compel us to confess that which they should teach by reason [...].

Cap. 7 (Of Logic)
[...] If therefore the principles of demonstration be very ill understood, and the circumstance shall not be admitted, certes hereof can be had none but very slender and uncertain knowledge: for we must believe things showed by certain weak principles, to the which we agree either for the forepassed authority of the wise, as it were to known limits, or else with experience we allow them by the senses. For every knowledge (as they say) hath his beginning of the senses, and the proof of true speeches (as Averroes saith) is that they agree with sensible things. And that thing is better known and truer whereupon most minds and senses do agree. Through the knowledge then of sensible things we are led by the hand to all such things that may be known by us. But sith that oftentimes all the senses are deceived, doubtless they cannot prove to us any certain experience. Furthermore, sith that the senses cannot attain to the intellectual nature, and the causes of the inferior things (of which their natures, ef-

fects, and properties or rather passions should be declared) by the consent of all men be altogether unknown to our senses, is it not manifest that the way of the truth is shut up from the senses? Wherefore all these derivations and sciences which are fast rooted in the senses shall be uncertain, erroneous, and deceitful. What then is the profit of logic, and what fruit cometh of that learned demonstration, by principles and proofs, to the which we shall of necessity assent as it were to known limits?

Cap. 42 (Of Natural Magic)
Men think that natural magic is nothing else but a singular power of natural knowledges which therefore they call the greatest profoundness of natural philosophy, and absolute perfection thereof [...], which with the aid of natural virtues, according to the mutual and convenient applying of them, doth publish works exceeding all the capacity of admiration: the which magic was much used of the Egyptians and of the Indians, where there was abundance of herbs, of stones, and other things thereunto belonging. They say [...] that the magicians were of this sort which went to worship Christ when he was born, visiting him with gifts, which the interpreters of the gospel do expound the philosophy of the Chaldees; such as were Hiarchus among the Brachmans, Thespion among the Gymnosophists, Buda among the Babylonians, Numa Pompilius among the Romans, Zamolxides among the Thracians, Abbaris among the Hyperboreans, Hermes among the Egyptians, Zoroastes son of Oromasus among the Persians. For the Indians, Ethiopians, Chaldeans, and Persians were very excellent in this magic [...].

Natural magic then is that which, having intentively beheld the forces of all natural things, and celestial, and with curious search sought out their order, doth in such sort publish abroad the hidden and secret powers of nature, coupling the inferior things with the qualities of the superior, as it were certain enticements, by a natural joining of them together, that thereof oftentimes do arise marvellous miracles, not so much by art as nature, whereunto this art doth proffer herself a servant when she worketh these things. For the magicians, as very diligent searchers of nature, bringing the things which be prepared by nature, applying and setting active things to passive, very oftentimes before the time by nature appointed do bring forth effects which of the common sort be accounted miracles [...]: as if a man in the month of March would cause roses to spring, and ripe grapes [...], and greater things than these, as clouds, rain, thunder, beasts of divers sorts, and infinite transformations of things, of which kind Roger Bacon doth boast that he hath done many with pure and natural magic. Of the works thereof

have written Zoroastes, Hermes, Evantes King of the Arabians [...].
But of the later writers few have written in natural magic, and they
few things: as Albert, Arnold of Villanova, Raymond Lully, Bacon,
Apponus, and the author of the book to Alphonsus published under the
name of *Picatrix*, which notwithstanding intermeddleth much superstition with natural magic, which others have done also.

Cap. 43 (Of Mathematical Magic)
There be moreover other very prudent and adventurous searchers of nature which, without natural virtues, with the mathematical disciplines
alone, the influences of the heavens being put thereto, do promise that
they are able to bring forth things like to the works of nature, as bodies
that go and speak, which for all that have not the virtues of the soul:
as the wooden dove of Archytas was, which flew, and the image of
Mercury that spake, and the brazen head forged by Albert the great,
which as it is said did speak [...]. I suppose that is spoken of these skills,
which Plato saith in the [tenth] book of his *Laws*: Men have an art,
whereby they brought forth certain latter things, not partaking of the
verity, and divinity, but made certain semblances much like to themselves: and the magicians, very presumptuous persons, have gone so far
to do all things, especially with the favor of that ancient and terrible
serpent the promiser of sciences, that like to him, as apes they endeavor
to counterfeit God and nature.

Cap. 44 (Of Witching Magic)
[...] it is no doubt that magicians alone also with words and affections
and other like things oftentimes do bring forth some marvellous effect
not only in themselves, but also in strange things: all which operations
they suppose to spread abroad upon other things the force engraffed
in them and to draw these unto them [...]: and so by this orderly and
linked composition of things Iamblichus, Proclus and Sinesius, according to the opinion of the magicians, do confirm that not only the natural
and celestial gifts but the intellectual and heavenly also may be received
from above: the which Proclus confesseth in the book *Of Sacrifice and
Magic*; to wit, that by such consent of things magicians were wont to
bind spirits. For some of them are fallen into so great a madness that
they believe that with divers constellations of stars rightly observed by
distance of time, and with a certain order of proportions, by the consent
of heavenly sprites an image made may receive the sprite of life, and
understanding, whereby he giveth answer to them that will demand any
thing, and revealeth the secrets of hidden verity. Hereby it is manifest

that this natural magic sometimes inclineth to Goecie and Theurgy; oftentimes it is entangled in the crafts and errors of the devils of hell.

Cap. 45 (Of Goecie and Necromancie)

The parts of ceremonial magic be Goecie and Theurgy. Goecie is grounded upon the intercourse of wicked sprites made with the rites of detestable curiosity, with unlawful conjurations, and with defensive prayers, banished and accursed by the decrees of all laws. Of this kind be they which at this day we call necromancers and enchanters [...] and at this day also there are books carried about with feigned titles under the names of Adam, Abel, Enoch, Abraham, Solomon [...], which books yet do openly declare to him that doth subtly consider the order of their precepts, the usage of their ceremonies, their kind of words and characters, their order of construction, their foolish phrase, to contain nothing else but mere trifles and falsehood, and to be made in these latter times by men ignorant in ancient magic, most damnable artificers of damnation [...].

Cap. 46 (Of Theurgy)

Many think that Theurgy is not prohibited, as who saith it were governed by good angels, and by the divine power, whereas yet oftentimes under the name of God and the angels it is bound with wicked deceits of the devils, for not only with natural forces, but with certain solemnities and ceremonies also, we win and draw unto us heavenly things, and through them the divine virtues [...]. The greatest part of all ceremonies consisteth in keeping cleanliness, first of the mind, afterward of the body and of the things which are about the body [...]. Notwithstanding sometimes the unclean spirits and the deceiving powers do require also this cleanness, that they may be worshipped and adored for gods, and therefore we ought here to be very circumspect, whereof largely we have spoken in our books *Of Hidden Philosophy* [i.e., *De occulta philosophia*]. But Porphyry, who doth much dispute of this theurgy or magic of things divine, doth finally conclude that with theurgical consecrations man's mind may be made apt to receive sprites and angels, and to see the gods, but that by this art there may any man come to God, he altogether denieth it [...].

Cap. 47 (Of Cabala)

[...] But as I doubt not that God hath revealed to Moses and other of the prophets many mysteries not to be disclosed to the ignorant people, which were covered under the bark of the words of the Law, so I know that this art Cabala, whereof the Hebrews do so much boast, and I with great labour have in time past searched out, to be nothing else but a mere agreement of superstition and a certain theurgical magic [...]. Therefore this Jewish Cabala is nothing else but a certain most pestilent superstition, wherewith at their will they do gather, divide, and transpose the words, names, and letters dispersed in the scripture, and making one of another do unbind the members of the truth [...]. From this Jewish heap of Cabalistic superstition proceeded (I suppose) the Ophites, the Gnostics, and Valentinian heretics [...].

Cap. 48 (Of Juggling)
But let us return to magic, whereof the juggler's skill is a part also; that is, illusions, which are only done according to the outward appearance: with these the magicians do show vain visions, and with juggling casts do play many miracles, and cause dreams [...]. By these things then which are already spoken, it is evident that magic is nothing else but a containing of idolatry, astrology, and superstitious physic. Of the magicians also is sprung in the Church a great rout of heretics, which as Iamnes and Iambres have rebelled against Moses, so they have resisted the apostolic truth [cf. 2 *Tim*: 3: 8]: the chief of these was Simon [the] Samaritan, who for this art had an image erected at Rome in the time of Claudius Caesar with this inscription: To Simon the holy God. His blasphemies be written at large by Clement, Eusebius, and Irenaeus. Out of this Simon, as out of a seed-plot of all heresies, have proceeded by many successions the monstrous Ophites, the filthy Gnostics, the wicked Valentinians, the Cerdonians, the Marcionists, the Montanians, and many other heretics, for gain and vain glory speaking lies against God, availing nor profiting men, but deceiving and bringing them to ruin and destruction; and they which believe in them shall be confounded in God's judgment. I being also a young man wrote of magical matters three books in a sufficient large volume, which I have entitled *Of Hidden Philosophy*, in which books whatsoever was then done amiss through curious youth, now being more advised I will that it be recanted with this retractation, for I have in times past consumed very much time and substance in these vanities. At the length I got this profit thereby, that I know by what means I should discourage and dissuade others from this destruction. For all they that presume to divine and prophesy, not in the truth, not in the virtue of God, but in the elusion [i.e., deception] of devils, according to the operation of wicked sprites, and exercising deceits of idolatry, and showing illusions and vain visions, the which suddenly ceasing, they avaunt that they can work miracles [...]: all these, with Iamnes and Iambres and Simon Magus, shall be condemned to the pains of everlasting fire.

Cap. 55 (Of Politic Governance)
[...] But they which nowadays be called kings, emperors and princes suppose that they be born and created not for the people, for the citizens, for the common sort, for justice, but to defend and preserve the nobility: and do rule in such sort that they seem that the wealth of all the citizens is not committed to their custody, but given them to spoil and sack, taking all things from all men; and use their subjects according to their will and pleasure, and do abuse the authority given them from above towards their subjects [...].

Cap. 61 (Of the Magistrates of the Church)
[...] whosoever shall not be called by the spirit of God to the great office of God and to the apostolic dignity as Aaron was, and he that shall not enter through the gate which is Christ, but by some other place shall climb into the Church, through the window, through the favor of men, through voices bought, through the rule of princes, verily he is not the Vicar of Christ and the apostles, but a thief and a robber, the Vicar of Judas Iscariot and Simon the Samaritan [...] many such bishops and apostles have climbed up to the seat of Christ [...], laying grievous burdens upon the shoulders of the people [...] not esteeming the true temple of God, and the lively images of Christ and the altars of the people's souls [...]. But do utterly neglect the weightiest and the best works of the gospel, of the law, and of Christian righteousness, judgment, mercy, and faith. They strain a gnat through their teeth and swallow down a camel, they stumble at a straw and leap over a block, blind guides, false and deceitful, the generation of vipers, scoured cups, whited sepulchres outwardly showing holiness in their mitres, in their caps, in their rachets, in their apparel, in their hoods: within they are full of filthiness, of hypocrisy, of iniquity; whore-hunters, dancers, stage players, bawds or whore-merchants, dicers, gluttons, drunkards, poisoners, which [...] have climbed and ascended not by the virtue of their merits, but either by filthy flattery, or by gifts, or by the favor of princes, or by force of arms to priesthoods, benefices, and bishoprics [...].

Cap. 82 (Of Physic)
But now let us pass from warfare and nobility to Physic, which also is a certain art of manslaughter altogether servile, although it presume to pass under the title of philosophy, and above the knowledge of the law doth seek to have the next place to divinity, wherefore there is great contention between physicians and lawyers [...].

Cap. 83 (Of Physic, that consisteth in practice)
[...] Pindarus saith also that Esculapius, father of physic, was by Jupiter stricken with lightning for a due desert of covetousness, because wickedly and to the damage of the commonwealth he had practised physic. And if by any chance the diseased shall happily recover in their hands, they rejoice without measure; no man will be able to set forth the glory of so great a miracle. They will say that he hath raised Lazarus from death, that he gave him his life, that he is bound to thank them that he is alive: and by and by (attributing that to themselves, which belongeth only unto God), they avaunt that they have drawn him out of hell [...]. I put the case that the physicians know (and I would to God they knew) all the virtues and operations of the elements, roots, herbs, flowers, fruits, seeds, of living creatures also and minerals, and of all things which nature, the mother of them, hath brought forth; yet they cannot with all these virtues not only make man immortal, but which is less, not always cure him that is sick of every light disease [...].

Cap. 91 (Of the Law and Statutes)
[...] Behold now ye perceive how this knowledge of the law presumeth to bear sway over all other arts, and exerciseth tyranny, and how, preferring itself before all other disciplines as it were the first begotten of the gods, doth despise them as vile and vain, although it be altogether made of nothing else but of frail and very weak inventions and opinions of men, which things be of all other the weakest [...].

Cap. 97 (Of Scholastical Divinity)
Lastly it resteth to speak of divinity [...]. But let us speak first of scholastical divinity, which doctrine was first made by the Sorbonists of Paris, with a certain mixture of God's word and philosophical reasons, fashioned like two bodies, as if it were of the centaur's kind [...]. Hereupon scholastical divinity in the end by little and little was turned to sophisms, whilest that these divine sophisters of latter time and hucksters of God's word (which be not divines, except the title be bought) of so high a science they have made a certain logomachy, that is, an undiscreet altercation [...]. And in this manner [...] they have picked out very many apt questions to dispute upon divinity, in the which they, exercising their wit and consuming their time, have placed all the doctrine of divinity in them alone; against which if any will resist with the authority of the holy scriptures, forthwith he shall here say: The letter killeth, it is deadly, it is unprofitable [...]. Afterward they, having recourse to interpreting, to expounding, to glossing, and to syllogizing, do rather give

it some other sense than the proper meaning of the letter [...]. Hereof it is come to pass that the high science of school divinity is not free from error and naughtiness, so many sects, so many heresies have the wicked hypocrites and hair-brained sophisters brought up: which, as Paul saith, preach Christ not for good will but for contention [...].

Cap. 101 (Of Masters of Arts)

[...] in the time past this was the superstition of the gentiles, which with divine honors worshipped the inventors of things [...], and placed them in the number of their gods [...]. And this is that [dei]fication, and no other, of sciences: which that ancient serpent, the shaper of such gods, promised to our first parents, saying to them: Ye shall be as gods, knowing the good and the evil [...]. It is better therefore and more profitable to be idiots and know nothing, to believe by faith and charity, and to become next unto God, than being lofty and proud through the subtleties of sciences to fall into the possession of the serpent. So we read in the gospel how Christ was received of idiots, of the rude people, and of the simple sort: who was contemptuously rejected, despised, and persecuted even to the death by the high Priests, by the Lawyers, by the Scribes, by the Masters and Rabbins. For this cause Christ himself also chose his apostles, not Rabbins, not Scribes, not Masters, nor Priests, but unlearned persons of the rude people, void well near of all knowledge, unskilful, and asses.

The Conclusion of the work

Wherefore O ye asses, which are now with your children, under the commandment of Christ by his apostles, the messengers and readers of true wisdom in his holy gospel, be you loosed from the darkness of the flesh and blood. If ye desire to attain to this divine and true wisdom, not of the tree of the knowledge of good and ill, but of the tree of life, [cast aside the sciences of men]...; now entering not into the schools of philosophers and sophisters, but into your [own] selves, ye shall know all things: for the knowledge of all things is compact in you, which (as the Academics confess) the holy scriptures do so witness, because God created all things very good, that is to say in the best degree wherein they might abide. Even as he then hath created trees full of fruits, so also hath he created the souls as reasonable trees full of forms and knowledges; but through the sin of the first parent all things were [concealed], and oblivion the mother of ignorance [entered] in. Set you then now aside, which may, the veil of your understanding, [you] which are wrapped in the darkness of ignorance. Cast out the drink of Lethe, you which have made yourselves drunken with forgetfulness, await for the true light, you which have suffered yourselves to be taken with unreasonable sleep; and forthwith when your face is discovered ye shall pass from the light to the light: for (as John saith) Ye are annointed by the holy Ghost, and have known all things; and again, Ye need not to be taught of any, because his annointing teacheth you all things [...]. O ye fools and wicked ones, which setting apart the gifts of the holy Ghost, endeavor to learn those things of faithless philosophers and masters of errors which ye ought to receive of God and the holy Ghost. Will you believe that we can get knowledge out of the ignorance of Socrates? [....] But descend into yourselves, you which are desirous of the truth, depart from the clouds of man's traditions, and cleave to the true light: behold, a voice from heaven, a voice that teacheth from above, and showeth you more clearly than the sun [that you are] your own enemies and prolong time to receive wisdom. Hear the oracle of Baruch: God is, [he says], and no other shall be esteemed with him; he hath found out all manner of learning, and hath given [it] to Jacob, his child, and Israel, his beloved, giving laws and commandments, and ordaining sacrifices; after this he was seen on the earth, and was conversant with men [cf. *Baruch* 3: 36-38]; that is to say, taking flesh, and with an open mouth teaching those things which under dark questions he hath taught in the Law and Prophets. And to the end that you may not think that these things be referred to divine things only, and not [also] to natural, hear what the wise man witnesseth of himself: It is He that hath given me the true knowledge of those things which are, that I might know the dispositions of the compass of the earth, the virtue of the elements, the beginning, consummation, middle, and revolutions of times, the course of the year, the dispositions of the stars, the natures of living creatures, the anger of beasts, the force of the winds, the thoughts of men, the differences of plants, the virtues of roots, and finally I have learned all the things which be hidden and unknown, for the Artificer of all things hath taught me wisdom [*Wisdom of Solomon* 7: 17-21]....

De occulta philosophia

De occulta philosophia, *Author's Preface*
I do not doubt but that the title of our book of Occult philosophy, or of Magic, may by its rarity entice a large number to read it, among whom some twisted, feeble-minded people, and also many ill-disposed and hostile to my talents, will approach: these, in their rash ignorance taking the name of magic in the worse sense, will cry out, hardly having

beheld the title, that I teach forbidden arts, sow the seed of heresy, am an offense to pious ears and to outstanding minds a stumbling block; that I am a sorcerer, a superstitious man, and a demoniac, because I am a magician. To these people I would reply that *magus* among learned men does not signify a sorcerer, nor a superstitious man, nor one possessed, but one who is a wise man, a priest, a prophet. The Sibyls were magicians; hence they prophesied most plainly of Christ. And indeed the Magi knew by the wonderful secrets of the world that Christ the author of the world itself was born, and were the first of all to come and worship him. And the name itself of magic was accepted by philosophers, extolled by theologians, and was also not displeasing to the gospel itself. Yet I believe those censors to be of such steadfast arrogance that they will forbid themselves the Sibyls and the holy magicians, and even the gospel itself, sooner than that the name of magic should be admitted into favor; to such a degree are they careful of their conscience, that neither Apollo, nor all the Muses, nor an angel from heaven would be able to deliver me from their curse. And I advise them now that they neither read, nor understand, nor remember our treatise, for it is harmful, it is poisonous, the gate of Acheron is in this book, it speaks stones: let them take heed lest it beat out their brains [...].

Book III, Dedicatory Epistle
[...] The understanding of divine things purges the mind from errors and renders it divine, gives an infallible virtue to our works, and drives far away the deceits and hindrances of all evil demons. And at the same time it subjects them to our command, and even compels the good angels and the universal virtues of the world into our service; that is to say, the virtue of our works being drawn from the archetype himself, when we ascend to him all creatures necessarily must obey us, and all the choir of the heavenly beings follow us [...].

Book III, Chap. 1.
[...] We cannot obtain a firm and solid intellect (as Hermes says) otherwise than by integrity of life, by piety, and finally, by divine religion. For holy religion purges the intellect and renders it divine [...]

Book III, Chap. 3.
[...] now truly I will recount a mysterious, necessary and secret thing [...] which is the principle and complement and key of all magical operations: it is the dignification of man to this so very exalted virtue and power [...] Indeed, the apprehension and power of all things inheres

in our own selves. We are prevented, however, from having full use of these, through passions hindering us from our begetting, through deceptive imaginations and immoderate desires: which being expelled, divine knowledge and power suddenly arrive [...].

Book III, Chap. 6.
[...] Our mind, pure and divine, burning with religious love, adorned by hope, and directed by faith, placed in the height and summit of the human soul, attracts the truth, and suddenly comprehending, beholds in the divine truth itself, as though in a certain mirror of eternity, all the conditions, reasons, causes and sciences of things both natural and immortal [...]. Hence it comes to us, who are established in nature, sometimes to rule over nature, and to accomplish operations so wonderful, so sudden, and so difficult, whereby the spirits of the dead may obey, the stars be disordered, the divine powers compelled, and the elements enslaved: so men devoted to God, and elevated by these theological virtues, command the elements, drive away mists, summon winds, collect clouds into rain, cure diseases, raise the dead [...].

Book III, Chap. 36.
[...] even our words can bring forth very many miracles, provided that they be shaped by the Word of God. In these miracles also our single generation is perfected, just as Isaiah says: We have conceived by thy face, O Lord, as women rightly conceive by the face of their husbands, and have brought forth spirit [...].

Book III, Chap. 44.
[...] The soul which is united to the mind is therefore called the soul standing and not falling: but not all men have obtained mind, because (as Hermes says) God the Father wanted to set it forth just as a contest and prize of souls. Those who, devoid of mind, despise this prize, being given over to bodily senses, are made like the irrational brutes, and share the same annihilation with them [...]. There is no work in the whole succession of the world so admirable, so excellent, so marvellous, that the human soul, embracing its image of divinity (which the magicians call the soul standing and not falling) cannot accomplish by its own virtue without any external assistance. The form, therefore, of all magical virtue is from man's soul standing, and not falling [...].

De occulta philosophia, Appendix

[To the first edition of this book Agrippa appended chapters 41 to 48 of *De vanitate*—those chapters which deal with the various magical arts. The book therefore concludes with the following sentences, which I offer this time in my own translation.]

[...] At last I advanced to this, that I might know by what reasons it might be proper to dissuade others from this ruin. For all who presume to divine and to prophesy, not in the truth, nor in the power of God, but in the deception of demons, according to the operation of evil spirits, and by means of magical vanities, practising exorcisms, incantations, love-potions, conjurings, and other demoniacal works and idolatrous deceits, presenting their short-lived deceptions and apparitions, boast that they work miracles: all these shall be destined, with Iannes and Mambres and Simon Magus, to be tortured by eternal fires.

Appendix D: *Excerpts from Jean Calvin,* The Institution of Christian Religion, *trans. Thomas Norton (1561, rpt. 1587)*

[Jean Calvin (1509-64), the most influential of the second-generation Protestant reformers and the great systematizer among sixteenth-century theologians, was a powerful presence in Elizabethan England. As A.D. Nuttall has remarked, the nearly one hundred English-language editions of his writings printed by 1640 far outnumber those of any other author (Calvin's close associate Theodore de Bèze stands in second place with fifty editions, followed by Luther and Bullinger with thirty-eight each.) Not until the early seventeenth century was Calvin's rate of publications in English overtaken—"and then it was by William Perkins and Henry Smith, both Calvinists" (Nuttall 1980: 21). Calvin's thought formed part of the dominant ideology of Elizabethan England, for although the Church of England retained an episcopal structure, its theology was strongly Calvinistic (Sinfield 1983: 12-14). This fact, Alan Sinfield observes, "has fascinating consequences for the study of literature of the period. It obliges us to entertain the thought, for instance, that Marlowe's Faustus is not damned because he is wicked, but wicked because he is damned" (14).

Calvin published the first edition of his most important work, the *Institutio christianae religionis,* in 1536. Revised and expanded texts were printed in 1539, 1543, 1545, 1550, 1553, 1554, and 1559, and French versions in 1541 and 1560. Thomas Norton's English translation of the final Latin version appeared in 1561, and was frequently reprinted; the selections which follow are taken from the edition of 1587. The standard editions of Calvin's *Institutes* are those of Jean-Daniel Benoît (1957-63) and John T. McNeill and Ford Lewis Battles (1960). Important critical studies of Calvin's influence in England include A. D. Nuttall's *Overheard by God* (1980), Alan Sinfield's *Literature in Protestant England 1560-1660* (1983), and John Stachniewski's *The Persecutory Imagination* (1991), as well as recent articles by Andrew Pettegree and Dan Danner.

Some current interpretations of Calvin's thought, among them William J. Bousma's very perceptive *John Calvin: A Sixteenth Century Portrait* (1988), have tended to emphasize Calvin's affiliations with widely shared Christian traditions, both theological and humanist, and consequently to soften or obscure the distinctive turns in his arguments which are largely responsible for their persuasive power, and which made them seem to sixteenth-century readers either incontrovertible or

highly disturbing—or both at once. The excerpts given here are chosen with a different end in mind. In highlighting the harshest aspects
of Calvin's thought, they may help to suggest why, after six years of
advanced study at Cambridge, Christopher Marlowe reacted with such
violence against Christianity.

Calvin's starting point is a firm belief in the absolute sovereignty of
God's will. He is, in many respects, a ruthlessly honest thinker. But
whereas the thought of Luther or Pascal is dialectical in nature, Calvin's
can more properly be described as equivocating. Dialectical thought,
whether Platonic, scholastic, or post-Hegelian, requires the operation of at
least two distinct terms. But because Calvin regards all actions and events,
from Adam's fall to that of a sparrow, as being wholly determined by God's
inscrutable will, and all categories and agents in creation as subsumed by
that same will, a recurrent feature of his arguments is a reduction of all issues to the basic principle of the absolute monarchy of God. The dominant
mode of his argumentation is thus, necessarily, equivocation—for when
the reality of one term so wholly absorbs that of all others, an extended and
serious discourse can only be constructed out of equivocations.

The most disturbing of Calvin's equivocations, and those of most
relevance to *Doctor Faustus*, have to do with the relation between the
divine will and human wills.]

I. xvi. 3
[...] there is not in creatures a wandering power, working or motion,
but [...] they are governed by the secret counsel of God, so that nothing
can chance but that which is decreed by him both witting and willing
it to be.

I. xvi. 4
God doth so give heed to the government of the successes of all things,
and [...] they all do so proceed from his determinate counsel, that nothing happeneth by chance.

I. xvi. 6
It is a fond madness that men will take upon themselves to do things
without God, which cannot so much as speak but what he will.

I. xvii. 5
The same men do unorderly and unadvisedly draw the chances of time
past to the naked providence of God. For because upon it do hang all
things whatsoever happen, therefore (say they) neither robberies nor adul-

teries nor manslaughters are committed without the will of God. Why then (say they) shall a thief be punished, for that he spoiled him whom the Lord's will was to punish with poverty? Why shall the murderer be punished which hath slain him whose life the Lord hath ended? If all such men do serve the will of God, why shall they be punished? But I deny that they serve the will of God. For we may not say, that he which is carried with an evil mind doth service unto God as commander of it, where indeed he doth but obey his own wicked lust. He obeyeth God, which being informed of his will doth labor to that end whereunto God's will calleth him. But whereby are we informed of his will, but by his Word? Therefore in doing of things we must see that same will of God which he declareth in this word. God requireth of us only that which he commandeth. If we do anything against his commandment, it is not obedience but obstinacy and transgression. But unless he would [i.e., unless he willed it], we should not do it. I grant. But do we evil things to this end, to obey him? But he doth not command us to do them, but rather we run on headlong, not minding what he willeth, but so raging with the intemperance of our own lust, that of set purpose we bend our travail against him. And by these means in evil-doing we serve his just ordinance, because according to the infinite greatness of his wisdom he hath good skill to use evil instruments to do good. And see how foolish is their manner of arguing. They would have the doers unpunished for mischievous acts, because they are not committed but by the disposition of God.

I grant more: that thieves and murderers and other evil-doers are the instruments of God's providence, whom the Lord doth use to execute those judgments which he hath with himself determined. But I deny that their evil doings ought to have any excuse thereby. For why? Shall they either entangle God in the same wickedness with them, or shall they cover their naughtiness with his righteousness? They can do neither of both. Because they should not be able to excuse themselves, they are accused by their own conscience. And because they should not be able to blame God, they find all the evil in themselves, and in him nothing but a lawful use of their evilness. But he worketh by them. And whence, I pray you, cometh the stink in a dead carrion, which hath been both rotted and disclosed by the heat of the sun? All men do see that it is raised by the beams of the sun. Yet no man doth therefore say that the sunbeams do stink. So when there resteth in an evil man the matter and guiltiness of evil, what cause is there why it should be thought that God is any thing defiled with it, if he use their service at his pleasure? Away therefore with this doggish frowardness, which may indeed afar off bark at the justice of God, but cannot touch it.

I. xvii. 11

[...] when [the saints] call to mind that the devil and all the rout of the wicked are so every way holden in by the hand of God as with a bridle, that they can neither conceive any mischief against us, nor go about it when they have conceived it, nor if they go never so much about it, can stir one finger to bring it to pass but so far as he shall suffer, yea, so far as he shall command, and that they are not only holden fast bound with fetters, but also compelled with bridle to do service: here have they abundantly wherewith to comfort themselves. For as it is the Lord's work to arm their fury and to turn and direct it whither it pleaseth him, so is it his work also to appoint a measure and end, that they do not after their own will licentiously triumph.

II. ii. 6-7

[...] For I do much farther differ from the later Sophisters, even so much as they be farther gone from the ancient time. But yet somewhat, after such a sort as it is, we perceive by this division, after what manner they have given free will to man. For at length Lombard saith that we have not free will therefore, because we are alike able either to do or to think good and evil, but only that we are free from compulsion: which freedom is not hindered, although we be perverse and the bondmen of sin, and can do nothing but sin.

Therefore man shall be said to have free will after this sort, not because he hath a free choice as well of good as of evil, but because he doth evil by will, and not by compulsion. That is very well said: but to what purpose was it to garnish so small a matter with so proud a title? A goodly liberty forsooth, if man be not compelled to serve sin: so is he yet a willing servant that his will is holden fast bound with the fetters of sin. Truly I do abhor striving about words, wherewith the Church is vainly wearied, but I think that such words are with great religious carefulness to be taken heed of, which sound of any absurdity, especially where the error is hurtful. How few, I pray you, are there, which when they hear that free will is assigned to man, do not by and by conceive that he is lord both of his own mind and will, and that he is able of himself to turn himself to whether part he will?

II. iii. 5

[...] Therefore [if] this, that it is of necessity that God do well, does not hinder the free will of God in doing well; if the devil, which cannot do but evil, yet willingly sinneth; who shall then say that a man doth therefore less willingly sin for this, that he is subject to [the] necessity of sinning?

II. iv. 1

The blinding of the wicked, and all the wicked deeds that follow thereupon, are called the works of Satan, of which yet the cause is not to be sought elsewhere than in the will of man, out of which ariseth the root of evil, wherein resteth the foundation of the kingdom of Satan, which is sin.

II. iv. 3

The old writers [...] are sometime precisely [i.e. scrupulously] afraid simply to confess the truth, because they fear lest they should so open a window to wickedness, to speak irreverently of the works of God [...]. Augustine himself sometime was not free from the superstition, as where he saith that hardening and blinding pertain not to the work of God, but to his foreknowledge. But the phrases of Scripture allow not these subtleties [...]. It is oftentimes said that God blindeth and hardeneth the reprobate, that he turneth, boweth, and moveth their hearts, as I have elsewhere taught more at large. But of what manner that is, it is never expressed, if we flee to free foreknowledge or sufferance. Therefore we answer that it is done after two manners. For first, whereas when his light is taken away, there remaineth nothing but darkness and blindness: whereas when his spirit is taken away, our hearts wax hard and become stones: whereas when his direction ceaseth, they are wrested into crookedness. It is well said that he doth blind, harden and bow them from whom he taketh away the power to see, obey and do rightly. The second manner, which cometh near to the property [i.e. proper meaning] of the words, is that for the executing of his judgments by Satan, the minister of his wrath, he both appointeth their purposes to what end it pleaseth him, and stirreth up their wills, and strengtheneth their endeavors.

II. viii. 58–59

In weighing of sins (saith Augustine) let us not bring false balances to weigh what we list and how we list at our own pleasure, saying: this is heavy, this is light. But let us bring God's balance out of the holy Scriptures, as out of the Lord's treasury, and let us therein weigh what is heavy: rather, let us not weigh, but reknowledge things already weighed by the Lord. But what saith the Scripture? Truly, when Paul saith that the reward of sin is death [*Romans* 6: 23], he showeth that he knew not this stinking distinction [i.e., between venial and mortal sins]. Sith we are too much inclined to hypocrisy, this cherishment thereof ought not to have been added to flatter our slothful consciences.

I would to God they would consider what that saying of Christ meaneth: He that transgresseth of one of the least of these commandments, and teacheth men so, shall be counted none in the kingdom of heaven [*Matthew* 5: 19]. Are not they of that sort, when they dare so extenuate the transgression of the law, as if it were not worthy of death? [....] Is it a small matter with them, that God's majesty be offended in any thing? Moreover, if God hath declared his will in the law, whatsoever is contrary to the law displeaseth him. Will they imagine the wrath of God to be so disarmed, that punishment of death shall not forthwith follow upon them? And he himself hath pronounced it plainly, if they would rather find in their hearts to hear his voice than to trouble the clear truth with their unsavory subtleties of argument. The soul (saith he) that sinneth, the same shall die [*Ezekiel* 18: 4, 20]. Again, which I even now alleged: the reward of sin is death [*Romans* 6: 23]. But albeit they grant it to be a sin, because they cannot deny it, yet they stand stiff in this, that it is no deadly sin. But sith they have hithertoo too much borne with their own madness, let them yet at length learn to wax wiser. But if they continue in their dotage, we will bid them farewell: and let the children of God learn this: that if all sin is deadly, because it is a rebellion against the will of God, which of necessity provoketh his wrath, because it is a breach of the law, upon which the judgement of God is pronounced without exception: and that the sins of the holy ones are venial and pardonable, not of their own nature, but because they obtain pardon by the mercy of God.

II. xvi. 2-3

[...] God, which prevented us with his mercy, was our enemy until he was reconciled to us by Christ [...]. In a sum: because our mind can neither desirously enough take hold of life in the mercy of God, nor receive it with such thankfulness as we ought, but when it is before stricken and thrown down with the fear of the wrath of God and dread of eternal death, we are so taught by holy Scripture, that without Christ we may see God in manner wrathfully bent against us, and his hand armed to our destruction: and that we may embrace his goodwill and fatherly kindness no otherwise, but in Christ.

And although this be spoken according to the weakness of our capacity, yet it is not falsely said. For God, which is the highest righteousness, cannot love wickedness, which he seeth in us all. Therefore we all have in us that which is worthy of the hatred of God.

III. iii. 10-11

[...] this image or shadow of faith, as it is of no value, so it is not worthy of the name of faith [...]. It is said that Simon Magus believed, which yet within a little after bewrayed his own unbelief. And whereas it is said that he believed, we do not understand it as some do, that he feigned a belief when he had none in his heart: but we rather think that, being overcome with the majesty of the Gospel, he had a certain faith, such as it was, and so acknowledged Christ to be the author of life and salvation that he willingly professed himself to be one of his [...].

I know that some think it hard that we assign faith to the reprobate, whereas Paul affirmeth faith to be the fruit of election [cf. 1 *Thessalonians* 1: 4-5]. Which doubt yet is easily dissolved: for though none receive the light of faith, nor do truly feel the effectual working of the Gospel, but that they are foreordained to salvation, yet experience showeth that the reprobate are sometime moved with the same feeling that the elect are, so that in their own judgement they nothing differ from the elect. Wherefore it is no absurdity that the apostle ascribeth to them the taste of the heavenly gifts [*Hebrews* 6: 4-6], that Christ: ascribeth to them faith for a time [*Luke* 8: 13]: not that they soundly perceive the spiritual force of grace and assured light of faith, but because the Lord, the more to condemn them and make them inexcusable, conveyeth himself into their minds so far forth as his goodness may be tasted without the spirit of adoption.

III. iii. 21

[...] The Apostle also meaning to exclude apostates from hope of salvation, appointeth this reason, that it is impossible for them to be renewed unto repentance [*Hebrews* 6: 4-6]: because God, in renewing them whom he will not have perish, showeth a token of his fatherly favour, and in a manner draweth them unto him with the beams of his cheerful and merry countenance: on the other side, with hardening them, he thundereth against the reprobate, whose wickedness is unpardonable. Which kind of vengeance the Apostle threateneth to wilful apostates, which when they depart from the faith of the gospel do make a scorn of God, reproachfully despise his grace, and defile and tread under feet the blood of Christ, yea as much as in them is they crucify him again. For he doth not (as some fondly rigorous men would have it) cut off hope of pardon from all wilful sins: but teacheth that apostasy is unworthy of all excuse: so that it is no marvel that God doth punish a contempt of himself so full of sacrilege, with unappeasable rigor.

III. iii. 22

[...] This therefore is the spirit of blasphemy, when man's boldness of set purpose leapeth forth to reproach of the name of God. Which Paul signifieth when he saith that he obtained mercy because he had ignorantly committed those things through unbelief [1 *Timothy* 1: 13], for which otherwise he had been unworthy of God's favor. If ignorance joined with unbelief was the cause that he obtained pardon, thereupon followeth, that there is no place for pardon where knowledge is joined to unbelief.

III. iii. 24

But whereas some do think it too hard, and too far from the tender mercifulness of God, that any are put away that flee to beseeching the Lord's mercy: that is easily answered. For he doth not say that pardon is denied them if they turn to the Lord: but he utterly denieth that they can rise unto repentance, because they are by the just judgment of God stricken with eternal blindness for their unthankfulness. And it maketh nothing to the contrary that afterward he applieth to this purpose the example of Esau, which in vain attempted with howling and weeping to recover his right of the first begotten [*Hebrews* 12: 16-17]. And no more doth that threatening of the Prophet: When they cry, I will not hear [*Zechariah* 7: 13]. For in such phrases of speech is meant neither the true conversion, nor calling upon God, but that carefulness of the wicked, wherewith being bound, they are compelled in extremity to look unto that which before they carelessly neglected, that there is no good thing for them but in the Lord's help. But this they do not so much call upon, as they mourn that it is taken from them. Therefore the Prophet meaneth nothing else by crying, and the Apostle nothing else by weeping, but that horrible torment which by desperation fretteth and vexeth the wicked. This it is good to mark diligently, for else God should disagree with himself, which crieth by the Prophet that he will be merciful so soon as the sinner turneth [*Ezekiel* 18: 21-22]. And as I have already said, it is certain that the mind of man is not turned to better, but by God's grace preventing [i.e., pre-arranging] it. Also his promise concerning calling upon him will never deceive. But that blind torment wherewith the reprobate are diversely drawn when they see that they must needs seek God, that they may find remedy for their evils, and yet do flee from his presence, is unproperly called conversion and prayer.

III. xxiii. 3-4

[...] if any man assail us with such words: why God hath from the beginning predestinate some to death, which when they were not, could not yet deserve the judgment of death, we instead of answer may again on our side ask of them, what they think that God oweth to man, if he will judge him by his own nature. In such sort as we be all corrupted with sin, we cannot but be hateful to God: and that not by tyrannous cruelty, but by most upright reason of justice. If all they whom the Lord doth predestinate to death are by the estate of nature subject to the judgment of death, of what injustice against themselves, I beseech you, may they complain? Let all the sons of Adam come: Let them strive and dispute with their creator, for that by his eternal providence they were before their generation condemned to everlasting misery. What shall they be able once to mutter against this defence, when God on the other side shall call them to reknowledging of themselves? If they be all taken out of a corrupt mass, it is no marvel if they be subject to damnation. Let them not therefore accuse God of injustice, if by his eternal judgment they be appointed to death, to which they themselves do feel, whether they will or no, that they are willingly led of their own nature. Whereby appeareth how wrongful is the desire of their murmuring, because they do of set purpose hide the cause of damnation which they are compelled to acknowledge in themselves, that the laying of the blame upon God may acquit them. But although I do a hundred times confess, as it is most true, that God is the author of it, yet they do not by and by wipe away the guiltiness which, being engraved in their consciences, from time with oft recourse presenteth itself to their eyes.

Again they except and say: were they not before predestinate by the ordinance of God to the same corruption which is now alleged for the cause of damnation? When therefore they perish in their corruption, they do nothing but suffer the punishment of that misery into which, by his predestination, Adam fell and drew his posterity headlong with him. Is not he therefore unjust, which doth so cruelly mock his creatures? I grant indeed that all the children of Adam fell by the will of God into that misery of state wherein they be now bound: and this is it that I said at the beginning, that at length we must always return to the determination of the will of God, the cause whereof is hidden in himself. But it followeth not by and by that God is subject to this slander. For we will with Paul answer them in this manner: O man, what art thou that contendest with God? Doth the thing formed say to him that formed it, Why hast thou formed me so? Hath not the potter power to make of the same lump one vessel to honor, and another to dishonor [*Romans* 9: 20-21]?

III. xxiii. 7
It is a terrible decree, I grant: yet no man shall be able to deny, but that God foreknew what end man should have ere he created him, and therefore foreknew it because he had so ordained by his decree.

III. xxiii. 8
Here they run to the distinction between will and permission, by which

they will have it granted that the wicked do perish, God only permitting but not willing it. But why should we say that he permitteth it, but because he so willeth? Howbeit it is not likely that man by himself, by the only permission of God, without any his ordinance, brought destruction to himself: as though God appointed not of what condition he would have the chief of his creatures to be. I therefore will not doubt to confess simply with Augustine that the will of God is a necessity of things, and that what he willeth, it must of necessity come to pass: as those things shall truly come to pass which he hath foreseen [...]. Man therefore falleth, the providence of God so ordaining it: but he falleth by his own fault. The Lord had a little before pronounced that all the things which he had made were very good [*Genesis* 1: 31]. Whence therefore cometh that perverseness to man, to fall away from his God? Lest it should be thought to be of creation, the Lord with his commendation allowed [i.e., approved] that which came from himself. Therefore by his own evilness he corrupted the nature which he had received pure of the Lord, and by his fall he drew his whole posterity with him into destruction. Wherefore let us rather behold an evident cause of damnation in the corrupted nature of mankind, which is nearer to us, than search for a hidden and utterly incomprehensible cause thereof in the predestination of God.

III. xxiv. 12
As the Lord by the effectualness of his calling toward the elect maketh perfect the salvation whereunto he had by eternal counsel appointed them, so he hath his judgments against the reprobate, whereby he executeth his counsel of them. Whom therefore he hath created unto the shame of life, and destruction of death, that they should be instruments of his wrath, and examples of his severity. From them, that they may come to their end, sometime he taketh away the power to hear his word, and sometime by the preaching of it he more blindeth and amazeth them [...]. He shall trouble himself in vain that shall here search for a cause higher than the secret and unsearchable counsel of God.

III. xxiv. 14
[...] Whereas therefore the reprobate do not obey the word of God opened unto them, that shall be well imputed to the malice and perverseness of their heart, so that this be therewithal added: that they are therefore given into this perverseness because by the righteous but yet unsearchable judgment of God they are raised up to set forth his glory with their damnation.

Works Cited and Recommended Reading

Early editions

A1

THE / TRAGICALL / History of D. Faustus. /*As it hath bene Acted by the Right* / *Honorable the Earle of Nottingham his seruants.* / Written by Ch. Marl. / [Device] / LONDON / Printed by V.S. for Thomas Bushell. 1604. (Bodleian Library, shelf-mark Malone 233 [3]; STC 17429; facsimile rpt. in *Christopher Marlowe: Doctor Faustus 1604 and 1616* [Menston, England: Scolar Press, 1970].)

A2, A3

Reprints of A1, printed by George Eld for John Wright in 1609 and 1611 respectively.

B1

The Tragicall History / of the Life and Death / of *Doctor Faustus.* / Written by *Ch. Mar.* / [Woodcut of Faustus conjuring a devil] / *LONDON,* / Printed for *Iohn Wright,* and are to be sold at his shop / without Newgate, at the si[gne] of the / Bibl[e.] 1616. (British Library, shelf-mark C. 34. d. 26; STC 17432; facsimile rpt. in *Christopher Marlowe: Doctor Faustus 1604 and 1616* [Menston, England: Scolar Press, 1970].)

B2, B3, B4

Reprints of the B text, for John Wright, in 1619, 1620, and 1624 respectively. The title pages of these editions contain the words "With new Additions." (Wright published two further reprints, B5 and B6, in 1628 and 1631.)

Editions Containing Both Versions

Bevington and Rasmussen

Bevington, David, and Eric Rasmussen, eds. *Christopher Marlowe and his collaborators and revisers: Doctor Faustus: A and B texts (1604, 1616).* The Revels Plays. Manchester: Manchester UP, 1993.

Burnett

Burnett, Mark Thornton, ed. *Christopher Marlowe: The Complete Plays.* The Everyman Library. London: Dent, 1999.

Dyce

Dyce, Alexander, ed. *The Works of Christopher Marlowe: with some account of the author.... A new edition, revised and corrected.* 1858; rpt. London: George Routledge and Sons, n.d. [c. 1860].

Greg

> Greg, W.W., ed. *Marlowe's "Doctor Faustus" 1604-1616: Parallel Texts.*
> Oxford: Clarendon Press, 1950.

Kastan

> Kastan, David Scott, ed. *Christopher Marlowe: Doctor Faustus. A Two-Text*
> *Edition (A-Text, 1604; B-Text, 1616), Contexts and Sources, Criticism.* New
> York and London: W.W. Norton, 2005.

Keefer 2007

> Keefer, Michael, ed. *Christopher Marlowe: The Tragical History of Doctor*
> *Faustus: a critical edition of the 1604 version, with a full critical edition of the*
> *revised and censored 1616 text and selected source and contextual materials.*
> Peterborough: Broadview Press, 2007.

A-version Editions

Bullen

> Bullen, A.H., ed. *The Works of Christopher Marlowe.* 3 vols.; London:
> Nimmo, 1885.

Ellis

> Ellis, Havelock, ed. *Christopher Marlowe.* The Mermaid Series; London,
> Vizetelly, 1887.

Gill 1989

> Gill, Roma, ed. *Dr Faustus / Christopher Marlowe. 2nd edition based on the*
> *A text.* The New Mermaids. London: Black; New York: Norton, 1989.

Gill 1990

> —. ed. *The Complete Works of Christopher Marlowe, vol. 2: Doctor Faustus.*
> Oxford: Clarendon Press, 1990.

Keefer 1991

> Keefer, Michael, ed. *Christopher Marlowe's Doctor Faustus: a 1604-version*
> *edition.* Peterborough: Broadview Press, 1991.

Kocher

> Kocher, Paul H., ed. *The Tragical History of Doctor Faustus.* New York:
> Appleton-Century-Crofts, 1950.

Ormerod and Wortham

> Ormerod, David, and Christopher Wortham, eds. *Christopher Marlowe:*
> *Dr Faustus: The A-Text.* Nedlands: U of Western Australia P, 1985.

Romany and Lindsey

> Romany, Frank, and Robert Lindsey, eds. *Christopher Marlowe: The*
> *Complete Plays.* London: Penguin, 2003.

Tucker Brooke

> Tucker Brooke, C.F., ed. *The Works of Christopher Marlowe.* 1910; rpt.
> Oxford: Clarendon Press, 1941.

Ward

> Ward, A.W., ed. *Marlowe: "Tragical History of Dr. Faustus"; Greene: "Honourable History of Friar Bacon and Friar Bungay."* 4th ed.; Oxford: Clarendon Press, 1901.

B-version Editions

Barnet

> Barnet, Sylvan, ed. *Christopher Marlowe: Doctor Faustus.* New York: New American Library, 1969.

Boas

> Boas, F.S., ed. *The Tragical History of Doctor Faustus.* In *The Works and Life of Christopher Marlowe*, General Editor R. H. Case. 1932; rpt. London: Methuen, 1949.

Bowers

> Bowers, Fredson, ed. *The Complete Works of Christopher Marlowe.* 2 vols.; Cambridge: Cambridge UP, 1973.

Gill 1965

> Gill, Roma, ed. *Doctor Faustus / Christopher Marlowe.* The New Mermaids. London: Benn, 1965.

Jump

> Jump, John D., ed. *Doctor Faustus / Christopher Marlowe.* The Revels Plays. 1962; rpt. London: Methuen, 1974.

Kirschbaum

> Kirschbaum, Leo, ed. *The Plays of Christopher Marlowe.* 1962; rpt. Cleveland: Meridian Books, 1968.

Steane

> Steane, J.B., ed. *Christopher Marlowe: The Complete Plays.* Harmondsworth: Penguin, 1969.

Works Cited

[Citations from classical and patristic writers are in most cases keyed to the editions in the Loeb Classical Library and the Ante-Nicene Christian Library respectively. With the exception of certain patristic writings of particular importance in the development of the Faustus legend, these texts are not cited here. Unless otherwise indicated, Shakespeare is quoted from *The Norton Shakespeare*, and biblical quotations are given in the wording of the Geneva Bible.]

Agrippa 1530

> Agrippa, Henricus Cornelius. *Splendidae nobilitatis viri et armatae militiae equitis aurati ac utriusque Iuris doctoris sacrae caesareae maiestatis a consilijs et*

archiuis iniditiarij Henrici Cornelij Agrippae ab Nettesheym De Incertitudine et Vanitate Scientiarum et Artium atque excellentia Verbi Dei declamatio. Antwerp, 1530.

Agrippa 1533

—. *Henrici Cornelii Agrippae ab Nettesheym a consiliis & archiuis iniditiarii sacrae caesareae maiestatis: De occulta philosophia libri res.* [Cologne], 1533.

Agrippa 1575

—. *Henrie Cornelius Agrippa, of the Vanitie and vncertaintie of Artes and Sciences: Englished by Ia[mes]. San[ford]. Gent.* 1569; rpt. London, 1575.

Agrippa 1970

—. *Opera.* Ed. R.H. Popkin. 2 vols.; c. 1600; facsimile rpt. Hildesheim and New York: Georg Olms, 1970.

Agrippa 1974

—. *Of the Vanitie and Vncertaintie of Artes and Sciences.* Ed. Catherine M. Dunn. Northridge: California State UP, 1974.

Agrippa 1992

—. *De Occulta Philosophia Libri Tres.* Ed. Vittoria Perrone Compagni. Leiden, New York, Köln: E. J. Brill, 1992.

Agrippa 1993

—. *Three Books of Occult Philosophy.* Trans. James Freake, ed. Donald Tyson. St. Paul, MN: Llewellyn Publications, 1993.

Agrippa 1996

—. *Declamation on the Nobility and Preeminence of the Female Sex.* Trans. and ed. Albert Rabil, Jr. Chicago: U of Chicago P, 1996.

Allen

Allen, Marguerite de Huszar. *The Faust Legend: Popular Formula and Modern Novel.* Frankfurt, Bern, New York: Peter Lang, 1985.

Aristotle

The Complete Works of Aristotle. The Revised Oxford Translation. Ed. Jonathan Barnes. 2 vols. Princeton: Princeton UP, 1984.

Astington

Astington, John H. "Descent Machinery in the Playhouse." *Medieval and Renaissance Drama in England* 2 (1985): 119-33.

Augustine

Augustine, St. *Confessions.* Trans. Henry Chadwick. 1991; rpt. Oxford and New York: Oxford UP, 1992.

Bacon

Bacon, Sir Francis. *A Harmony of Lord Bacon's Essays, &c. 1597-1638.* Ed. Edward Arber. London: Arber's English Reprints, 1871.

Bakeless

Bakeless, John. *The Tragicall History of Christopher Marlowe.* 2 vols.; 1942; rpt. Hamden, CT.: Archon Books, 1964.

Barber

> Barber, C.L. "'The form of Faustus' fortunes good or bad'." *Tulane Drama Review* 8 (1963-64): 92-119.

Barnes

> Barnes, Celia. "Matthew Parker's Pastoral Training and Marlowe's *Doctor Faustus*." *Comparative Drama* 15 (981): 258-67.

Baron 1978

> Baron, Frank. *Doctor Faustus from History to Legend*. Munich: Wilhelm Fink, 1978.

Baron 1982

> —. *Faustus: Geschichte, Sage, Dichtung*. Munich: Winkler, 1982.

Baron 1985

> —. "The Faustbook's Indebtedness to Augustin Lercheimer and Wittenberg Sources." *Daphnis* 14 (1985): 517-45.

Baron 1989

> —. "Who was the Historical Faustus? Interpreting an Overlooked Source." *Daphnis* 18 (1989): 297-302.

Baron 1992a

> —. *Faustus on Trial: The Origins of Johann Spies's "Historia" in an Age of Witch Hunting*. Tübingen: Max Niemeyer, 1992.

Baron 1992b

> —. "The Precarious Legacy of Renaissance Humanism in the Faust Legend." In *The Harvest of Humanism in Central Europe: Essays in Honor of Lewis W. Spitz*, ed. Mannfred P. Fleischer. St. Louis: Concordia, 1992. 303-15.

Baskervill

> Baskervill, C.R. *The Elizabethan Jig and Related Song Drama*. 1929; rpt. New York: Dover, 1965.

Becon

> Becon, Thomas. *The Catechism of Thomas Becon [...] with other pieces written by him in the reign of King Edward the Sixth*. Ed. John Ayre. Cambridge: Parker Society, 1844.

Behringer

> Behringer, Wolfgang. *Witchcraft Persecutions in Bavaria: Popular Magic, Religious Zealotry and Reason of State in Early Modern Europe*. Trans. J.C. Grayson and David Lederer. Cambridge: Cambridge UP, 1997.

Bevington 1991

> Bevington, David. "Marlowe and God." *Explorations in Renaissance Culture* 17 (1991): 1-38.

Boas 1940

> Boas, F.S. *Christopher Marlowe: A Biographical and Critical Study*. Oxford: Clarendon Press, 1940.

Bodin

Bodin, Jean. *De la démonomanie des sorciers [...] par I. Bodin Angevin*. Paris, 1581.

Bouswma

Bouwsma, William J. *John Calvin: A Sixteenth Century Portrait*. New York: Oxford UP, 1988.

Bowers, "Additions"

Bowers, Fredson. "Marlowe's *Doctor Faustus*: The 1602 Additions." *Studies in Bibliography* 26 (1973): 1-18.

Brann

Brann, Noel L. *The Abbot Trithemius (1462-1516): The Renaissance of Monastic Humanism*. Leiden: E.J. Brill, 1981.

Bray

Bray, Alan. *Homosexuality in Renaissance England*. 2nd ed. New York: Columbia UP, 1995.

Brown

Brown, Peter. *Augustine of Hippo: A Biography*. 1967; rpt. London: Faber and Faber, 1975.

Bruno 1964

Bruno, Giordano. *The Expulsion of the Triumphant Beast*. Ed. and trans. Arthur D. Imerti. New Brunswick, NJ: Rutgers UP, 1964.

Bruno 1995

—. *The Ash Wednesday Supper*. Ed. and trans. Edward A. Gosselin and Lawrence A. Lerner. 1977; rpt. Toronto: U of Toronto P, 1995.

Buridan

Buridan, John. *Sophisms on Meaning and Truth*. Trans. Theodore Kermit Scott. New York: Appleton-Century Crofts, 1966.

Burke

Burke, Peter. *Popular Culture in Early Modern Europe*. 1978; revised ed. Aldershot: Scolar P, 1994.

Butler 1948

Butler, E.M. *The Myth of the Magus*. Cambridge: Cambridge UP, 1948.

Butler 1950

—. *Ritual Magic*. Cambridge: Cambridge UP, 1950.

Butler 1952

—. *The Fortunes of Faust*. Cambridge: Cambridge UP, 1952.

Calvin 1587

Calvin, Jean. *The Institution of Christian Religion, written in Latine by M. John Caluine, and translated into English according to the Authors last edition [...] by Thomas Norton*. 1561; rpt. London, 1587.

Calvin 1957–63

—. *Institution de la religion chrestienne*. Ed. Jean-Daniel Benoît. 5 vols. Paris: Vrin, 1957–63.

Calvin 1960

—. *Institutes of the Christian Religion*. Ed. John T. McNeill, trans. Ford Lewis Battles. 2 vols. Philadelphia: Westminster P, 1960.

Castiglione

Castiglione, Baldassare. *The Book of the Courtier*. Trans. Thomas Hoby. In Burton A. Milligan, ed., *Three Renaissance Classics: The Prince, Utopia, The Courtier*. New York: Scribner's, 1953.

Cavendish

Cavendish, George. *Life and Death of Cardinal Wolsey*. In *Two Early Tudor Lives*, ed. Richard S. Sylvester and Davis P. Harding. New Haven: Yale UP, 1962.

Chapman 1962

Chapman, George. *The Poems of George Chapman*. Ed. Phyllis Bartlett. 1941; rpt. New York: Russell and Russell, 1962.

Chapman 1964

—. *Bussy d'Ambois*. Ed. N.S. Brooke. The Revels Plays. 1964; rpt. Manchester: Manchester UP, 1979.

Cheney

Cheney, Patrick. *Marlowe's Counterfeit Profession: Ovid, Spenser, Counter-Nationhood*. Toronto: U of Toronto P, 1997.

Cicero

M. Tulli Ciceronis De natura deorum. Ed. A.S. Pease. 2 vols. Cambridge, MA: Harvard UP, 1955–58.

Clare 1990

Clare, Janet. *'Art made tongue-tied by authority': Elizabethan and Jacobean Dramatic Censorship*. Manchester: Manchester UP, 1990.

Clare 1997

—. "Historicism and the Question of Censorship in the Renaissance." *English Literary Renaissance* 27.2 (Spring 1997): 155–76.

Clark

Clark, Stuart. *Thinking with Demons: The Idea of Witchcraft in Early Modern Europe*. Oxford and New York: Oxford UP, 1997.

Cornelius

Cornelius, R. M. *Christopher Marlowe's Use of the Bible*. Frankfurt, Bern, New York: Peter Lang, 1984.

Couliano

Couliano, Ioan P. *Eros and Magic in the Renaissance*. Trans. Margaret Cook. Chicago: U of Chicago P, 1987.

Crane

Crane, Hart. *The Complete Poems and Selected Letters and Prose of Hart Crane*. Ed. Brom Weber. Garden City, NY: Anchor, 1966.

Danner

Danner, Dan G. "The Later English Calvinists and the Geneva Bible." In W. Fred Graham, ed., *Later Calvinism: International Perspectives*. Kirksville: Sixteenth Century Essays and Studies, vol. 22, 1994. 489-504.

Dee

Dee, John. *John Dee's Five Books of Mystery [Mysteriorum libri quinque]*. Ed. Joseph H. Peterson. Boston: Weiser Books, 2003.

Dekker 1904

Dekker, Thomas. *The Guls Hornbook and The Belman of London in Two Parts*. Ed. Oliphant Smeaton. London: Dent, 1904.

Dekker 1905

—. *The Seven Deadly Sinnes of London*. Cambridge and London: Cambridge UP, 1905.

Dent

Dent, R.W. *Proverbial Language in English Drama Exclusive of Shakespeare, 1495-1616*. Berkeley: U of California P, 1984.

Dido

Marlowe, Christopher. *Dido Queen of Carthage* and *The Massacre at Paris*. Ed. H.J. Oliver. The Revels Plays. London: Methuen, 1968.

Dollimore 1991

Dollimore, Jonathan. *Sexual Dissidence: Augustine to Wilde, Freud to Foucault*. Oxford: Clarendon Press, 1991.

Dollimore 1993

—. *Radical Tragedy: Religion, Ideology and Power in the Drama of Shakespeare and his Contemporaries*. 2nd ed. 1989; rpt. Durham: Duke UP, 1993.

Donne

Donne, John. *The Complete Poetry of John Donne*. Ed. John T. Shawcross. New York: Anchor Books, 1967.

Du Plessis-Mornay

Du Plessis-Mornay, Philippe. *A Woorke concerning the trewnesse of the Christian Religion*. Trans. Sir Philip Sidney and Arthur Golding. London, 1587.

Dutton

Dutton, Richard. "Marlowe and Shakespeare: Censorship and Construction." *The Yearbook of Engish Studies* 23 (1993): 1-29.

Edward II

Marlowe, Christopher. *Edward the Second*. Ed. Charles R. Forker. The Revels Plays. Manchester: Manchester UP, 1994.

Ellis-Fermor

Ellis-Fermor, Una. *Christopher Marlowe*. London: Methuen, 1927.

EFB

The English Faust Book: A critical edition based on the text of 1592. Ed. John Henry Jones. Cambridge: Cambridge UP, 1994.

EFB 1592

The Historie of the damnable life, and deserued death of Doctor Iohn Faustus, Newly imprinted, and in conuenient places imperfect matter amended: according to the true Copie printed at Franckfort, and translated into English by P.F. Gent. [...] London: Thomas Orwin, for Edward White, 1592. (British Library, shelf mark C. 27 b. 43)

Empson

Empson, William. *Faustus and the Censor: The English Faustbook and Marlowe's "Doctor Faustus"*. Ed. John Henry Jones. Oxford: Blackwell, 1987.

Eriksen 1981

Eriksen, Roy T. "The Misplaced Clownage-scene in *The Tragedie of Doctor Faustus* (1616) and its Implications for the Play's Total Structure." *English Studies* 62 (1981): 249-58.

Eriksen 1985

—. "Giordano Bruno and Marlowe's *Doctor Faustus* (B)." *Notes and Queries* 32 (1985): 463-65.

Eriksen 1986

—. "Marlowe's Petrarch: *In Morte di Madonna Laura*." *Cahiers Élizabéthains* 29 (1986): 13-25.

Eriksen 1987

—. *"The Forme of Faustus Fortunes": A Study of The Tragedie of Doctor Faustus (1616)*. Oslo: Solum Forlag; Atlantic Highlands, NJ: Humanities Press, 1987.

First Folio

Mr. William Shakespeares Comedies, Histories, & Tragedies. Ed. Helge Kükeritz, intro. C.T. Prouty. Facsimile rpt. New Haven and London: Yale UP, 1954.

Fitzmyer

Fitzmyer, Joseph, ed. *The Gospel According to Luke*. 2 vols. Anchor Bible 28-28A. Garden City, NY: Doubleday, 1981-85.

Forsyth

Forsyth, Neil. *The Old Enemy: Satan and the Combat Myth*. Princeton: Princeton UP, 1987.

Foxe

Foxe, John. *Acts and Monuments.* 3 vols. Ed. George Townsend. London: Seeley and Burnside, 1841.

Freedman

Freedman, Barbara. "Elizabethan Protest, Plague, and Plays: Rereading the Documents of Control." *English Literary Renaissance* 29 (1996): 17-45.

Füssel and Kreutzer

Füssel, Stephan, and Hans Joachim Kreutzer, eds. *Historia von D. Johann Fausten: Text des Druckes von 1587.* Stuttgart: Philipp Reclam Jun., 1988.

Garin

Garin, Eugenio. *Medioevo e Rinascimento: studi e ricerche.* 1954; rpt. Bari: Laterza, 1966.

Geneva Bible

The Geneva Bible: A Facsimile of the 1560 Edition. Eds. Lloyd Eason Berry and William D. Whittingham. Madison: U of Wisconsin P, 1969.

Gill 1987

Gill, Roma, ed. *The Complete Works of Christopher Marlowe, vol. I. All Ovids Elegies, Lucans First Booke, Dido Queene of Carthage, Hero and Leander.* Oxford: Clarendon Press, 1987.

Gill 1988

—. "*Doctor Faustus*: The Textual Problem." *University of Hartford Studies in Literature* 20 (1988): 52-60.

Girouard

Girouard, Mark. *Life in the English Country House: A Social and Architectural History.* New Haven and London: Yale UP, 1978.

Grafton

Grafton, Anthony. *Cardano's Cosmos: The Worlds and Works of a Renaissance Astrologer.* Cambridge, MA and London: Harvard UP, 1999.

Grande

Grande, Troni Y. *Marlovian Tragedy: The Play of Dilation.* Lewisberg: Bucknell UP, 1999.

Grantley and Roberts

Grantley, Darryll, and Peter Roberts, eds. *Christopher Marlowe and English Renaissance Culture.* Aldershot: Scolar Press; Brookfield, VT: Ashgate, 1996.

Greene 1923

Greene, Robert. *The Repentance of Robert Greene.* Ed. G.B. Harrison. The Bodley Head Quartos. London: John Lane, 1923.

Greene 1963

—. *Friar Bacon and Friar Bungay.* Ed. Daniel Seltzer. Regents Renaissance Drama Series. Lincoln: U of Nebraska P, 1963.

Greene 1996

—. *Menaphon*. Ed. Brenda Cantar. Ottawa: Dovehouse Editions, 1996.

Greg 1946

Greg, W.W. "The Damnation of Faustus." *Modern Language Review* 41 (1946): 97-107; rpt. in Bluestone, Max, and Norman Rabkin, eds., *Shakespeare's Contemporaries*. Engelwood Cliffs, NJ: Prentice-Hall, 1961. 90-103.

Greville

Greville, Fulke. *Selected Writing of Fulke Greville*. Ed. Joan Rees. London: Athlone Press, 1973.

Hamlet Q1

Shakespeare, William. *Shakespeare's Hamlet: The First Quarto, 1603. Reproduced in facsimile from the copy in the Henry E. Huntington Library.* Cambridge, MA: Harvard UP, 1931.

Hamlet Q2

—. *Hamlet: Second Quarto: 1605*. Facsimile rpt. London: Scolar Press, 1969.

Happé 1972

Happé, Peter, ed. *Tudor Interludes*. Harmondsworth: Penguin, 1972.

Hamlin

Hamlin, William M. "'Swolne with Cunning of a Selfe Conceit': Marlowe's Faustus and Self Conception." *English Language Notes* 34.2 (December 1996): 7-12.

Happé 1979

—. ed. *Four Morality Plays*. Harmondsworth: Penguin, 1979.

Hattaway

Hattaway, Michael. "The Theology of Marlowe's *Doctor Faustus*." *Renaissance Drama* 3 (1970): 51-78.

Headley

Headley, John M. *Luther's View of Church History*. New Haven and London: Yale UP, 1963.

Henslowe

Henslowe, Philip. *Henslowe's Diary*. Eds. R.A. Foakes and R.T. Rickert. Cambridge: Cambridge UP, 1961.

Herbert

Herbert, George. *The English Poems of George Herbert*. Ed. C.A. Patrides. 1974; rpt. London: Dent, 1977.

Hermetica

Hermetica: The Greek Corpus Hermeticum *and the Latin* Asclepius *in a new English translation*. Ed. and trans. Brian P. Copenhaver. Cambridge: Cambridge UP, 1992.

Historia
> See entry for Füssell and Kreutzer.

Hooker
> Hooker, Richard. *Of the Laws of Ecclesiastical Polity*. Ed. Christopher Morris. 2 vols. London: Dent, 1954.

Horace, *Ars poetica*
> Q. *Horati Flacci De arte poetica liber*. In *Horace: The Epistles*. Ed. F.G. Plaistowe and A.F. Watt. London: University Tutorial Press, n.d.

Hotine
> Hotine, Margaret. "The Politics of Anti-Semitism: *The Jew of Malta* and *The Merchant of Venice*." *Notes and Queries* 38 (1991): 35-38.

Housman
> Housman, A.E. *The Name and Nature of Poetry and Other Selected Prose*. Ed. John Carter. 1961; rpt. New York: New Amsterdam Books, 1989.

Hunter
> Hunter, R.G. *Shakespeare and the Mystery of God's Judgments*. Athens, Georgia: U of Georgia P, 1976.

Irenaeus
> Irenaeus, Bishop of Lyons. *Against Heresies*. In *The Writings of Irenaeus*, vol. 1. Trans. A. Roberts and W.H. Rambaut. Ante-Nicene Christian Library, vol. 5. Edinburgh: T. and T. Clark, 1868.

James
> James VI and I. *Daemonologie*. Edinburgh: R. Waldengrave, 1597.

Jew of Malta
> Marlowe, Christopher. *The Jew of Malta*. Ed. N.W. Bawcutt. The Revels Plays. Manchester: Manchester UP; Baltimore: Johns Hopkins UP, 1978.

Johnson 1945
> Johnson, F. R. "Marlowe's 'Imperiall Heaven'." *ELH (English Literary History)* 12 (1945): 35-44.

Johnson 1946
> —. "Marlowe's Astronomy and Renaissance Skepticism." *ELH (English Literary History)* 13 (1946): 241-54.

Jonson
> Jonson, Ben. *Ben Jonson*. Ed. C.H. Herford and Percy and Evelyn Simpson. 11 vols. Oxford: Clarendon Press, 1925-1952.

Keefer 1983
> Keefer, Michael H. "Verbal Magic and the Problem of the A and B Texts of *Doctor Faustus*." *Journal of English and Germanic Philology* 82 (1983): 324-46.

Keefer 1985-86
> —. "Misreading Faustus Misreading: The Question of Context." *The Dalhousie Review* 65.4 (Winter 1985-86): 511-33.

Keefer 1987

—. "History and the Canon: The Case of *Doctor Faustus*." *University of Toronto Quarterly* 56.4 (1987): 498-522.

Keefer 1988

—. "Agrippa's Dilemma: Hermetic 'Rebirth' and the Ambivalences of *De vanitate* and *De occulta philosophia*." *Renaissance Quarterly* 41 (1988): 614-53.

Keefer 1989

—. "Right Eye and Left Heel: Ideological Origins of the Legend of Faustus." *Mosaic* 22 (1989): 79-94.

Keefer 2002

—. "Text, Apparatus, History." In A. Lynne Magnusson and C.E. McGee, eds., *Elizabethan Theatre XV.* Toronto: P.D. Meany, 2002. 131-57.

Keefer 2004

—. "'Fairer than the evening air': Marlow's Gnostic Helen of Troy and the Tropes of Belatedness and Historical Mediation." In Alan Shepard and Stephen D. Powell, eds., *Fantasies of Troy: Classical Tales and the Social Imaginary in Medieval and Early Modern Europe.* Toronto: Centre for Reformation and Renaissance Studies, 2004. 39-62.

Keefer 2006

—. "The A and B Texts of Marlowe's *Doctor Faustus* Revisited." *Papers of the Bibliographical Society of America* 100.2 (June 2006): 227-57.

Kirschbaum 1943

Kirschbaum, Leo. "Marlowe's Faustus: A Reconsideration." *Review of English Studies* 19 (1943): 225-41.

Kirschbaum 1946

—. "The Good and Bad Quartos of *Doctor Faustus*." *The Library* 2nd series, 26 (1946): 272-94.

Klaits

Klaits, Joseph. *Servants of Satan: The Age of the Witch Hunts.* Bloomington: Indiana UP, 1985.

Kuriyama 1975

Kuriyama, Constance Brown. "Dr. Greg and *Doctor Faustus*: The Supposed Originality of the 1616 Text." *English Literary Renaissance* 5 (1975): 171-97.

Kuriyama 1988a

—. "Marlowe's Nemesis: The Identity of Richard Baines." In Kenneth Friedrich, Roma Gill, and Constance B. Kuriyama, eds., *"A Poet and a filthy Play-maker": New Essays on Christopher Marlowe.* New York: AMS Press, 1988. 343-60.

Kuriyama 1988b

—. "Marlowe, Shakespeare, and the Nature of Biographical Evidence."
University of Hartford Studies in Literature 20 (1988) 1-12.

Kuriyama 2002

—. *Christopher Marlowe: A Renaissance Life.* Ithaca: Cornell UP, 2002.

Kyd

Kyd, Thomas. *The First Part of Hieronymo and The Spanish Tragedy.* Ed.
Andrew S. Cairncross. Lincoln: U of Nebraska P, and London: Arnold,
1967.
A Companion to Shakespeare. Oxford: Blackwell, 1999. 57-84.

Lake, D.

Lake, David J. "Three Seventeenth-Century Revisions: *Thomas of
Woodstock, The Jew of Malta,* and *Faustus B.*" *Notes and Queries* 30 (April
1983): 133-43.

Lake, P.

Lake, Peter. "Religious Identities in Shakespeare's England." In *A
Companion to Shakespeare.* Ed. David Scott Kastan. Oxford: Blackwell,
1999. 57-84.

Lecky

Lecky, W.E.H. *History of the Rise and Influence of the Spirit of Rationalism in
Europe.* 2 vols. 2nd ed., New York: Appleton, 1898.

Leech

Leech, Clifford. *Christopher Marlowe: Poet for the Stage.* Ed. Anne
Lancashire. New York: AMS Press, 1986.

Liber XXIV philosophorum

Il libro dei ventiquattro filosofi. Ed. and trans. Paolo Lucentini. Milan:
Adelphi Edizioni, 1999.

Lily and Colet

Lily, William, and John Colet. *A Short Introduction of Grammar.* 1549;
facsimile rpt. Menston: Scolar Press, 1970.

Looking-Glass

Lodge, Thomas, and Robert Greene. *A Looking-Glass for London and
England.* Ed. W.W. Greg. Malone Society Reprints. 1932; rpt. New York:
AMS Press, 1985.

Lucian

The Works of Lucian of Samosata. Trans. H.W. and F.G. Fowler. 4 vols.
Oxford: Clarendon Press, 1905.

Luther

See entry for *WA.*

Lyly

    The Complete Works of John Lyly. Ed. R.W. Bond. 3 vols. 1902; rpt.
    Oxford: Clarendon Press, 1967.

Maclure

    Maclure, Millar, ed. *Marlowe: The Critical Heritage 1588-1896.* London:
    Routledge & Kegan Paul, 1979.

Maguire

    Maguire, Laurie. *Shakespearean suspect texts: The 'bad' quartos and their
    contexts.* Cambridge: Cambridge UP, 1996.

Malleus

    Kramer, Heinrich, and James Sprenger. *Malleus maleficarum.* Trans.
    Montague Summers. 1928; rpt. London: Arrow Books, 1971.

Marcus

    Marcus, Leah. *Unediting the Renaissance: Shakespeare, Marlowe, Milton.*
    London and New York: Routledge, 1996.

Massacre at Paris

    See entry for *Dido.*

McAdam

    McAdam, Ian. *The Irony of Self and Imagination in the Drama of Christopher
    Marlowe.* Newark: U of Delaware P, 1999.

McAlindon 1994a

    McAlindon, T. *Doctor Faustus: Divine in Show.* New York: Twayne, 1994.

McAlindon 1994b

    —. "Doctor Faustus: Grounded in Astrology." *Literature and Theology* 8
    (1994): 384-93.

McDaniel

    McDaniel, W. B. "An Hermetic Plague-Tract by Johannes Mercurius
    Corrigiensis." *Transactions and Studies of the College of Physicians of
    Philadelphia* 4th series 9 (1941-42): 96-111, 217-25.

Mebane

    Mebane, John S. *Renaissance Magic and the Return of the Golden Age.*
    Lincoln and London: U of Nebraska P, 1989.

Monter

    Monter, E. Wiliam, ed. *European Witchcarft.* New York: Wiley, 1969.

Nashe

    Nashe, Thomas. *The Works of Thomas Nashe.* Ed. Ronald B. McKerrow,
    revised by F.P. Wilson. 5 vols. 1958; rpt. Oxford: Blackwell, 1966.

Nauert

    Nauert, Charles G., Jr. *Agrippa and the Crisis of Renaissance Thought.*
    Urbana: U of Illinois P, 1965.

Neill

    Neill, Michael. *Putting History to the Question: Power, Politics, and Society in English Renaissance Drama*. New York: Columbia UP, 2000.

Nicholl

    Nicholl, Charles. *The Reckoning: The Murder of Christopher Marlowe*. 1992; rpt. London: Picador, 1993.

Norton-Smith

    Norton-Smith, John. "Marlowe's *Faustus* (I. iii, 1-4)." *Notes and Queries* 25 (1978): 436-37.

Nuttall 1980

    Nuttall, A. D. *Overheard by God: Fiction and Prayer in Herbert, Milton, Dante and St. John*. London: Methuen, 1980.

Nuttall 1998

    —. *The Alternative Trinity: Gnostic Heresy in Marlowe, Milton, and Blake*. Oxford: Clarendon Press, 1998.

Oberman

    Oberman, Heiko. *Masters of the Reformation: The Emergence of a New Intellectual Climate in Europe*. Trans. Dennis Martin. Cambridge: Cambridge UP, 1981.

Oliver

    Oliver, L.M. "Rowley, Foxe, and the *Faustus* Additions." *Modern Language Notes* 60 (1945): 391-94.

Owens

    Owens, Margaret E. "Desperate Juggling Knacks: The Rehearsal of the Grotesque in *Doctor Faustus*." *Medieval and Renaissance Drama in England* 8 (1996): 63-93.

Palmer and More

    Palmer, P.M., and R.P. More, eds. *The Sources of the Faust Tradition from Simon Magus to Lessing*. 1936; rpt. New York: Haskell House, 1965.

Patterson

    Patterson, Annabel. *Censorship and Interpretation: The Conditions of Writing and Reading in Early Modern England*. Madison: U of Wisconsin P, 1984.

Peele

    Peele, George. *The Arraignment of Paris*. Ed. Oliphant Smeaton. London: J.M. Dent, 1905.

Perkins

    Perkins, William. *The Works ... of Mister William Perkins*. Cambridge, 1605.

Pettegree

    Pettegree, Andrew. "The Reception of Calvinism in Britain." In

Wilhelm H. Neuser and Brian G. Armstrong, eds., *Calvinus Sincerioris Religionis Vindex: Calvin as Protector of the Purer Religion*. Kirksville: Sixteenth Century Essays and Studies, vol. 36, 1997. 267-89.

Pico

Pico della Mirandola, Giovanni. *Syncretism in the West: Pico's 900 Theses (1486). The Evolution of Traditional Religious and Philosophical Systems. With Text, Translation, and Commentary*. Ed. and trans. S.A. Farmer. Tempe. Arizona: Medieval & Renaissance Texts & Studies, 1998.

Prayer Book

The Prayer-Book of Queen Elizabeth, 1559. London, 1890.

Puttenham

Puttenham, George. *The Arte of English Poesie*. Ed. Edward Arber. London: Constable, 1906.

Pymander

[Hermes Trismegistus, pseud.] *Mercurii Trismegisti Pymander, de potestate et sapientia dei. Eiusdem Asclepius, de voluntate dei*. Trans. Marsilio Ficino. Ed. Jacques Lefèvre d'Étaples. Basel, 1532.

Rasmussen

Rasmussen, Eric. *A textual companion to Doctor Faustus*. Manchester and New York: Manchester UP, 1993.

Recognitions

Clement I (Pope, pseud.). *Recognitions of Clement*. In *The Writings of Tatian and Theophilus; and The Clementine Recognitions*. Trans. B.P. Pratten, M. Dods, and T. Smith. Ante-Nicene Christian Library, vol. 3. Edinburgh: T. and T. Clark, 1867.

Richardson

Richardson, E. C. "Faust and the Clementine Recognitions." *Papers of the American Society of Church History* 6 (1894): 133-45.

Riggs

Riggs, David. *The World of Christopher Marlowe*. London: Faber and Faber, 2004.

Roberts

Roberts, Gareth. "Necromantic Books: Christopher Marlowe, *Doctor Faustus* and Agrippa of Nettesheim." In Grantley and Roberts, 148-71.

Robbins

Robins, R.H. *The Encyclopedia of Witchcraft and Demonology*. 1959; rpt. London: Spring Books, 1967.

Russell

Russell, Jeffrey Burton. *Mephistopheles: The Devil in the Modern World*. Ithaca: Cornell UP, 1986.

Scholem
>Scholem, Gershom. *Kabbalah.* New York: Quadrangle/The New York Times Books, 1974.

Scot
>Scot, Reginald. *The Discoverie of Witchcraft.* Ed. Brinsley Nicholson. 1886; rpt. East Ardsley, Wakefield: EP Publishing 1973.

Searle
>Searle, John. "Marlowe and Chrysostom." *Times Literary Supplement* (15 February 1936): 139.

Shakespeare Apocrypha
>Tucker Brooke, C.F., ed. *The Shakespeare Apocrypha.* Oxford: Clarendon Press, 1908.

Shapiro
>Shapiro, James. *Rival Playwrights: Marlowe, Jonson, Shakespeare.* New York: Columbia UP, 1991.

Sharpe
>Sharpe, James. *Instruments of Darkness: Witchcarft in Early Modern England.* Philadelphia: U of Pennsylvania P, 1996.

Shepherd
>Shepherd, Simon. *Marlowe and the Politics of Elizabethan Theatre.* Brighton: Harverter, 1986.

Sinfield 1983
>Sinfield, Alan. *Literature in Protestant England, 1550-1650.* London: Croom Helm; Totowa, NJ: Barnes & Noble, 1983.

Sinfield 1992
>—. *Faultlines: Cultural Materialism and the Politics of Dissident Reading.* Berkeley: U of California P, 1992.

Smith
>Smith, Bruce R. *Homosexual Desire in Shakespeare's England: A Cultural Poetics.* Chicago: U of Chicago P, 1991.

Snow
>Snow, Edward A. "Marlowe's *Doctor Faustus* and the Ends of Desire." In Alvin Kernan, ed., *Two Renaissance Mythakers: Christopher Marlowe and Ben Jonson.* Baltimore: Johns Hopkins UP, 1977. 70-110.

Snyder 1965
>Snyder, Susan. "The Left Hand of God: Despair in Medieval and Renaissance Tradition." *Studies in the Renaissance* 12 (1965): 18-59.

Snyder 1966
>—. "Marlowe's *Doctor Faustus* as an Inverted Saint's Life." *Studies in Philology* 63 (1966): 565-77.

Spenser

Spenser, Edmund. *Spenser: Poetical Works*. Ed. J.C. Smith and E. de Selincourt. 1912; rpt. London: Oxford UP, 1966.

Stachniewski

Stachniewski, John. *The Persecutory Imagination: English Puritanism and the Literature of Religious Despair*. Oxford: Clarendon Press, 1991.

Strauss

Strauss, Gerald. "How to Read a *Volksbuch*: The *Faust Book* of 1587." In Peter Boerner and Sidney Johnson, eds., *Faust through Four Centuries: Retrospect and Analysis/Vierhundert Jahre Faust: Rückblick und Analyse*. Tübingen: Max Niemeyer, 1989. 27-39.

Tamburlaine 1593

Marlowe, Christopher. *Tamburlaine the Great*. Ed. Roma Gill. Facsimile rpt. of the 1593 edition. Menston, Yorkshire: Scolar Press, 1973.

Tamburlaine 1967

——. *Tamburlaine the Great Parts I and II*. Ed. John D. Jump. Regents Renaissance Drama Series. Lincoln: U of Nebraska P, 1967.

Thevet

Thevet, André. *Les vrais pourtraits et vies des hommes illustres*. 2 vols. Paris, 1584.

Thomas

Thomas, Keith. *Religion and the Decline of Magic*. 1971; rpt. Harmondsworth: Penguin, 1973.

Thomas and Tydeman

Thomas, Vivien, and William Tydeman, eds. *Christopher Marlowe: The plays and their sources*. London and New York: Routledge, 1994.

Thorndike

Thorndike, Lynn. *A History of Magic and Experimental Science During the First Thirteen Centuries of Our Era*. 6 vols. 1923; rpt. New York: Columbia UP, 1964.

Tille

Tille, Alexander. *Die Faustsplitter in der Literatur des sechzehnten bis achtzehnten Jahrhunderts*. Berlin: Emil Felber, 1900.

Tilley

Tilley, M. P. *A Dictionary of the Proverbs in England in the Sixteenth and Seventeenth Centuries*. Ann Arbor: U of Michigan P, 1950.

Tomlinson

Tomlinson, Gary. *Music in Renaissance Magic: Toward a Historiography of Others*. Chicago: U of Chicago P, 1993.

Tromly

    Tromly, Fred B. *Playing with Desire: Christopher Marlowe and the Art of Tantalization*. Toronto: U of Toronto P, 1998.

Tyndale *NT*

    Tyndale, William, trans. *The New Testament: The text of the Worms edition of 1526 in original spelling*. Ed. W.R. Cooper, preface by David Daniell. London: The British Library, 2000.

Urry

    Urry, William. *Christopher Marlowe and Canterbury*. Ed. Andrew Butcher. London: Faber and Faber, 1988.

WA

    D. Martin Luthers Werke. Ed. P. Pietsch et al. 93 vols.; Weimar: Hermann Bühlaus, 1883-1987. (*WA* = Weimarer Ausgabe; *WATr* = Tischreden; *WABr* = Briefwechsel.)

Walker 1972

    Walker, D.P. *The Ancient Theology: Studies in Christian Platonism from the Fifteenth to the Eighteenth Century*. London: Duckworth, 1972.

Walker 1975

    —. *Spiritual and Demonic Magic from Ficino to Campanella*. 1958; rpt. Notre Dame: Notre Dame UP, 1975.

Warren

    Warren, Michael J. "*Doctor Faustus*: The Old Man and the Text." *English Literary Renaissance* 11 (1981): 111-47.

Wentersdorf

    Wentersdorf, Karl P. "Some Observations on the Historical Faust." *Folklore* 89 (1978): 201-23.

Weyer

    Weyer, Johann. *De praestigiis daemonum*. English translation in Mora, George, et al., eds., John Shea, trans. *Witches, Devils, and Doctors in the Renaissance: Johann Weyer, "De praestigiis daemonum."* Tempe, Arizona: Medieval & Renaissance Texts & Studies, 1998.

Whitney

    Whitney, Geoffrey. *A Choice of Emblemes*. Leiden: F. Raphelengius, 1586.

Williams

    Williams, George Huntsdon. *The Radical Reformation*. 3rd ed. Kirksville, Missouri: Truman State UP, 2000.

Wilson

    Wilson, Richard. "Introduction," and "Visible Bullets: *Tamburlaine the Great* and Ivan the Terrible." In Richard Wilson, ed., *Christopher Marlowe*. London and New York: Longman, 1999. 1-29, 120-39.

Yates 1964
> Yates, Francis A. *Giordano Bruno and the Hermetic Tradition*. London: Routledge and Kegan Paul, 1964.

Yates 1979
> —. *The Occult Philosophy in the Elizabethan Age*. London: Routledge & Kegan Paul, 1979.

Zambelli
> Zambelli, Paola. "Magic and Radical Reformation in Agrippa of Nettesheim." *Journal of the Warburg and Courtauld Institutes* 39 (1976): 104-38.

Other Works on *Doctor Faustus*

[In addition to the critical studies by Barber, Cheney, Dollimore, Grande, Hunter, Kuriyama, Leech, Marcus, McAdam, McAlindon, Mebane, Nuttall, Owens, Rasmussen, Riggs, Roberts, Shapiro, Sinfield, Snow, Tromly, and R. Wilson listed among the Works Cited above, the following books, articles, and collections of essays offer valuable critical insights into this play and its principal author.]

Barber, C.L. *Creating Elizabethan Tragedy: The Theater of Marlowe and Kyd*. Ed. Richard P. Wheeler. Chicago: U of Chicago P, 1988.

Barker, Francis. *The Culture of Violence: Tragedy and History*. Manchester: Manchester UP, 1993.

Bartels, Emily C. *Spectacles of Strangeness: Imperialism, Alienation, and Marlowe*. Philadelphia: U of Pennsylvania P, 1993.

—. ed. *Critical Essays on Christopher Marlowe*. New York: G.K. Hall; London: Prentice Hall, 1997.

Bevington, David. *From "Mankind" to Marlowe*. Cambridge, MA: Harvard UP, 1962.

—. "Staging the A- and B-Texts of *Doctor Faustus*." In Deats and Logan, 43-60.

Birringer, Johannes H. "Between Body and Language: 'Writing' the Damnation of Faustus." *Theatre Journal* 36 (1984): 335-55.

Bloom, Harold, ed. *Christopher Marlowe*. New York: Chelsea House, 1986.

Bredbeck, Gregory W. *Sodomy and Interpretation: Marlowe to Milton*. Ithaca and London: Cornell UP, 1991.

Brockbank, J.P. *Marlowe: Dr. Faustus*. London: Arnold, 1962.

Cartelli, Thomas. *Marlowe, Shakespeare, and the Economy of Theatrical Experience*. Phildelphia: U of Pennsylvania P, 1991.

Cheney, Patrick, ed. *The Cambridge Companion to Christopher Marlowe.* Cambridge: Cambridge UP, 2004.

Cox, John D. *The Devil and the Sacred in English Drama, 1350-1642.* Cambridge: Cambridge UP, 2000.

Deats, Sara Munson. *Sex, Gender, and Desire in the Plays of Christopher Marlowe.* Newark: U of Delaware P, 1997.

—. and Robert A. Logan, eds. *Marlowe's Empery: Expanding his Critical Contexts.* Newark: U of Delaware P, 2002.

DiGangi, Mario. *The Homoerotics of Early Modern Drama.* Cambridge: Cambridge UP, 1997.

Downie, J.A., and J.T. Parnell, eds. *Constructing Christopher Marlowe.* Cambridge: Cambridge UP, 2000.

Forsyth, Neil. "Heavenly Helen." *Études de lettres* 4 (1987): 11-21.

Friedenrich, Kenneth, Roma Gill, and Constance B. Kuriyama, eds. *"A Poet & a Filthy Play-Maker": New Essays on Christopher Marlowe.* New York: AMS Press, 1988.

Gatti, Hilary. *The Renaissance Drama of Knowledge: Giordano Bruno in England.* London and New York: Routledge, 1989.

Geckle, George L. "The 1604 and 1616 Versions of *Dr. Faustus*: Text and Performance." In David G. Allen and Robert A. White, eds., *Subjects on the World's Stage: Essays on British Literature of the Middle Ages and the Renaissance.* Newark: U of Delaware P, and London: Associated U Presses, 1995.

Hamlin, William M. "Casting Doubt in Marlowe's *Doctor Faustus*." *Studies in English Literature* 41.2 (Spring 2001): 257-75.

Hammer, Paul E.J. "A Reckoning Reframed: The 'Murder' of Christopher Marlowe Revisited." *English Literary Renaissance* 26.2 (Spring 1996): 225-42.

Hammill, Graham L. *Sexuality and Form: Caravaggio, Marlowe, and Bacon.* Chicago: U of Chicago P, 2000.

Harraway, Clare. *Re-citing Marlowe: Approaches to the Drama.* Aldershot: Ashgate, 2000.

Healy, Thomas. *Christopher Marlowe, Writers and their Work.* Plymouth: Northcote House, 1994.

Hopkins, Lisa. *Christopher Marlowe: A Literary Life.* Basingstoke and New York: Palgrave, 2000.

Keiper, Hugo. *Studien zur Raumdarstellung in den Dramen Christopher Marlowes: Dramaturgie und dargestellte Wirklichkeit.* Essen: Verlag die blaue Eule, 1988.

Kendall, Roy. "Richard Baines and Christopher Marlowe's Milieu." *English Literary Renaissance* 24.3 (Autumn 1994): 507-52.

Kuriyama, Constance Brown. *Hammer or Anvil: Psychological Patterns in the Christopher Marlowe's Plays*. New Brunswick, NJ: Rutgers UP, 1980.

Levin, Harry. *The Overreacher: A Study of Christopher Marlowe*. 1952; rpt. Boston: Beacon P, 1964.

Lunney, Ruth. *Marlowe and the Popular Tradition: Innovation in the English Drama Before 1595*. Manchester: Manchester UP, 2002.

Neill, Michael. *Putting History to the Question: Power, Politics, and Society in English Renaissance Drama*. New York: Columbia UP, 2000.

Pinciss, G.M. "Marlowe's Cambridge Years and the Writing of *Doctor Faustus*." *Studies in English Literature* 33 (1993): 249-64.

Prieto-Pablos, Juan A. "'What Art Thou Faustus?' Self-Reference and Strategies of Identification in Marlowe's *Doctor Faustus*." *English Studies* 74.1 (February 1993): 66-83.

Proser, Matthew N. *The Gift of Fire: Aggression and the Plays of Christopher Marlowe*. New York: Peter Lang, 1995.

Ricks, Christopher. "*Doctor Faustus* and Hell on Earth." *Essays in Criticism* 35 (1985): 101-20.

Sales, Roger. *Christopher Marlowe*. New York: St. Martin's P, 1991.

Simkin, Stevie. *A Preface to Marlowe*. New York: Longman, 2000.

—. *Marlowe: The Plays*. Basingstoke: Palgrave, 2001.

Steane, J.B. *Marlowe: a critical study*. Cambridge: Cambridge UP, 1964.

Szonyi, Gyorgy. *John Dee's Occultism: Magical Exaltation through Powerful Signs*. Albany: SUNY P, 2005.

Waswo, Richard. "Damnation, Protestant style: Macbeth, Faustus, and Christian tragedy." *Journal of Medieval and Renaissance Studies* 4 (1974): 63-99.

Weil, Judith E. *Christopher Marlowe: Merlin's Prophet*. Cambridge: Cambridge UP, 1977.

White, Paul Whitfield, ed. *Marlowe, History, and Sexuality: New Critical Essays on Christopher Marlowe*. New York: AMS Press, 1998.

Zunder, William. *Elizabethan Marlowe: Writing and Culture in the English Renaissance*. Cottingham, Hull: Unity Press, 1994.